Introduction to Object-Oriented Databases

Computer Systems
Herb Schwetman, editor

Metamodeling: A Study of Approximations in Queueing Models, Subhash Chandra Agrawal, 1985

Logic Testing and Design for Testability, Hideo Fujiwara, 1985

Performance and Evaluation of LISP Systems, Richard P. Gabriel, 1985

The LOCUS Distributed System Architecture, edited by Gerald Popek and Bruce J. Walker, 1985

Performance Models of Multiprocessor Systems, M. Ajmone Marsan, G. Balbo, and G. Conte, 1986

Analysis of Polling Systems, Hideaki Takagi, 1986

A Commonsense Approach to Theory of Error-Correcting Codes, Benjamin Arazi, 1987

Microprogrammable Parallel Computer: MUNAP and Its Applications, Takanobu Baba, 1987

Simulating Computer Systems: Techniques and Tools, M. H. MacDougall, 1987

Research Directions in Object-Oriented Programming, edited by Bruce Shriver and Peter Wegner, 1987

Object-Oriented Concurrent Programming, Edited by Akinori Yonezawa and Mario Tokoro, 1987

Networks and Distributed Computation: Concepts, Tools, and Algorithms, Michel Raynal, 1988

Fault Tolerance Through Reconfiguration of VLSI and WSI Arrays, R. Negrini, M. G. Sami, and R. Stefanelli, 1989

Queueing Networks-Exact Computational Algorithms: A Unified Theory Based on Decomposition and Aggregation, by Adrian Conway and Nicholas Georganas, 1989

ABCL: An Object-Oriented Concurrent System, edited by Akinori Yonezawa, 1989

Interpretation and Instruction Path Coprocessing, by Eddy H. Debaere and Jan M. Van Campenhout, 1990

Introduction to Object-Oriented Databases, by Won Kim, 1990

Introduction to Object-Oriented Databases

Won Kim

The MIT Press
Cambridge, Massachusetts
London, England

Second printing, 1991

This book was set in Times Roman by Chiron, Inc. and printed and bound in the United States of America.

Library of Congess Cataloging-in-Publication Data

Kim, Won.
Introduction to object-oriented databases / Won Kim.
p. cm.—(Computer systems)
Includes bibliographical references.
ISBN 0-262-11124-1
1. Object-oriented data bases. 1. Title. II. Series: Computer systems (Cambridge, Mass.)
QA76.9.D3K54 1990
005.75—dc20 90-5779
CIP

This book is dedicated to three people in my life who have loved me and endured through my free-spirited ways.

Eul-Kyo Kim, my mother
Jae-Sun Kim, my father
Hyun-Kyung Kim, my wife

Contents

Series Foreword

This series is devoted to all aspects of computer systems. This means that subjects ranging from circuit components and microprocessors to architecture to supercomputers and systems programming will be appropriate. Analysis of systems will be important as well. System theories are developing, theories that permit deeper understanding of complex interrelationships and their effects on performance, reliability, and usefulness.

We expect to offer books that not only develop new materials but also describe projects and systems. In addition to understanding concepts, we need to benefit from the decision making that goes into actual development projects; selection from various alternatives can be crucial to success. We are soliciting contributions in which several aspects of systems are classified and compared. A better understanding of both the similarities and the differences found in systems is needed.

It is an exciting time in the area of computer systems. New technologies mean that architectures that were at one time interesting but not feasible are now feasible. Better software engineering means that we can consider several software alternatives, instead of "more of the same old thing," in terms of operating systems and system software. Faster and cheaper communications mean that intercomponent distances are less important. We hope that this series contributes to this excitement in the area of computer systems by chronicling past achievements and publicizing new concepts. The format allows publication of lengthy presentations that are of interest to a select readership.

Herb Schwetman

Preface

This book is my attempt to consolidate much of the recent results of research into object-oriented databases. My hope is that this book will help to define object-oriented databases and to suggest a host of important additional research issues that I believe should receive attention from database researchers. This book is based significantly on the published results of the ORION next-generation databases project in the Advanced Computer Technology (ACT) Program at Microelectronics and Computer Technology Corporation (MCC) in Austin, Texas. I had the privilege of starting the project at the end of 1985 and leading it until its successful completion at the end of 1989. The ORION project prototyped a family of three next-generation database systems, each of which was object-oriented; concurrently with the prototyping efforts, the project identified a rich set of database architectural issues and extensively published results of research into these issues.

I have elected to base this book on the results of the ORION project. The reason is basically that, of all the systems, I am most intimately familiar with ORION. In particular, there is no standard object-oriented data model at this point in time. A data model determines a database language, which in turn determines the implementation of a database system; as such, a data model is the starting point for discussing a database system. Since I had to select some data model for the purposes of illustrating the architectural issues in object-oriented databases, it was natural for me to select the ORION data model. Further, the extensive set of research papers on a broad spectrum of architectural issues in object-oriented and next-generation databases that the ORION project has published during the past few years makes the ORION architecture and implementation an ideal basis for a book on object-oriented database architecture. The architectural issues for object-oriented databases which the ORION project has addressed include dynamic schema evolution, query model, automatic query optimization, secondary indexing, concurrency control, authorization, multimedia data management, versions, composite objects, and notions of private and shared databases. The ORION project was the first to publish detailed foundational papers on many of these topics.

I believe that the fact that this book is based on the ORION data model and the ORION solutions to various architectural issues does not compromise its generality and relevance to students and professionals interested in understanding object-oriented databases and even building object-oriented database systems. Although there is no standard object-oriented data model, most object-oriented database systems that are operational or under development today share a set of fudamental object-oriented concepts. The architectural issues in object-oriented databases which this book deals with are issues that arise due to these common fundamental object-oriented concepts; that is, the issues are universal, and solutions outlined in the book from the ORION research are generally applicable to object-oriented databases.

About half the chapters of this book contain polished materials I have taken from research papers I have (co-)authored in the recent past. I have woven these materials and new materials which I have written expressely for this book in order to reflect my personal perspectives about what is and what is not an object-oriented database, what are relevant research issues in object-oriented databases, and the position of object-oriented database systems in the history of evolution of database systems.

This book consists of 16 chapters. The seven chapters after Introduction (Chapters 2 through 8) deal with data modeling and semantics of database facilities in an object-oriented context. Chapter 2 presents an object-oriented data model. The model consists of a small set of core object-oriented concepts and semantic modeling concepts. The core object-oriented concepts are common to most object-oriented programming languages and database systems currently operational; and the semantic modeling concepts are versions and composite objects (part hierarchies) which are common in many types of next-generation database applications. Chapter 3 makes the data model concrete by presenting a somewhat restricted programmatic interface for defining and manipulating an object-oriented database. Chapter 4 explores similarities and differences between object-oriented databases and other databases, such as design databases, extensible databases, hierarchical and network databases. Chapter 5 examines the semantics and implementation of dynamic changes to the database schema; the richness of an object-oriented data model (in particular, the model developed in Chapter 2) gives rise to a significantly larger set of meaningful changes to the database schema. Chapter 6 develops a model of queries as one crucial element of a formal foundation for object-oriented database systems. The model is consistent with the object-oriented data model presented in Chapter 2; further, it bridges the gap between object-oriented databases and relational databases by introducing object-oriented equivalents of the relational join and set operations. Chapter 7 makes the query model concrete by providing a concrete query language. Chapter 8 develops a model of authorization. Again, the model is consistent with the object-oriented data model presented in Chapter 2. The object-oriented data model necessitates significant extensions to the relational model of authorization. In particular, the concept of implicit authorization is extended to provide a basis for authorization on an individual object, a set of versions of an object, and a set of objects in a composite object.

The next six chapters (Chapters 9 through 14) are concerned with architecture and implementation issues for object-oriented database systems. Chapter 9 examines storage structures, including the disk and page layout, clustering of related objects, and access methods for navigational accesses and set-oriented queries. Chapter 10 discusses query optimization and processing. The techniques used in relational database systems to optimize and process queries are directly applicable for optimizing and processing queries in object-oriented database systems. They include the enumeration of all reasonable combinations of classes involved in a query, construction of a query-execution plan in terms of the best access method for evaluating each of the classes, and cost estimation for a query-execution plan for each of these combinations. Chapter 11 presents transaction management, including concurrency control and recovery.

Except for some changes in concurrency control to account for the object-oriented concept of inheritance along a class hierarchy, the concurrency control and recovery techniques used in conventional database systems are directly applicable for object-oriented database systems. Chapter 12 further presents the semantics of versions and composite objects (introduced in Chapter 2), and explores the impacts of versions and composite objects on the architecture of an object-oriented database system, including query processing, concurrency control, and authorization. Chapter 13 describes extensions to the database system architecture to support persistent programming, that is, to integrate a programming language and a database system. The essence of the architectural extensions is the support of an object buffer pool in addition to the traditional page buffer pool. The database system must manage migration of objects between the buffer pools. Chapter 14 presents the architecture of an object-oriented database system (ORION) to tie together the architectural and implementation considerations in preceding chapters.

Chapter 15 is a survey of a representative subset of the currently operational object-oriented database systems. The survey includes commercial systems, and prototypes from both industrial research laboratories and universities. Chapter 16 closes out the book with directions for future research and development in object-oriented databases. Important challenges that remain include standardization and formalization, performance enhancement, migration path from conventional databases (especially relational databases), database design tools, user-friendly interfaces, additional database facilities such as views and deductive capabilities, and extensible architecture to allow the customization of semantic modeling concepts and to support multiple object-oriented programming languages.

I have assumed that the reader is familiar with basic database concepts discussed in standard database textbooks, including data models, query languages, storage structures, transaction management, concurrency control, recovery, and authorization. My hope is that this book will be used as a textbook for a graduate or advanced undergraduate course on object-oriented database systems for students who have taken a course on relational database systems; as a reference book for an advanced course on database systems in general; as a reference book for designers and implementors of object-oriented database systems; and as a reference book for designers and implementors of object-oriented applications. I have included a list of recommended readings at the end of each chapter for those readers interested in a deeper understanding of the subject matter of the chapter. I fully expect that additional research will enhance the current understanding of the object-oriented database theory and architecture, that existing object-oriented database systems will evolve and/or go out of existence, and new object-oriented database systems will be introduced. However, this book deals with issues of object-oriented data models, and semantics and architectures for a broad range of database features for object-oriented database systems. As such, I do not expect that such future developments will make this book obsolete in the foreseeable future; of course, Chapters 15 (survey of the current systems) and 16 (directions for future R/D) will need to be adjusted to reflect any major changes in the object-oriented database landscape. I may include in a new edition new results in some of the areas of future research I outlilne in Chapter 16; for example, views, integration of rules and objects, database design tools, and user-friendly interfaces to object-oriented database systems.

Won Kim
Austin, Texas

Acknowledgments

The ORION next-generation databases project at MCC started at the end of 1985, and successfully concluded at the end of 1989. During the span of four years, the members of the ORION project identified and resolved various research issues in object-oriented databases and next-generation databases, and designed and implemented a series of three database systems. The three systems the project prototyped are ORION-1, ORION-1SX, and ORION-2. ORION-1 is a single-processor-based system. ORION-1SX is an object server that manages a shared persistent database on behalf of a number of client workstations which do not have their own persistent databases. ORION-2 is a fully distributed, and federated, database system.

The original members of the ORION project, who brought up the ORION-1 prototype from scratch, included Nat Ballou, Jay Banerjee (now with the Unisys Corporation), Hong-Tai Chou (now with Object Sciences Corporation), Jorge Garza, and Darrell Woelk. The project later had Wan-Lik Lee. Jorge Garza, Nat Ballou, and Darrell Woelk contributed to the implementation of all three systems (in fact, together they implemented about 75% of the ORION code, with Jorge Garza being the biggest contributor); Hong-Tai Chou on ORION-1 and ORION-1SX; and Jay Banerjee on ORION-1. Further, Fausto Rabitti and Elisa Bertino (both of CNR, Italy), as visiting scientists, made outstanding research contributions in the areas of authorization and queries. Kyung-Chang Kim, Paul Jenq, Hyung-Joo Kim, Don Stuart, Janet Miller, Martin Carter, and Dawn Cizmar—all as limited-duration participants (3 months to 12 months)—also helped the ORION project.

The materials presented in this book are based on the results of the ORION project, and about half the chapters of this book contain materials taken from previously published research papers which I had co-authored with members of the ORION project.

The three reviewers of this book made many helpful comments on the presentation and contents of the book. I have incorporated most of their comments in the final version of the manuscript.

Special Acknowledgments

If I am asked to express in one word how I feel about my life and career, the word I will choose without hesitation is *gratitude*. I am grateful to all those who came into my life to help me to grow professionally and personally. I have special places in my heart for three of them: the late Mr. James K. Kernan, Prof. David J. Kuck, and Dr. Donald D. Chamberlin, in the order in which they came into my life. They truly set the course of my career. I hope to never betray their confidence in me, and to be able to help others in the magnanimous ways in which they helped me.

Mr. James K. Kernan was my English teacher at Forest Hills High School in New York City. He encouraged me to cultivate my (what he perceived to be) talents in writing English, and opened the door to the Massachusetts Institute of Technology for me.

Mr. Kernan even showed some of my classroom writings to Mrs. Kernan—that was the highest form of compliment he reserved for his students. To this day I am sorry that Mr. Kernan passed away before I graduated from high school.

Prof. David J. Kuck was my Ph.D. dissertation advisor at the University of Illinois at Urbana-Champaign. He taught me that I should always strive for excellence and for solutions to real-world problems in choosing and pursuing research topics. He also taught me, through his own deeds, that I should always be fair to people. His teachings shaped and articulated a lot of my good side. Further, even though the area of my dissertation was of remote relevance to his area of research and he was always impossibly busy, Prof. Kuck always made time for me and extended financial support to me during my dissertation research.

Dr. Donald D. Chamberlin of IBM's Almaden Research Center gave me a start in the field of databases. He started by helping me to publish my very first paper, a survey paper on relational database systems, which appeared in the ACM Computing Surveys. Then, when I was still in graduate school, he offered me a summer internship at IBM's San Jose Research laboratory, where I was exposed to a magnificent relational database prototype, System R. The experience led to my Ph.D. dissertation on query processing in relational database systems, and subsequently to employment at IBM, where I learned very much about databases. Dr. Chamberlin also graciously extended friendship to me and my family while I was with IBM.

Introduction to Object-Oriented Databases

1 Introduction

1.1 Evolution of Database Technology

During the past three decades, the database technology for information systems has undergone four generations of evolution, and the fifth generation database technology is currently under development. The transition from one generation to the next has always been necessitated by the ever-increasing complexity of database applications and the cost of implementing, maintaining, and extending these applications. The first generation was file systems, such as ISAM and VSAM. The second generation was hierarchical database systems, such as IMS and System 2000. The third generation was CODASYL database systems, such as IDS, TOTAL, ADABAS, IDMS, etc. The second and third generation systems realized the sharing of an integrated database among many users within an application environment. The lack of data independence and the tedious navigational access to the database gave rise to the fourth-generation database technology, namely, relational database technology. Relational database technology is characterized by the notion of a declarative query. Fifth-generation database technology will be characterized by a richer data model and a richer set of database facilities necessary to meet the requirements of applications beyond the business data-processing applications for which the first four generations of database technology have been developed.

The transition from one generation to the next of the database technology has been marked by the offloading of some tedious and repetitive bookkeeping functions from the applications into the database system. This has made it easy for the application programmers to program database applications; however, it made the performance of database systems a major problem, and required considerable research and development to increase the performance of the new generation database systems to an acceptable level. This point was particularly true with the transition into the era of relational databases. The introduction of declarative queries in relational databases relieved application programmers of the tedious chore of programming navigational retrieval of records from the database. However, a major new component, namely the query optimizer, had to be added to the database system to automatically arrive at an optimal plan for executing any given query, such that the plan will make use of appropriate access methods available in the system. The evolution in database technology is analogous to the evolution in programming languages from machine languages, to assembly languages, and to high-level languages; this series of evolutions has facilitated the task of programming increasingly complex applications, but required the introduction of increasingly sophisticated language processors, that is, assemblers and compilers.

During the 1970s research and development activities in databases were focused on realizing the relational database technology. These efforts culminated in the introduction of commercially available systems in late 70s and early 80s, such as Oracle, SQL/DS and DB2, and INGRES. However, relational database technology, just as each of the previous generation database technology, was developed for the conventional business data-processing applications, such as inventory control, payroll, accounts, and so on. Attempts to make use of relational database technology in a wide variety of other types of application have quickly exposed several serious shortcomings of the relational and past-generation database technology. These applications include computer-aided design, engineering, software engineering, and manufacturing (CAD, CAE, CASE, and CAM) systems and applications that run on them; knowledge-based systems (expert systems and expert system shells); multimedia systems which deal with images, voice, and textual documents; and programming language systems. Relational and past-generation database systems will henceforth be called conventional database systems; the data model for a conventional database system a conventional data model; and the database technology incorporated into conventional database systems the conventional database technology.

Let us review several of the well-known shortcomings of the conventional database technology.

(1) A conventional data model, especially the relational model, is too simple for modeling complex nested entities, such as design and engineering objects, and complex documents; conventional database systems do not provide mechanisms, such as configuration management, to represent and manage such entities.

(2) Conventional database systems support only a limited set of atomic data types, such as integer, string, etc.; they do not support general data types found in programming languages. In particular, they do not even allow the storage and retrieval of long unstructured data (long data) such as images, audio, and textual documents.

(3) The conventional data model does not include a number of frequently useful semantic concepts, such as generalization and aggregation relationships; this

means that application programmers must explicitly represent and manage such relationships in their programs, since the database system does not provide the necessary functions.

(4) The performance of conventional database systems, especially relational database systems, is unacceptable for various types of compute-intensive applications, such as simulation programs in computer-aided design and programming language environments.

(5) Application programs are implemented in some algorithmic programming language (such as COBOL, FORTRAN, or PL/1) and some database language embedded in it (such as SQL, DL/1, or CODASYL DML). Database languages are very different from programming languages, in both data model and data structures. This impedance-mismatch problem motivated the development of fourth-generation languages (4GLs).

(6) The model of transactions supported in conventional database systems is inappropriate for long-duration transactions necessary in interactive, cooperative design environments. Conventional database systems do not support facilities for representing and managing the temporal dimension in databases, including the notion of time and versions of objects and schema, and change notification.

The discovery of the shortcomings of conventional database technology has provided impetus for database professionals for the most part of the 1980s to pave the way for the fifth-generation of database technology. The next-generation database technology must necessarily build on conventional database technology and incorporate solutions to many of the problems outlined above in order to meet the requirements of current and newly emerging database applications. There are currently at least two proposed approaches for transitioning from fourth-generation database technology to the fifth-generation technology: extended relational database technology and object-oriented database technology. The fundamental differences between them are the basic data model and the database language. The extended relational approach starts with the relational model of data and a relational query language, and extends them in various ways to allow the modeling and manipulation of additional semantic relationships and database facilities. POSTGRES is the best-known next-generation database system which is based on the extended relational approach. The object-oriented approach, adopted in MCC's ORION system and a number of other systems (such as Ontos (formerly VBase), GemStone, IRIS, O2, etc.), starts with an object-oriented data model and a database language that captures it, and extends them in various ways to allow additional capabilities.

One important point which we must recognize is that an object-oriented data model is a more natural basis than an extended relational model for addressing some of the deficiencies of the conventional database technology previously outlined; for example, support for general data types, nested objects, and support for compute-intensive applications. We note that the underlying data model has nothing to do with other deficiencies, such as long-duration transactions, support for long data, and temporal data.

There are important differences between an object-oriented data model and the relational data model. An object-oriented data model includes the object-oriented concepts of encapsulation, inheritance, and polymorphism; these concepts are not part of the conventional models of data. The difference between an object-oriented database system and a non-object-oriented database system is that an object-oriented database system can directly support the needs of the applications that create and manage objects that have the object-oriented semantics, namely, object-oriented programming languages or applications designed in an object-oriented style.

Further, an object-oriented programming language may be extended into a unified programming and database language. The resulting language is subject to the problem of impedance mismatch to a far less extent than the approach of embedding a current-generation database language in one of the conventional programming languages. The reason is that an object-oriented programming language is built on object-oriented concepts, and object-oriented concepts consist of a number of data modeling concepts, such as aggregation, generalization, and membership relationships. An object-oriented database system which supports such a unified object-oriented programming and database language will be a better platform for developing object-oriented database applications than an extended relational database system which supports an extended relational database language (assuming that it is not augmented with a 4GL).

We believe that both the extended relational and object-oriented approaches are viable, and that most likely systems adopting either approach will co-exist. The case for the extended relational approach is based largely on the fact that it is rooted on the familiar current-generation database technology; for current-generation database technology, there is already a large user/customer base, and there is a mathematical foundation for the query language and even an industry-wide standard for the database language. This is something that proponents of the object-oriented next-generation database technology cannot claim. However, object-oriented programming and object-oriented approach to designing complex software systems are to date the most promising approach to coping with the increasingly complex software systems and the corresponding costs of developing, maintaining, and evolving such software systems. If the object-oriented approach truly fulfills its promises in the design and implementation of software and representation of knowledge in future knowledge-based systems, object-oriented database systems will become crucial as the platform for object-oriented applications and application development environments.

1.2 Next-Generation Databases

Commercial relational database systems provide various facilities, including queries and automatic query optimization, access methods to support efficient evaluation of queries. short-duration transactions, concurrency control, recovery, limited semantic integrity control, and authorization. Next-generation database systems must include all (or most) of the features found in conventional database systems, since the features supported in conventional database systems have proven to be useful for both the current classes of applications and most of the emerging classes of applications. However, next-generation database systems should include additional facilities, regardless of whether the underlying data model is object-oriented or extended relational. In this section, we will review the database features found in conventional database systems, and discuss several additional features that will be important in next-generation database systems.

1.2.1 Features of the Conventional Database Systems

Conventional database systems provide database languages to allow application programmers or end-users to define and manipulate the database. A conventional database language consists of three components (or sublanguages): a data definition language, a data manipulation language, and a data control language.

The data definition language (DDL) allows the specification of the database schema. In relational databases, the schema of a database is the specification of a set of relations: the name of each relation, the name of each column of a relation, the domain (data type) of each column, and integrity constraints on the domain.

The data manipulation language (DML) includes facilities to express queries and updates (replace, insert, delete) against the database. In relational databases, a query is an expression of a subset of the database to be retrieved which satisfies user-specified search conditions.

The data control language (DCL) includes facilities for protecting the integrity of the database and for managing resources of the system. The integrity feature of a DCL includes transactions; a limited form of semantic integrity constraints, for most systems; and authorization. A transaction is a sequence of reads and writes against a database, such that the sequence is treated as an atomic action against the database. If a transaction does not successfully complete, the system automatically backs out any change that may have been made to the database within the transaction. If a transaction successfully completes, all writes into the database become permanent. Semantic integrity constraints are conditions imposed on the contents of the database; because of the performance overhead for updates, most systems do not support automatic checking of general integrity constraints.

The resource management feature of a DCL is the specification of the creation and deletion of database schema elements (such as relations and columns) and access methods to the database (e.g., B+ tree secondary indexes, physical clustering of records, etc.).

Beyond the features expressed in these database languages, database systems provide various facilities, including concurrency control, recovery, and various utilities. The objective of concurrency control is to protect the integrity of a database in the face of simultaneous accesses to the same data by multiple users. Recovery is necessary to restore the database to a consistent state after crashes. A crash may be a soft crash which destroys the contents of main memory, or a hard crash which destroys the contents of the disk. Utilities include error reporting, performance monitoring, application program tracing, etc.

Further, relational database systems automatically determine an optimal plan for evaluating a given query; it generates a number of reasonable alternative plans for a given query, and on the basis of a cost estimation for each of these plans, selects one optimal plan. The programmer need not provide any hint to aid the system.

1.2.2 Additional Features for the Next-Generation Database Systems

The following list of useful additional database features is not meant to be exhaustive, since the exhaustiveness of such a list necessarily depends on the applications. The database language must be designed to allow the users to make use of these database features; further, the database architecture must be significantly changed to efficiently support these features. The discussion of these issues will not be included here. The primary objective of this section is to differentiate next-generation databases and object-oriented databases. Any conventional database system may be extended with many of these features; the resulting data model need not include the object-oriented concepts of encapsulation, inheritance, and polymorphism.

(1) The ability to represent and manipulate complex nested objects to allow the successive refinement of complex entities. It should be possible to fetch an entire complex object or a subset of it as a single unit, or incrementally one component object at a time. A complex nested object may be stored in one physical cluster for storage and retrieval efficiency. A nested object may be a unit of concurrency control.

(2) The ability to store and retrieve arbitrarily long data. It should be possible to store and retrieve long data in small segments. Effective techniques must be supported to minimize storage space for long data and the time for transferring long data between main memory and secondary storage. The ability to search for desired string patterns in textual documents should be

supported; and it may even be combined with the conventional query capability against short formatted records.

(3) The ability to define and manipulate arbitrary data types. The definition and manipulation languages should extend in a natural way an underlying programming language. Efficient storage and access methods must be supported for these data types to expedite the processing of queries on them.

(4) The ability to represent and manage changes in the database over time, including the notions of time and time interval, versions of single objects, versions of complex nested objects, and versions of the schema entities. There is no consensus on the semantics of versions; as such, a worthwhile approach may be to provide a two-layered architecture for a version manager. The lower level may support a basic mechanism for low-level version semantics that are common to various proposals; the higher level may be made extensible to allow easy tailoring of installation-specific version semantics.

(5) The ability to represent and manipulate various semantic modeling concepts that are useful for applications. One such concept is the assembly-part hierarchy in the context of computer-aided manufacturing, compound document composition, etc. It is very difficult to correctly capture the full semantics of these modeling concepts, since different users prefer different semantics. Like the version manager, the components of a database system that support semantic modeling concepts may best be made extensible.

(6) The ability to specify rules and extended constraints to support inferencing and constraint management which are necessary as basic mechanisms for supporting knowledge-based applications. The database system must support an efficient unification mechanism to support forward and backward rule processing, and efficient implementation of highly flexible constraints on the contents of data and the relationships among data.

(7) The ability to manage long-duration cooperative transactions. In interactive, cooperative work environments, the notion of serializability is an inappropriate definition of database consistency. A less stringent definition of database consistency is necessary, which nonetheless satisfies the practical need for flexible and concurrent sharing of common information among multiple users.

1.3 Object-Oriented Approach and Databases

We will now define object-oriented databases on the basis of the rationale for the object-oriented approach to the design and programming of software, and to model the entities and relationships among entities in an application (environment).

1.3.1 Object-Oriented Approach

Object-oriented programming languages, such as Smalltalk, C++, Objective C, Eiffel, and Common LISP Object System (CLOS), are now in fairly wide use. Frame-based knowledge representation systems, such as KEE and ART, offer object-oriented features in knowledge representation and manipulation. Apple's MacIntosh MacDraw and Hypercard are popular object-oriented user interface applications. Tektronix and Data General offer object-oriented computer-aided design and engineering systems. These are but a small sampling of object-oriented concepts in use. Indeed, the underlying object-oriented concepts are the common thread linking frame-based knowledge representation and reasoning systems, object-oriented programming (application development) environments, and object-oriented advanced human interface systems. Therefore, they may be the key to building one type of intelligent high-performance programming system in the foreseeable future. The growing popularity and importance to software of object-oriented concepts is evidenced in the new conferences that have started during the past several years, including Object-Oriented Programming Systems, Languages and Applications (OOPSLA), the European Object-Oriented Programming (ECOOP) Conference, the Conference on Deductive and Object-Oriented Databases (DOOD), and the Workshop on Object-Oriented Databases (OODB). Even a new journal, *Journal of Object-Oriented Programming*, started a few years ago.

Object-oriented concepts have evolved in three different disciplines: first in programming languages, then in artificial intelligence, and then in databases. Simula-67 is generally regarded as the first object-oriented programming language. Since Simula-67, researchers in programming languages have taken two different paths to promote object-oriented programming. One is the development of new object-oriented languages, most notably Smalltalk, and such languages as Traits, Eiffel, and Trellis/Owl, among others. Another is the extension of conventional languages: Flavors, Object LISP, OakLisp, LOOPS, and Common LOOPS as extensions of LISP; Objective C and C++ as extensions of C; CLASCAL as an extension of PASCAL; and so on. After Marvin Minsky's introduction of frames as a knowledge representation scheme, researchers in artificial intelligence have developed such frame-based knowledge representation languages as KEE (from Intellicorp), ART (from Inference), and so on. In the database area, research into semantic data models has led to data modeling concepts similar to those embedded in object-oriented programming and knowledge representation languages. The class concept captures the instance-of relationship between an object and the class to which it belongs; the concept of a subclass specializing its superclass captures the generalization (IS-A) relationship; and the composition of an object in terms of attributes captures the aggregation relationship. Some of the better-known semantic data models include E/R (entity-relationship), SDM (semantic data model), and DAPLEX.

An object-oriented approach to programming is based on the concepts of encapsulation and extensibility. A program in general consists of data and code that operates on the data. Object-oriented programming encapsulates in an object some data and, and programs to operate on the data: the data is the state of the object, and the code is the behavior of the object. The state of an object is the set of values of the attributes defined for the object, and the behavior is a set of programs with a well-defined interface for their invocation. Object-oriented programming requires the invocation of the behavior of an object via message passing to the object through the interface defined for the behavior of the object. For example, one may define a Shape object, whose state consists of the values of the attributes Center-Point and Bounding-Box for the object, and whose behavior includes a program called Display-Shape to display the object on a screen. One may cause a Shape object to display itself on a screen by sending a message to invoke the Display-Shape behavior of the object. The notion of encapsulation has proven to be a natural and easy paradigm for various application environments, such as graphical user-interface systems.

Extensibility refers to the ability to extend an existing system without introducing changes to it. Extensibility is an especially powerful concept for building and evolving very large and complex software systems. An object-oriented approach to programming offers extensibility in two ways: behavioral extension and inheritance. The behavior of an object may be extended by simply including additional programs. A behavioral extension of an object does not affect the validity of any existing program. For example, a new program named Rotate-Shape may be added to the Shape object defined above. An object-oriented approach further promotes extensibility through reuse or inheritance. The behavior, and even the attributes, defined for an object may be reused in the definition of more specialized objects, that is, they are inherited into the new objects. For example, a new object named Triangle may be defined as a specialized Shape object. The Triangle object inherits (reuses) the behavior (Display-Shape and Rotate-Shape) and attributes (Center-Point and Bounding Box) defined for the Shape object. Further, one may define additional behavior and attributes for the Triangle object, and even re-define some of the inherited behavior and attributes.

1.3.2 Object-Oriented Databases

A data model is a logical organization of the real-world objects (entities), constraints on them, and relationships among objects. A data model that captures object-oriented concepts is an object-oriented data model. An object-oriented database is a collection of objects whose behavior and state, and the relationships are defined in accordance with an object-oriented data model. An object-oriented database system is a database system which allows the definition and manipulation of an object-oriented database. Object-oriented concepts form a good basis for a rich data model for the next-generation database applications, such as CAD/CAE/CASE/CAM systems, knowledge-based systems, multimedia information systems, and advanced human-interface systems. The reason is that object-oriented concepts already include such data modeling concepts, found in conventional database languages, as grouping objects into a class (corresponding to grouping records into a record type, or tuples into a relation), aggregation relationships between an object and objects it consists of (nested objects), and generalization relationships between a class of objects and classes of objects specialized from it. The fact that an object-oriented data model includes the aggregation and generalization relationships means that an object-oriented database system provides a user interface for the definition and manipulation of the relationships among objects. This in turn means that application programmers need not explicitly program and manage these relationships. For example, the aggregation relationship is the basis of the recursive definition of a complex object in terms of other objects. This makes it possible to successively refine the representation of complex objects often found in such applications as computer-aided design and engineering and compound documents.

Despite the surging interest in object-oriented programming and object-oriented databases, the programming language, knowledge representation, and database disciplines, and even any one of them by itself, presently do not agree on a single standard for object-oriented concepts. This may lead one to question the merit of building object-oriented database systems, especially for commercial purposes. Relational database systems are now firmly taking root, and object-oriented database systems must carve out new market niches. However, many believe that object-oriented programming will be further developed and accepted widely in the future, and that there will emerge a standard object-oriented data model to make it possible for object-oriented next-generation database systems to take root in the foreseeable future. This optimism is based on the current trends in the marketplace and on the proven feasibility of constructing a core object-oriented data model which can be the basis of building object-oriented database systems even in the absence of a single standard.

Many expect that in the foreseeable future a small number of de facto standards will emerge, based largely on the commercial success of some of the programming languages, knowledge representation languages, and database systems.

Further, if one examines existing object-oriented programming languages, knowledge representation languages, and semantic data models, one can identify a small set of fundamental concepts whose primary semantics are common to almost all of them. A standard object-oriented data model will most certainly include these concepts, because these concepts have proven useful already. A useful launching point for research and development in object-oriented databases today is an object-oriented data model which includes at a minimum the core object-oriented concepts. An object-oriented database language may then be specified for the data model. An object-oriented database system may then be constructed to support the language. This is essentially the approach taken in all currently operational object-oriented database systems; although they differ in varying degrees, they share the same set of core concepts. We emphasize that, even if the eventual object-oriented model standard differs in various minor ways from the core model, the technology for implementing a database system which supports the core model will still be fairly straightforwardly applicable to a database system which will support the eventual standard. The reason is that the technology is based on only the primary semantics of the core object-oriented concepts.

Recommended Readings

Simula-67 is discussed in [BIRT72]. Smalltalk is described in [GOLD81, GOLD83], Traits in [CURR82, CURR84], Eiffel in [MEYE85], Trellis/Owl in [SCHA86], Flavors in [MOON86, KEEN85], Object LISP in [LMI85], LOOPS in [BOBR83], Common LOOPS in [STEF86, BOBR86], CLOS in [MOON89] Objective C in [COX84] and C++ in [STRO86]. [SMIT77] and [HULL88] discuss semantic modeling concepts. The E/R model is presented in[CHEN76], SDM in [HAMM81], and DAPLEX in [SHIP81].

2 Data Model

An object-oriented data model, simply put, is a set of object-oriented concepts for modeling data. Object-oriented concepts have been embedded in various programming languages and knowledge-representation languages. Unfortunately, different languages have adopted somewhat different interpretations of the concepts, and indeed a universal consensus does not yet exist about object-oriented concepts, and therefore, about an object-oriented data model. However, a survey of object-oriented programming languages and knowledge-representation languages can bring out a set of commonly accepted and fundamentally important data modeling concepts. This set of modeling concepts forms a core object-oriented data model. The core model is sufficiently powerful to support data-modeling requirements of many types of application, and to shed insight into the changes an object-oriented data model forces on the architecture of a database system.

The core model, although powerful, simply does not capture some of the semantic-integrity constraints and semantic relationships that are important to many types of application. Examples of semantic-integrity constraints include specifications of the uniqueness of the values of an attribute, admissibility of a null value for an attribute, value range for an attribute, and so on. Examples of semantic relationships often found essential include the part-of relationship between a pair of objects, and the version-of relationship between a pair of objects.

An object-oriented data model then may be defined as a core model augmented with semantic-integrity constraints and a number of semantic relationships. The core model may have to be modified when a universal definition of object-oriented concepts is adopted sometime in the future; however, in view of the fact that the core model consists of a relatively small set of such fundamental and simple concepts, any future changes to the core model are likely to extend the core model by adding a number of second-order variations to the current interpretations of the core object-oriented concepts.

In this chapter we will present an object-oriented data model in two steps; first the core model, and then semantic extensions to the core model. The model is based on that implemented in the ORION system. In the discussions of the core model, we will emphasize the importance of each of the concepts that constitute the model, and compare the concepts with those found in the relational model of data, where applicable.

2.1 Core Model

In this section, we will first provide a concise summary of the data modeling concepts in the core model, and then examine and motivate the concepts in some detail.

2.1.1 Core Modeling Concepts

- **Object and Object Identifier**. Any real-world entity is an object, with which is associated a system-wide unique identifier.
- **Attributes and Methods**. An object has one or more *attribute*s, and one or more *method*s which operate on the values of the attributes.
  The value of an attribute of an object is also an object. An attribute of an object may take on a single value or a set of values.
- **Encapsulation and Message Passing**. Messages are sent to an object to access the values of the attributes and the methods encapsulated in the object. There is no way to access an object except through the public interface specified for it.
- **Class**. All objects which share the same set of attributes and methods may be grouped into a *class*.
  An object belongs to only one class as an instance of that class.
  A class is also an object; in particular, a class is an instance of a *metaclass*.
- **Class Hierarchy and Inheritance**. The classes in a system form a hierarchy or a rooted directed acyclic graph, called a *class hierarchy*, such that, for a class C and a set of lower-level classes {Si} connected to C, a class in the set {Si} is a specialization of the class C, and conversely the class C is the generalization of the classes in the set {Si}. The classes in {Si} are *subclass*es of the class C; and the class C is a *superclass* of the classes in {Si}.
  Any class in {Si} inherits all the attributes and methods of the class C and may have additional attributes and methods.
  All attributes and methods defined for a class C are inherited into all its subclasses recursively.
  An instance of a class S is also a logical instance of all superclasses of S.

2.1.2 Perspectives of the Core Concepts

Object and Object Identifier

The object identifier of an object is system-wide unique. The uniform treatment of any real-world entity as an object simplifies the user's view of the real world. An object is recursively related to any number of other objects through some semantic relationships. In object-oriented systems, the relationships between an object and other objects are represented in terms of references to the objects; the references are the values of the attributes of the object.

A reference to an object is implemented as the object identifier of the object. The object identifier is a convenient means of navigating through a complex network of objects. Historically, object-oriented systems and languages, and therefore object-oriented concepts, have been developed largely independently of any consideration of very large databases; that is, they have assumed that all objects reside in a large virtual memory. This means that object identifiers have been used as the sole means of specifying desired objects; the notion of a query for selecting an arbitrary set of objects that satisfy an arbitrary combination of search predicates has been an alien concept to the designers of object-oriented languages and systems.

The fact that an object consists logically of object identifiers and that object identifiers are the only means of specifying objects to access has naturally led to the navigational model of computation in most of the existing object-oriented applications. This of course does not imply that object-oriented systems cannot be augmented with non-navigational (declarative) manipulation of objects. In fact, an increasing number of object-oriented database systems support or plan to support queries, as we will see in Chaper 15. In view of the complex nested structure of an object (which we will discuss shortly), strictly non-navigational manipulation of objects is not likely to fully replace the navigational access. However, it is safe to presume that future object-oriented systems will use non-navigational manipulation of objects to complement the traditional navigational access to objects.

Attributes and Methods

The values of the attributes of an object constitute the state of the object, and the set of methods associated with an object operate on the state of the object. The attributes of an object are analogous to the attributes (columns) of a tuple of a relation in relational databases. The methods are analogous to the *attached procedures* supported in some hierarchical database systems.

The specification for an attribute may include, besides the name of the attribute, semantic integrity constraints. Integrity constraints include the uniqueness of the value, admissibility of the null value, the domain of the attribute, and so on. The *domain* of an attribute is the class to which the values of the attribute belong; and it is the basis of type checking. The domain of an attribute may be any class, including a primitive class (e.g., integer, string, etc.). Further, an attribute may have a single value or a set of values from its domain. The treatment of the domain of an attribute in the core object-oriented model is significantly different from that in the normalized relational model. In the relational model, an attribute may only have a single value belonging to a single primitive data type (equivalent to a single primitive class). In the core model, an attribute may have a set of values belonging to a class hierarchy rooted at a user-specified class. Let us consider an example to clarify this important point. The class Vehicle in Figure 2.1 has four attributes: ID, Weight, Drivetrain, and Manufacturer. The domains of the attributes ID and Weight are primitive classes, string and integer, respectively. The domains of the attributes Drivetrain and Manufacturer, however, are the classes VehicleDrivetrain and Company, respectively. The values of the Manufacturer attribute may be instances of the user-specified domain Company or any subclass of the class Company. Similarly, the values of the Drivetrain attribute may be instances of any class on the class hierarchy rooted at the class VehicleDrivetrain.

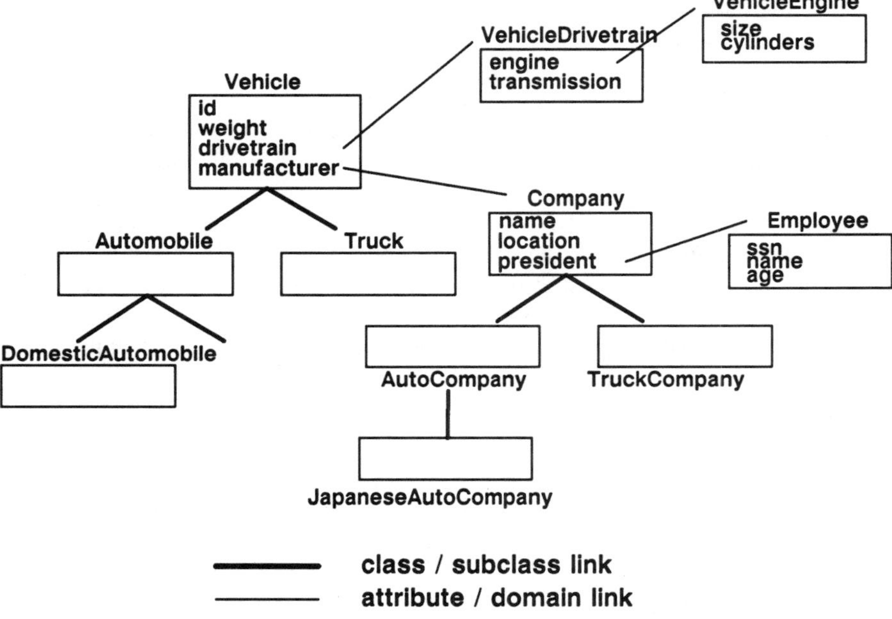

Figure 2.1
Class Hierarchy and Class-Composition Hierarchy

The fact that the domain of an attribute may be an arbitrary class has a major consequence on the core model; namely, it gives rise to the nested structure of the definition of a class. A class consists of a set of attributes; the domains of some or all of the attributes may be classes with their own sets of attributes; and so on. Then the definition of a class results in a directed graph of classes rooted at that class. If the graph for the definition of a class is restricted to a strict hierarchy, the class becomes a nested relation. The core model thus includes the nested-relational model. However, the nested relational model is not an object-oriented data model; rather it is an important aspect of an object-oriented model, as we will discuss in Chapter 4.

We emphasize that the above hierarchy of classes arises from the aggregation relationship between a class and its attributes and from the fact that the domain of an attribute may be an arbitrary class with its own set of attributes. This hierarchy, which we will call a *class-composition hierarchy*, is orthogonal to the concept of a class hierarchy. A class hierarchy captures the generalization relationship between one class and a set of classes specialized from it. A class-composition hierarchy has nothing to do with inheritance of attributes and methods. In Figure 2.1 the class Company is the root of a class hierarchy with subclasses AutomobileCompany, JapaneseAutocompany, and TruckCompany. It is also the root of a class-composition hierarchy involving the class Employee.

Class

In most object-oriented systems, classes are regarded as objects, just as instances of classes are objects. This is necessary mainly for uniformity in the handling of messages. Messages are supposed to be sent to objects; but to what objects must messages be sent to create objects? Obviously, messages cannot be sent to objects that do not exist. This problem is solved by treating a class as an object which has the method for creating instances of the class. Of course, to create a class, a message must be sent to a metaclass which has the method for creating the class, and so on. The class objects can have their own state and behavior, and a number of other situations arise to send messages to them, for example, to change the definition of a class.

The concept of a class is perhaps the most important link between object-oriented systems and databases. First, it directly captures the instance-of relationship between an instance and the class to which it belongs. Second, it provides the basis on which a query may be formulated. In relational databases, a query specifies search conditions and output attributes in the query result against a relation or a collection of relations. Similarly, the notion of a class is necessary for aggregating a collection of related objects in an object-oriented database as a target for the formulation of a query. Indeed, without the notion of a class, a query must be formulated against either all objects in the database or against some physical grouping of objects in the database (e.g., a segment of pages); a query would be not only difficult to formulate, but also expensive to evaluate. Third, the concept of a class can be used to enhance the semantic integrity of an object-oriented database. If it is not possible to specify the domain class for an attribute, integrity constraints would have to be specified in terms of an explicit set of values. Fourth, the notion of a class conveniently factors out the specifications of the attributes and methods from all instances of the class into a single object, namely, the class object for the class; obviously this results in the saving of storage space. The factoring out of redundant information into a single class object also makes dynamic changes to the database schema practical. If the specifications of the attributes and methods are not factored out, a schema change operation on a class would have to be applied to every instance of the class. For example, if an attribute is added to a class, the new name of the attribute would have to be included in every instance of the class; of course, every object in the database may have to be looked up first to identify only those instances that belong to the class.

A class is an object, and as such a set of attributes and methods may be associated with it which apply to the class object, rather than the instances of the class. Such attributes and methods are sometimes called *class attributes* and *class methods*, respectively. A class attribute of a class is often used to capture an aggregate property of the instances that belong to the class. An example of an aggregate property is the average weight of all Automobile instances.

There are two other types of attributes which apply to each instance of a class but which are specified in the class object: shared attributes, and default attributes. These attributes are logically a part of each instance of the class, but their values are kept in the class object. This means that their values are returned in response to messages to instances of the class. Further, the values of these attributes are inherited into the class objects for the subclasses. A *shared attribute* of a class is one whose value is used in each instance of the class. For example, we may add a shared attribute Number-of-Wheels to the class Automobile and specify the value 4 for it. All Automobile instances will share this value. We note that a shared attribute differs from a class attribute in that a class attribute represents an aggregate property of all instances of a class, while the value of a shared attribute applies to each and every instance of a class. A *default attribute* of a class is one whose value is used in each instance of the class, if the user does not explicitly provide a value for the attribute. As an example, let us suppose that the class Vehicle has a default attribute Number-of-Wheels, and the value is 4. If a new instance of Vehicle is created and the value for the Number-of-Wheels attribute is left unspecified, the system will use the default value 4; if a value 3 is specified for the attribute, the default value is not used.

It is sometimes useful to allow an instance to belong to more than one class. However, this generality causes performance degradation and increases system complexity. To allow an instance to belong to more than one class, the structure of an instance object has to be variable; that is, the identifiers of all classes to which an instance belongs must be stored with each and every instance. Only by examining the content of an instance object and determining the classes to which it belongs it is possible to determine its attributes and methods. For these reasons, in most systems, an instance belongs to only one class. Further, as we will show shortly, multiple inheritance makes it possible for an instance to logically belong to more than one class, without the performance overhead mentioned earlier.

If we enforce the principle that an object is an instance of a class, and a class is also an object, then we need the notion of a metaclass as the class of a class. Further, a metaclass is also an object, and it is an instance of a yet higher-level metaclass, and so on. Most object-oriented database systems do not support the strict notion of metaclasses. For example, in ORION, a system-defined class called CLASS is both the class of all other classes (i.e., the class CLASS is the metaclass of all other classes) and the root of the class hierarchy (i.e., it is the superclass of all other classes). This is not really proper; however, most object-oriented database systems operational today do not support metaclasses.

Class Hierarchy and Inheritance

In any object-oriented system, a class may have any number of subclasses. However, some systems allow a class to have only one superclass, while others allow a class to have any number of superclasses. In the former, a class inherits attributes and methods from only one class; this is called *single inheritance*. In the latter, a class inherits attributes and methods from more than one superclass; this is called *multiple inheritance*. In a system which supports single inheritance, the classes form a hierarchy. If a system supports multiple inheritance, the classes form a *rooted and connected directed acyclic graph* (DAG), sometimes called a class lattice. The class hierarchy (DAG) has only one root, a system-defined class called CLASS. The hierarchy (DAG) is connected, that is, there are no isolated nodes. Every node is reachable from the root. Every class on the class hierarchy (DAG) has a distinct name. Further, every attribute and method of a class, whether defined or inherited, has a distinct name. Henceforth, for simplicity, we will use the term class hierarchy to mean the more general directed acyclic graph of classes. Further, we note that, although most object-oriented languages support a single-root class hierarchy, some (notably C++) do not insist on it.

There has been some disagreement as to whether multiple-inheritance is really necessary. Although multiple-inheritance complicates the data model, it appears that multiple-inheritance is necessary and its acceptance is inevitable. CLOS and C++ release 2.0 include it. Single-inheritance often causes duplication of information and forces upon the users a less intuitive model of the database.

Let us consider the Submarine class of Figure 2.2. It is both a NuclearPoweredVehicle and a WaterVehicle, possessing properties common to both classes. If a class is not allowed to have multiple superclasses, an alternative class hierarchy must be constructed; Figures 2.3a and 2.3b are two of the alternative class hierarchies for the class hierarchy of Figure 2.2. The trouble with any of these alternatives is that the extra superclass ends up inheriting attributes and methods from semantically unrelated classes. For example, in Figure 2.3a, the class WaterVehicle inherits all the attributes and methods from the classes MotorizedVehicle and NuclearPoweredVehicle, although it is clear from Figure 2.2 that the class WaterVehicle is not a logical subclass of the classes MotorizedVehicle and NuclearPoweredVehicle. Figure 2.3c shows an alternative which solves this problem. However, the class Submarine must now be modeled in two different ways, corresponding to the two superclasses it has. Each type of Submarine now must replicate the attributes and methods that it would inherit from the extra superclasses if multiple inheritance is used.

A class hierarchy captures the generalization relationship between a class and its direct and indirect subclasses. The combined notions of a class, attributes, and a class hierarchy mean that the semantic data modeling concepts instance-of, aggregation, and generalization, are inherent in the object-oriented paradigm. This means that the gap between object-oriented applications and an object-oriented database is much narrower than that between object-oriented applications and a non-object-oriented database. The gap is also much narrower than that which exists between

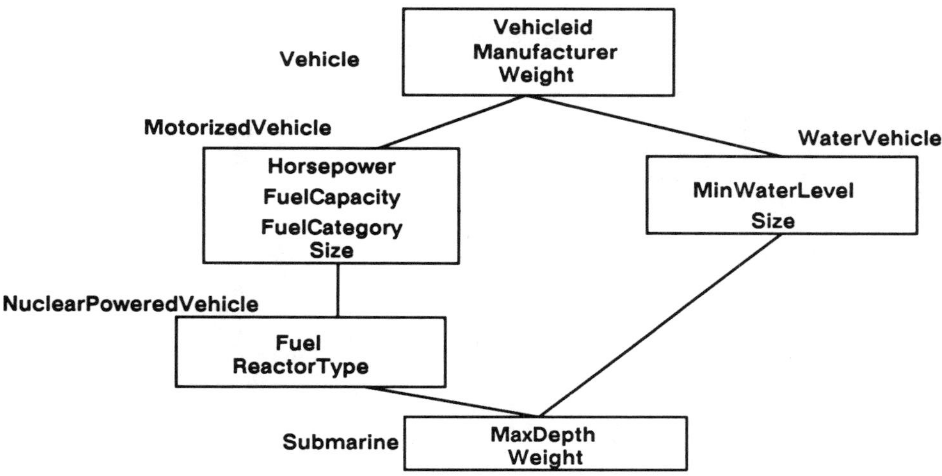

Figure 2.2
Multiple Inheritance

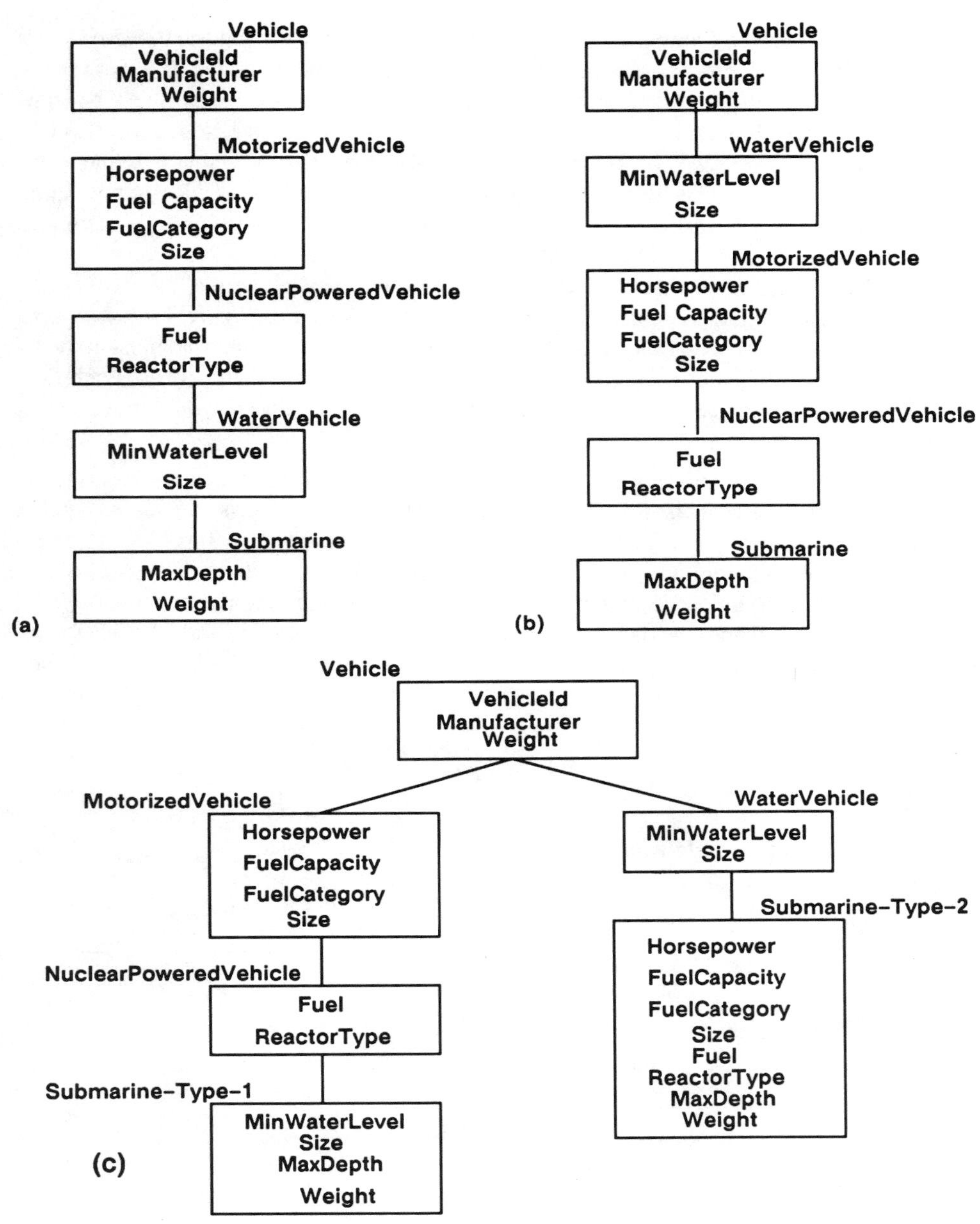

Figure 2.3
Alternative Class Hierarchies

conventional programming languages and conventional database systems, for example, between a PL/1 program and IBM's SQL/DS relational database system. Since object-oriented programmers or designers already model their application artifacts in the object-oriented paradigm, mapping them to objects supported in an object-oriented database system should not introduce a large measure of what has been labeled as 'impedance mismatch.'

The fact that the class hierarchy captures the IS-A relationship between a class and its superclass raises an issue regarding whether an instance of a class also belongs to the superclass of the class. A strong interpretation of the IS-A relationship leads to the view that indeed it does; while a weak interpretation leads to the contrary conclusion. The strong interpretation is that because of the IS-A relationship between a class and its superclass, an instance of a class also belongs to the superclass (and the superclass of that superclass, and so on, all the way up the class hierarchy); for example, in Figure 2.2, an instance of the class WaterVehicle is semantically an instance of the class Vehicle; after all, a water vehicle is a (IS-A) vehicle. This view introduces some serious difficulties with the deletion of instances. Even if an instance of a class is deleted, it must continue to exist as an instance of the superclass of the class. In fact, the instance cannot physically be deleted, until it percolates all the way to the root of the class hierarchy. The percolation of a deleted instance of a class to the superclasses of the class also means that the class identifier embedded in the instance must be changed to refer to the superclass. Further, since the superclass has fewer attributes than its subclass, the values of the attributes in the instance which are not defined for the superclass must be screened. Of course, if the class of the instance has more than one superclass, the instance needs to be replicated, one for each superclass.

The weak interpretation of the IS-A relationship differs from the strong interpretation only in the semantics for the deletion of instances. A query against a class may still be evaluated against all instances of the class hierarchy rooted at the class, rather than instances of just that class. However, for the purposes of deletion, an instance is physically deleted when it is deleted from the class. CLOS and ORION both take this view.

The concept of a class hierarchy and inheritance of attributes and methods along the class hierarchy is what distinguishes object-oriented programming from programming with abstract data types. The fact that a subclass may be specialized from an existing class can simplify the specification of the subclass, since the creator of a subclass can simply re-use the specification of the existing class. Of course, the specification of a class includes both the attributes (and any integrity constraints on them) and the methods which can operate on the class and the objects that belong to the class.

A class inherits methods from its superclasses. The inherited methods may be modifed even if their names are retained. When a message is sent to an object, the class of the object is looked up to determine a corresponding method. If the method is not associated with the class, the superclasses of the class are searched in a predefined order to locate the method; once the method is found, the program associated with it is executed. The use of a single name for more than one program is known as *overloading*.

The concept of inheritance presents some problems, including name conflicts, scope of inheritance, and violation of encapsulation. We will discuss the issues of name conflicts and scope of inheritance further in Chapter 5. Briefly, there are two types of name conflict: between a class and its superclass, and between superclasses of a class. In systems which support single-inheritance, only the first type of conflict occurs. If the name of an attribute or a method conflicts between a class and its superclass, the name used in the class takes precedence; that is, the attribute or method of the superclass is not inherited. In the case of a conflict between attributes or methods of superclasses, the usual solution is to select one superclass from which to inherit the attributes or methods on the basis of a precedence ordering. Most systems require the superclass-precedence ordering to be specified in each class; some systems determine the precedence ordering at run time. For example, the class Submarine in Figure 2.2 has to inherit the attribute Size either from the superclass WaterVehicle (which defines Size) or from NuclearPoweredVehicle (which inherits Size from its superclass MotorizedVehicle). If in the definition of the class Submarine, NuclearPoweredVehicle was specified as the first superclass, Size will be inherited from NuclearPoweredVehicle.

A second problem with inheritance is the scope of inheritance. One issue is whether to require full inheritance or allow selective inheritance. *Full inheritance* means that a subclass inherits all attributes and methods from all of its superclasses, except those attributes and methods involved in name conflicts. *Selective inheritance* allows a subclass not to inherit some of the attributes and methods from the superclasses. Although selective inheritance is sometimes convenient, almost all systems have adopted full inheritance; selective inheritance makes it difficult for both the user and the system to keep track of inheritance. Another issue is the inheritance of attributes when they have the same name but different specifications, in particular the domain specifications. A reasonable approach in this situation is to inherit the attribute with the most specific specification, provided that the domains of the attributes are compatible, that is, if they are all on one superclass chain. For example, in Figure 2.2, let us assume that the domain of the attribute Size in the class MotorizedVehicle is the class RealNumber, while the domain of Size in the class WaterVehicle is Integer. The class Integer is a subclass of RealNumber; that is, the attribute Size in WaterVehicle is more specific than that in MotorizedVehicle. Then the class Submarine will inherit the attribute Size from the superclass WaterVehicle.

A third problem with inheritance is the violation of the encapsulation principle. If one may directly access the attributes of a class from a subclass, such operations as the renaming or dropping of an attribute may invalidate the methods defined in the subclass which reference the attribute. One proposed solution is to restrict access to the attributes of a class through methods defined for them.

2.2 Semantic Extensions to the Core Model

The core model includes such semantic modeling concepts as instance-of, aggregation, and generalization concepts; and it is further augmented with the powerful concept of inheritance. The model is powerful enough to satisfy the data-modeling requirements of many types of applications. However, there are a number of important semantic modeling concepts which are essential for many types of applications but which the core model does not directly capture. Two of the most important of such modeling concepts are composite objects and versions. A composite object is a heterogeneous set of objects which form a part hierarchy; the part-of relationship is superimposed on the aggregation relationship between an object and other objects it references. A versioned object is a set of objects which are versions of the same conceptual object; a versioned object consists of a hierarchy of objects which captures the version-of relationship between an object and another object derived from the object.

The motivation for extending the core model with these additional modeling concepts is simply to provide a data model which is to be directly implemented in a database system. If these modeling concepts are not included in the data model directly supported by a database system, operations embedding the concepts must be performed in the applications, including such operations as the retrieval of an entire composite object from the database, finding the most recent version of a versioned object, deleting all components of an object if the object is deleted, and so on. Direct support of the extended model off-loads the implementation of operations embedding the data model from the applications. The database system can automatically enforce any integrity constraints associated with the operations and may also achieve higher performance for the operations.

In this section, we will outline the semantics of composite objects and versions; we defer more detailed discussions to Chapter 12. Since ORION is the only object-oriented database system which captures both these concepts in its data model, we will use the semantics of composite objects and versions as developed in the context of the ORION data model.

2.2.1 Composite Objects

As we have seen, in object-oriented systems, an object has a set of attributes, and the value of an attribute is another object which is an instance of the domain of the attribute. If the domain of an attribute is a primitive class (integer, string) , the value stored for the attribute is an instance or a set of instances of the domain. If the domain of an attribute is a non-primitive class, the value stored for the attribute is the object identifier(s) of the instance(s) of the domain. In this case, we say that an object *references* other objects, namely, the instances of the non-primitive domains of its attributes. The object identifiers of the instances of the non-primitive domains of its attributes are called *references* to those instances.

Since an object reference often implies the part-of (or consists-of) relationship between an object and another object which references it, it is often useful to make explicit the part-of relationship between a pair of objects. We will distinguish two types of reference: weak and composite. A *weak reference* is the object reference under the core model, that is, without the part-of semantics. A *composite reference* is a weak reference augmented with the part-of relationship. The semantics of a composite reference is further refined on the basis of whether an object is a part of only one object or more than one object. This consideration leads to two types of composite reference: exclusive and shared. An *exclusive composite reference* from an object X to another object Y means that Y is a part of only X; while a *shared composite reference* from X to Y means that Y is a part of X and possibly other objects.

We may further refine the semantics of a composite reference, either exclusive or shared, on the basis of whether the existence of an object depends on the existence of its parent object; that is, a composite reference may be dependent or independent. A *dependent composite reference* from X to Y means that the existence of Y depends on the existence of X; while an independent composite reference does not carry this additional semantics. The deletion of an object will trigger recursive deletion of all objects referenced by the object through dependent composite references (both exclusive and shared).

The above discussions lead us to four types of composite reference, as summarized below.

(1) exclusive dependent composite reference

(2) exclusive independent composite reference

(3) shared dependent composite reference

(4) shared independent composite reference

A composite object is in general a heterogeneous collection of objects, that is, the component objects from a number of different classes. The classes to which the component objects in a composite object belong are organized in a hierarchy called a *composite-attribute hierarchy*; each class in the hierarchy is called a *component class*. A composite-attribute hierarchy is merely a subset of a class-composition hierarchy. Further, a composite object is a nested instance of the schema represented by the composite-attribute hierarchy. If an attribute has a composite reference, the attribute is called a *composite attribute*. Figure 2.4 is an example composite-attribute hierarchy. The composite-attribute hierarchy rooted at the class Vehicle is a subhierarchy of the class-composition hierarchy rooted at Vehicle. In the figure, composite attributes are linked to their domains through thick lines, while thin lines are used to link non-composite attributes with their domains.

2.2.2 Versions

Version control is one of the most important data-modeling requirements in next-generation database applications. After the initial creation of an object, new versions of the object are derived from it, and new versions can in turn be derived from them, and so on. Versions give rise to (at least) two new types of relationship. One

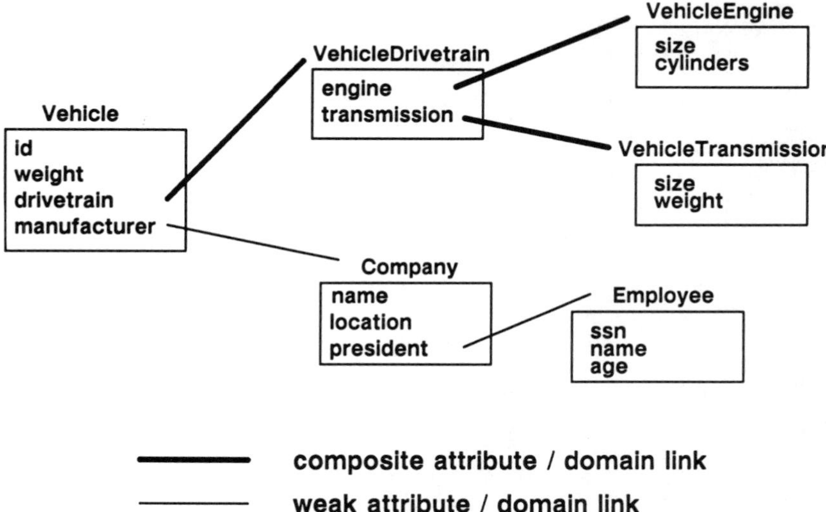

Figure 2.4
Composite Class Hierarchy

is the derived-from relationship between a new version of an object and an old version of the object from which the new version was derived. Another is the version-of relationship between each version of an object and an abstract object that represents the object. Figure 2.5 illustrates these relationships for an Engine object.

In general, versions of an object form a directed graph. Any number of new versions may be derived from any version at any time, and a version may be derived from more than one older versions. However, most proposed models of versions restrict the graph to a hierarchy, called a version hierarchy. The version graph, such as that shown in Figure 2.5, represents the history of evolution of a versioned object. The history information represented in a version graph is captured logically in the abstract object of a versioned object.

As we will show in Chapter 12, version support incurs storage and processing overhead, and it is desirable to distinguish *versionable* and *non-versionable* objects. Versionable objects are instances of a class which is declared to be versionable.

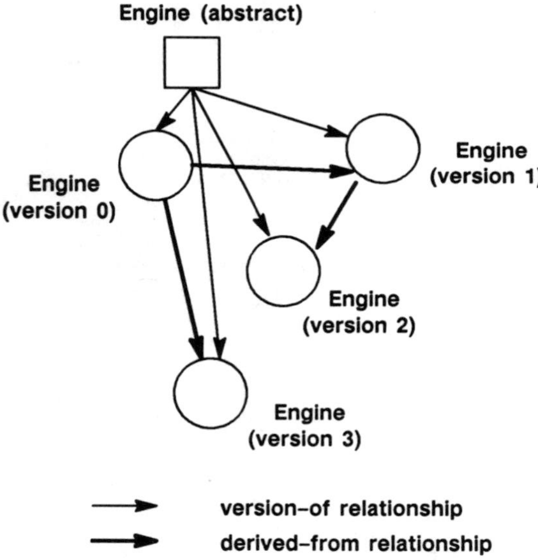

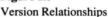

Figure 2.5
Version Relationships

Recommended Readings

The reader may gain a deeper understanding of the core object-oriented model from detailed descriptions of Smalltalk-80 [GOLD83], CLOS [MOON89], C++ [STRO86], and Objective C [COX84]. [STEF86] presents a good discussion of the similarities and differences in a number of object-oriented models. [STEI89] and [TOML89] compare classes and prototypes, and inheritance and delegation, as methodologies for organizing objects and sharing properties among objects, respectively. [KATZ86] and [CHOU86] provide models of versions. The semantics of composite objects are defined in [KIM88b] and [KIM89d]. The surveys of semantic data models in [HULL87] and [PECK88] may be a good starting point for those readers interested in understanding the similarities and differences between object-oriented data models and semantic data models.

3 Basic Interface

The designers of object-oriented database systems have adopted one of two distinct approaches to the design of the user interfaces to their systems. One is the traditional database approach of defining a database language to be embedded in host programming languages. The problem with this approach is that, as has been the case with conventional systems, the application programmers have to learn and use two different languages. Further, the application programmers have to negotiate the differences in the data models and data structures allowed in the two languages.

Another approach is to extend object-oriented programming languages with database-related constructs. A major advantage of this approach is that the application programmers only need to learn new constructs of the same language, rather than an entirely new language. Many of the currently operational object-oriented database systems have adopted this approach, including ORION (extending Common LISP), ZEITGEIST (extending Flavors) at Texas Instruments, GemStone from Servio Logic (extending Smalltalk), and AllTalk (also extending SmallTalk) at Eastman Kodak, among others. The database interface adopted in STATICE from Symbolics is based on the DAPLEX functional data model; however, the STATICE interface has been integrated into the programming language LISP.

A programmatic interface to an object-oriented database must include, as is the case for conventional databases, a data-definition sublanguage, a query and data manipulation sublanguage, and a data control sublanguage. These sublanguages must be designed to fully reflect the flexibilities and constraints inherent in the object-oriented data model. Further, in order to achieve seamless integration of an object-oriented programming language and a database language, it is necessary to design these sublanguages in a way which is consistent with the message-passing paradigm of object-oriented systems. In this chapter, we will provide a message-passing syntax for a basic subset of these sublanguages. A description of the query language is deferred to Chapter 7, and syntactical extensions necessary for composite objects and versions are provided in Chapter 12. The purpose of this brief chapter is to make concrete the discussion of the object-oriented data model in Chapter 2, and also to bring out the fact that an object-oriented data model can be cast into a data language which is comparable to relational data languages.

3.1 Message Passing

All operations on an object are performed by using the message interface of the object which is implemented with a method. A message can be sent to an object (a receiver) by using the following syntax.

(Selector Receiver [Arg1 Arg2 Arg3 ...])

Selector is the name of the message, and Receiver is the object to which the message is to be sent. The optional arguments, Arg1, Arg2, etc., are objects or can be evaluated to objects. Since a message returns an object, an argument may itself be a message. Similarly, the Receiver of a message may also be the result of some other message.

For example, to obtain the weight of an airplane object, the following message may be sent.

(Weight Airplane-Object),

where Weight is the attribute Weight of the class Airplane, and Airplane-Object is the identifier of the airplane object.

3.2 DDL

The DDL must allow the specification of the schema for an object-oriented database. The semantics that the DDL must support are the core object-oriented concepts discussed in Chapter 2.

A new class may be defined with the following message.

(**make-class** Classname [**:superclasses** ListofSuperclasses]
[**:attributes** ListofAttributes]
[**:methods** ListofMethodSpecs])

Classname is the name of the new class. Each of the keyword arguments following the Classname is optional. The ListofSuperclasses associated with the **:superclasses** keyword is a list of the superclasses of the new class (this simple construct captures the class-hierarchy concept). The ListofAttributes associated with the **:attribute** keyword is a list of attribute specifications (this is the familiar syntax for the definition of relations in relational databases). An attribute specification is a list consisting of an attribute name and keywords with associated values, as follows:

```
(AttributeName      [:domain  DomainSpec]
                    [:inherit-from  Superclass])
```

A DomainSpec specifies the type(s) of an attribute. The keyword **:inherit-from** is used to control inheritance. If the keyword is not provided, the attribute is a new attribute for the class being defined. If the keyword is provided, the Superclass specified is the name of the superclass from which the attribute will be inherited; if the Superclass is not given, the attribute is inherited from the first superclass in the ListofSuperclasses.

The ListofMethodSpecs associated with the **:methods** keyword is a list of pairs (MethodName Superclass). The MethodName is the name of a method to be inherited from the Superclass. If Superclass is not specified, the method is a new method for the class being defined.

The following example shows how the class Airplane may be defined.

```
(make-class  Airplane
     :superclasses (MotorizedVehicle  AirborneVehicle)
     :attributes ( (Capacity
                         :domain integer
                   (Weight
                         :inherit-from nil))
                   (Manufacturer
                         :domain AirplaneCompany
                         :inherit-from AirborneVehicle)
     :methods      ((PresentCoordinates  AirborneVehicle)))
```

3.3 DML

The DML must allow the creation, update, and deletion of individual instances of a class by sending an appropriate message to the class or the instance involved.

The syntax for object manipulation, that is for the creation, query, delete, and update, is very similar to that for relational database manipulation, although query expression is significantly different from that for relational databases. An instance can be created by sending a **make** message to the class to which the instance will belong.

```
(make Classname      :Attribute1  value1
                     ...
                     :AttributeN  valueN)
```

The following illustrates the **make** message to create an airplane object, using the airplane class object created with the **make-class** message in the previous example.

```
(make Airplane :Weight  1000
               :Manufacturer (make Company :Name Boeing))
```

Incidentally, the result of the second **make** is a new object which represents the company Boeing, and it is made the value of the attribute Manufacturer of the new instance of Airplane.

To select instances of a class that satisfy a given query expression, we may use a **select** message. A *set object* (possibly an empty set) containing these instances is returned.

```
(select    Class    QueryExpression)
```

where QueryExpression is a Boolean expression of predicates. We will present the syntax for the query expression in Chapter 7.

To delete all instances of a class that satisfy a given query expression, a **delete** message may be used.

```
(delete    Class    QueryExpression)
```

To delete a specific object, a **delete-object** message is used.

```
(delete-object  Object)
```

where Object is the object identifier.

Similarly, a **change** message may be used to replace the value of an attribute of all instances of a class that satisfy a given Boolean expression.

```
(change    Class    [QueryExpression]    AttributeName    NewValue)
```

3.4 DCL

The DCL must allow the specification of transactions, semantic integrity control, authorization, and management of access methods. The facilities for specifying transactions (transaction abort, and commit) are the same as those in conventional database systems (assuming that nested transactions or long-duration transactions are not supported). Semantic integrity constraints may be specified in methods associated with classes.

Recommended Readings

The designs of programmatic interfaces for object-oriented database systems exhibit the influence of object-oriented programming languages, notably CLU [LISK81]. Further, one common goal between object-oriented database systems and persistent programming languages is the removal of the distinction between non-persistent (memory-resident) objects and persistent (disk-resident) objects. Integration of a programming language and a database system is the subject of Chapter 13. A good reference on persistent programming is [ATKI87].

4 Relationships with Non-Object-Oriented Databases

There has been some degree of misunderstanding about object-oriented databases. There are two reasons for this. One is the absence of a standard object-oriented data model, and, even before that, a standard object-oriented programming language. Another is the existence of some of the fundamental object-oriented concepts in non-object-oriented databases. In this chapter, we will examine these sources of misunderstanding about object-oriented databases.

4.1 Conceptual Overlaps

4.1.1 Design Databases

As we have seen in Chapter 1, attempts to apply the relational database technology to computer-aided design, engineering, software engineering, and manufacturing applications (CAD, CAE, CASE, and CAM) and compound documents revealed various limitations of the data model and transaction model supported in conventional database systems. The relational model is not rich enough to admit the nested construction of complex designs or to properly capture the semantics of versions and representations (views) of a design. To allow the modeling of the nested construction of a complex design, a number of researchers proposed modifications to the relational model. These proposals include complex objects or nested relations (which formalizes the notion of complex objects). To capture the semantics of versions and representations of a design, a number of researchers have proposed models of design objects. Although they may be structurally similar to complex objects, versions or representations of a design object have very different semantics; for example, the versions of a design object are related through the version-of relationships and specific policies may be imposed on them with respect to their creation, update, and deletion. A complex object simply represents the nested composition of a complex artifact; the components of a complex object are related through the consists-of relationships.

Sometimes complex objects or design objects have been mistaken for objects from object-oriented programming languages. However, CAD/CAE/CASE/CAM systems and applications require databases and object-oriented concepts for very different purposes. The need for databases is largely to off-load the chore of managing complex interrelationships among many design components (version management, configuration management, and change notification). The object-oriented approach facilitates the development and maintenance of the CAD/CAE/CASE/CAM system software; and it is a rather natural paradigm for the end users (designers and engineers) to interact with the system. What these systems need is database support for objects which carry the object semantics found in object-oriented programming languages. On one hand, complex objects represent at best one aspect of an object-oriented data model. On the other hand, core object-oriented concepts are not by themselves sufficient for modeling all the relationships among design objects, either.

4.1.2 Hierarchical and Network Databases

There are at least two types of similarities between object-oriented and hierarchical (and network) databases. One important similarity is the nested structure of objects in object-oriented databases, and the nested structure of records in hierarchical databases. Although both databases admit objects (records) which refer to other objects (records) for the values of their attributes, there is an important difference. The nested object schema in object-oriented databases contains cycles, as we showed in Chapter 2; although hierarchical databases can admit cycles, they require artificial record types to be introduced in the schema.

Another similarity is between the object identifiers in object-oriented databases and the record pointers in hierarchical databases. However, an object identifier is a logical pointer and is never re-used, and as such it may be used for enforcing referential integrity. A record pointer is a physical pointer and is reused.

However, there are major differences that contrast object-oriented databases from hierarchical (and network) databases. Object-oriented databases support such concepts as a class hierarchy, inheritance, and methods; hierarchical (and network) databases obviously do not include these concepts.

4.1.3 Extensible Databases

Extensible databases share one thing with object-oriented databases, namely, extensibility. The goal of research into extensible database systems is to find approaches for building a database system such that the system may be easily extended to accommodate new functionality, or for building a database system by assembling components from a library of database-system building blocks. The notion of inheritance is what makes systems implemented in an object-oriented style (i.e., which make use of the data encapsulation and inheritance principles) rather extensible. If a database system is implemented in an object-oriented style or in an object-oriented programming language, then it tends to make it easier to add new database functionality (i.e., more extensible) than if it is implemented in conventional programming style. However, extensibility of a database system is merely a characteristic of the architecture of a database system, rather than a requirement for an object-oriented database system. Even if an object-oriented database system is not implemented in an object-oriented style, it will still be easy for the user to add new user-defined classes and data types to the system. To our knowledge, no object-oriented database systems operational today have been implemented entirely in object-oriented programming languages. Some systems have implemented some of their components in an object-oriented style or object-oriented programming language. For example, the multimedia data management subsystem of ORION has been implemented by making direct use of the message passing and class hierarchy (and inheritance) concepts to make it easy to add new types of multimedia data and devices to the system.

4.1.4 Semantic Databases

Semantic data models, such as the Entity-Relationship model, the DAPLEX functional model, and the Semantic Data Model, attempt to capture explicitly a rich set of semantic relationships among real-world entities. The generalization / specialization relationship between a superclass and its subclass, the aggregation relationship between a class and its attributes, and the instance-of relationship between an instance and its class (and the superclass of the class) are all included in semantic data models.

In terms of modeling power, we view a core object-oriented data model largely as a subset of a semantic data model; of course, semantic data models lack methods. For reasons of performance and ease of use, the core object-oriented model needs to be extended to include additional semantic modeling concepts for specific classes of applications. The most relevant of such concepts include versions and composite objects. These modeling concepts allow the user to deal with a collection of related objects as a single unit. For example, a composite object is a collection of objects related by the part-of relationship; and it may be used as a unit of access in a query and a unit of integrity.

4.1.5 Relational Databases

To the best of our knowledge, nobody mistakes a relational database for an object-oriented database. There are clear differences. An object-oriented data model has the notions of a class hierarchy, a class-composition hierarchy (for nested objects), and methods—none of which is a part of the normalized relational model. There are efforts to extend the relational model or language with these fundamental object-oriented concepts. POSTGRES is the best-known example of these efforts.

There have been a number of criticisms, some valid and some invalid, of object-oriented databases, relative to relational databases. Let us examine some of these points. The navigational model of computation and object access used in object-oriented applications apparently has given rise to the criticism that object-oriented databases represent a throwback to the days of hierarchical and network databases. This criticism focuses on only one aspect of object-oriented systems. One has to keep in mind that navigational access is used primarily to selectively traverse a set of complex nested objects (e.g., a constructive solid geometry tree), and that there is more to an object-oriented data model than just the nesting of an object. Further, there are important applications from computer-aided design and artificial intelligence which absolutely must navigate through a large database. For example, navigation and object identifiers make it possible to traverse a tree structure often used in such applications without resorting to value-based retrieval of objects (records) pointed to by a given object (record). Finally, as we will see in Chapters 6 and 7, an object-oriented equivalent of the relational query capability may be added to object-oriented database systems to complement the traditional navigational access. In fact, many of the currently operational object-oriented database systems either already support query languages or are in the process of implementing them.

Another criticism about object-oriented databases is that object-oriented data models proposed thus far are not based on an elegant mathematical theory. In contrast, the relational calculus and relational algebra provided theoretical underpinnings for queries in relational databases. However, we must realize that the relational calculus and relational algebra had nothing to do with various other aspects of database technology, including transaction management, authorization, concurrency control, recovery, automatic query optimization and processing, and semantic integrity control. Then a necessary element of a theoretical foundation for object-oriented databases comparable to that for relational databases is simply a formal model of queries. A number of researchers are currently attempting to define a query model and an 'object-oriented algebra' (corresponding to the relational algebra). Further, as observed above, many object-oriented database systems are starting to support query languages.

Object-oriented databases are sometimes criticized for the apparent complexity of inheritance. This is not a particularly useful criticism, if we recognize that one major objective of database systems is to directly support the data modeling requirements of their intended applications. In particular, one major objective of object-oriented database systems is to directly support object-oriented concepts, which are the data modeling requirements of object-oriented applications.

4.2 Lack of a Standard

The programming language, knowledge representation, and database disciplines, and even any one of them by itself, presently do not agree on a single standard set of semantics for object-oriented concepts. However, we expect that only a limited number of object-oriented data models will be widely accepted in the near future; in fact, efforts to agree on a standard object-oriented data model are already underway. Although there is indeed no consensus about *precisely* what object-oriented means, if one examines existing object-oriented programming languages, knowledge representation languages, and semantic data models, one can identify a set of core object-oriented concepts, as we described in Chapter 2. The trends today indicate that soon each discipline will adopt a small number of de facto standards, based largely on the commercial success of some of the programming languages, knowledge representation languages, and database systems. Recently, Common LISP Object System (CLOS) has been proposed as a standard object-oriented extension to Common LISP. Further, Objective C and C++ have become popular; and it appears that the popularity of C++ will significantly increase, now that AT&T has announced that it will market and support C++, and efficient compilers are becoming available, even in the public domain. It appears that the LISP community will adopt CLOS, and non-LISP community will adopt C++ in the near future. The knowledge representation languages may be standardized around such commercially successful products as KEE. A number of object-oriented database systems have become commercially available recently, including Ontos from Ontologic, GemStone from Servio-Logic, and Statice from Symbolics; several research prototypes are also being readied for entry into the marketplace, including IRIS from Hewlett-Packard, ZEITGEIST from Texas Instruments, O2 from Altair, and ORION from MCC. After a period of shakeout in the database marketplace, the data models supported in the survivors' products may form the basis for a future standard.

Recommended Readings

The interested reader will find [HASK82, IEEE82, IEEE84, ACM83, BATO85, KATZ86] good starting points for literature search on design databases; these bring out the data model and features requirements of computer-aided design systems. [LORI83, KIM87] focus on the implementation of complex objects. Theoretical foundations and implementation issues of nested relational databases are provided in [MAKI77, JAES82, ABIT84, DADA86, THOM86, DESH88, IEEE88].

[LIND87, CARE86, BATO88] represent the current approaches to building extensible database systems.

There is an extensive literature on semantic data models. [SMIT77] provides an in-depth discussion of the aggregation and generalization concepts. [CODD79] consolidates many of the semantic data modeling concepts that the original relational model does not capture. Some of the better-known semantic data models include E/R [CHEN76], SDM [HAMM81], and DAPLEX [SHIP81].

The reader interested in object-oriented programming languages which are expected to lead the standardization efforts should read [GOLD82] on Smalltalk-80, [MOON89] for an overview of CLOS, [STRO86] for a detailed description of C++, and [COX84] for Objective C.

5 Schema Modification

As we discussed in Chapter 1, one of the major advantages of an object-oriented approach to designing and implementing software systems is that the notions of inheritance and specialization allow existing systems to be easily extended. The semantics of inheritance and specialization defined in most object-oriented languages and systems are fairly simple and limited largely to single-user environments. In an integrated database environment where many users share a single database, different users often need to view the database schema differently; of course, the same user may have to view the schema differently at different times. This means that the users need to modify the database schema; further, it is highly desirable to be able to dynamically modify the schema, that is to modify the schema without forcing a system shutdown or incurring significant performance penalty. The ability to dynamically modify the schema is important during the exploratory phase in development environments; it is relatively less important in production environments where performance, rather than flexibility, is everything.

There are two dimensions to the dynamic modification of the schema of an integrated database: single-schema modification and schema versioning. *Single-schema modification* is the direct modification of a single logical schema. *Schema versioning* is the versioning of a single logical schema; it makes different views of the database visible to the users under different versions of schema. Any version of schema may be dynamically modified without causing the creation of a new version of schema; that is, schema evolution may be superimposed on schema versioning.

There are two issues in single-schema modification. One is to define a taxonomy and a model of changes to the schema; the taxonomy defines a set of meaningful schema changes, and the model provides a basis for specifying the semantics of schema changes. Another is the implementation of the schema changes that will not incur significant performance penalty. In this chapter, we will discuss these issues in some detail.

The problems of single-schema modification and schema versioning are part of a larger problem of logical database design. Logical database design is concerned with determining an optimal set of classes and their attributes and methods that will capture the semantics of the applications of a particular enterprise. At this time, adequate tools are not available that can aid the users with the logical design of an object-oriented database. The model of single-schema modification for an object-oriented database established in the ORION system is an important first step towards the development of tools for the logical design of an object-oriented database.

5.1 Taxonomy

The taxonomy of schema changes is closely tied to the data model. In normalized relational databases, because of the independence of relations, only a few types of schema change make sense, including adding a new relation to the database, dropping a relation from the database, adding a new column to an existing relation, and dropping a column from a relation. Further, a change to a relation does not impact other relations or their tuples.

There are two types of change to the schema of an object-oriented database. One is to the definition of a class. This includes changes to the attributes and methods defined for a class, such as changing the name or domain of an attribute, adding or dropping an attribute or a method. Another type of change is to the class-hierarchy structure. This includes adding or dropping a class, and changing the superclass / subclass relationship between a pair of classes.

Because of inheritance along the class hierarchy, a change to a class in general does impact other classes and their instances, as well as its own instances. For example, if an attribute is dropped from a class, the values of the attribute in all existing instances of the class must logically be dropped; and the attribute must also be dropped from all direct and indirect subclasses of the class which had inherited it, and of course the values of the attribute must also be dropped from the instances of the subclasses. Further, if a class is dropped, all its instances must be dropped; and all direct and indirect subclasses of the class lose all attributes of the class that they had inherited, and the values of these attributes in existing instances of these classes are dropped; and the direct subclasses of the class are made the direct subclasses of the direct superclasses of the class.

A change to a class in general logically requires database updates, that is, updates to the instances of the class and instances of the subclasses of the class. For many of the schema changes that logically require database updates, it is possible to avoid them indefinitely, in theory. However, for some of the schema changes, it is either impossible or impractical to avoid database updates. For example, if an attribute is dropped from a class, it is not necessary to immediately delete the values of the attribute in all existing instances of the class. It is sufficient to screen the value of the dropped attribute from any of the existing instances of the class before presenting the instance to the application (user). However, if a class is partitioned into two or more classes, the instances of the class must be reorganized to reflect their membership in new classes.

On the basis of the ORION experiences, for any schema change that does not require existing instances to change their classes, it is simple and practical to avoid database updates. We will call this type of schema change a *soft change*. However, for any schema change that forces existing instances to change their classes, which we will call a *hard change*, it is very difficult or impractical to avoid database updates. A hard change introduces two problems that a soft change does not present. One is of course that it forces potentially expensive database updates. Another is that, if the object identifier includes its class identifier, all existing references to the instances that migrated to new classes become invalid.

The ORION, GemStone, and Encore projects contributed to the understanding of the semantics and implementation of schema changes in object-oriented databases. The model of schema modification developed and implemented in ORION is by far the most comprehensive, and we will use it as the basis of discussion in this chapter.

The following is a simplified version of a taxonomy of schema changes. It is by no means comprehensive; however, it is adequate for the purposes of illustrating the problems of defining the semantics and implementation of schema changes. We defer discussions of schema changes involving composite objects and versions to Chapter 12.

1 Changes to the contents of a class

  1.1 Changes to an attribute

    1.1.1 add a new attribute to a class
    1.1.2 drop an existing attribute from a class
    1.1.3 change the name of an attribute of a class
    1.1.4 change the domain of an attribute of a class
    1.1.5 change the default value of an attribute

  1.2 Changes to a method

    1.2.1 add a new method to a class
    1.2.2 drop an existing method from a class
    1.2.3 change the name of a method of a class
    1.2.4 change the code of a method in a class

  1.3 change the name of a class

2 Changes to the superclass/subclass relationship

2.1 make a class S a superclass of a class C

2.2 remove a class S from the superclass list of a class C

2.3 change the order of superclasses of a class C

2.4 add a new class

2.5 drop an existing class

2.6 create a new class C as a generalized superclass of n existing classes

2.7 partition a class C into n new classes

2.8 coalesce n classes into one new class

Of the schema changes included in the above taxonomy, all except (2.7) and (2.8) are soft changes. ORION currently supports all soft changes, except (2.6).

A taxonomy of schema changes depends obviously on the underlying data model. The ORION data model supports multiple inheritance. This is reflected explicitly in schema changes (2.1), (2.2), and (2.3); and implicitly, as we will show, in the semantics of all schema changes. The GemStone data model supports single inheritance. A taxonomy of schema changes for a data model that supports single inheritance does not include schema changes (2.1), (2.2), (2.3), and (2.6). Multiple inheritance does complicate somewhat the semantics of some of the other schema changes; however, it does not affect the semantics of the schema changes (1.1.4), (1.1.5), (1.2.4), and (1.3).

5.2 Model

At this time, ORION, GemStone, and IRIS support single-schema modification. The model of schema modification developed for ORION is the first, and also most comprehensive. As such, in this section we will present the model of single-schema modification developed for ORION, and then, using the model, the semantics of single-schema modification implemented in ORION.

The model consists of a set of *invariants*, and a set of *rules*. The set of invariants provide the basis for the specification of the semantics of schema changes; that is, any schema change must preserve all invariants. However, for some schema changes, the schema invariants can be preserved in more than one way. The rules are used by the system to select one most meaningful way in which to preserve the invariants.

We note that, under a data model that is different from the ORION data model, a different set of invariants and rules may make sense. Further, even under the ORION data model, sometimes the distinction between a rule and an invariant is somewhat arbitrary. However, the approach of distinguishing a set of invariants and a set of rules is a worthwhile methodology for specifying the semantics of schema changes. We leave it as an exercise to the reader to derive an appropriate set of invariants and rules for a data model of the reader's choice.

5.2.1 Invariants of Schema Modification

The ORION model of schema modification includes four invariants that we outline below.

- **Class-Hierarchy Invariant.** The class hierarchy is a *rooted* and *connected directed acyclic graph (DAG).* The root of the DAG is the system-defined class, named CLASS.
- **Name Invariant.** All classes have unique names, and all attributes and methods defined within a class have unique names.
- **Origin Invariant.** All attributes, and methods, of a class have distinct origin.
- **Full-Inheritance Invariant.** A class inherits all attributes and methods from each of its superclasses, unless full inheritance violates the name and origin invariants.

Let us further examine these invariants. The class-hierarchy invariant means that the entire database schema consist of a single class hierarchy; that is, every class has a position in the class hierarchy, and every class is reachable from the class CLASS.

The name invariant says that different classes may have attributes or methods that have the same name. The origin invariant says that, if a class has more than one superclass with attributes or methods by the same name, the class may inherit only one such attribute or method. For example, in Figure 5.1, the classes WaterVehicle and NuclearPoweredVehicle both have the attribute Weight. The origin of the Weight attribute for both classes is the attribute Weight of the class Vehicle. Therefore, the class Submarine can inherit the attribute from only one of the superclasses.

The full-inheritance invariant basically further augments the origin invariant by saying that, if two attributes or methods have distinct origins but the same name in two different superclasses, one or both may be inherited. In case both are inherited, one of them must be renamed, so as not to violate the name invariant. For example, in Figure 5.1, the class Submarine may inherit the attribute Size from either or both of the classes MotorizedVehicle and WaterVehicle; if the attribute is inherited from both superclasses, one of them has to be renamed.

It is sometimes convenient if full-inheritance invariant is not enforced, that is, if partial inheritance is legal; this will make it easy to block unwanted attributes and methods

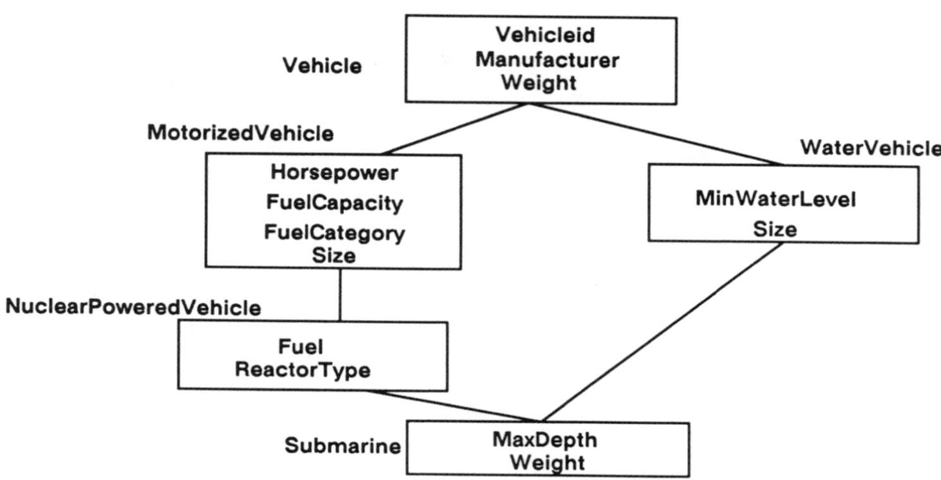

Figure 5.1
Example Class Hierarchy

from inheritance without having to redefine them. We leave it as an exercise to the reader to study the consequences of admitting partial inheritance on the semantics of schema changes.

The properties of an attribute includes its name, domain, and default value. The properties of an attribute, once defined or inherited into a class, can be modified. Further, the properties of a method belonging to a class may be modified by changing its name or code. The full-inheritance invariant implies that any changes in the properties of an attribute or a method propagate to all classes that had inherited the attribute or method.

5.2.2 Rules for Single-Schema Modification

Let us consider a name conflict among attributes to be inherited from superclasses. The full-inheritance invariant requires that at least one of the attributes be inherited; but it does not say which. This is an example of a schema change for which there is more than one way to preserve the schema invariants. For such schema changes, rules are needed to allow the system to select one way to preserve the invariants. The ORION schema model classifies these rules into four categories: conflict-resolution rules, inheritance rules, domain rules, and class-hierarchy rules.

Conflict-Resolution Rules

The following three rules are used whenever there is a name or origin conflict. They ensure that the name and origin invariants are satisfied in a deterministic way.

Rule 1: If the name of an attribute or method locally defined for a class conflicts with that of an inherited attribute or method, the locally defined attribute or method is selected. Further, if a new attribute or method locally defined for a class conflicts with an attribute or method already defined for the class, the new attribute or method is rejected.

Rule 2: If two or more superclasses of a class have an attribute or method with the same name but distinct origins, the attribute or method of the first superclass among conflicting superclasses is selected. (Each class has associated with it a list of superclasses; and the first superclass is the one that appears first in the list.)

Rule 3: If two or more superclasses of a class have attributes with the same origin, the class inherits the attribute with the most specialized domain. However, if the domains are the same, or if one domain is not a superclass of the other, the attribute is inherited from the first superclass among conflicting superclasses.

For example, in Figure 5.1, if the domain of Manufacturer of NuclearPoweredVehicle is Company, and the domain of Manufacturer of WaterVehicle is WaterVehicleCompany which is a subclass of Company, the class Submarine inherits the Manufacturer attribute from the class WaterVehicle.

Inheritance Rules

Properties of an inherited attribute or method may be redefined in a subclass. The following three rules refine the full-inheritance invariant.

Rule 4: Any change in the properties of an attribute or method in a class C is propagated recursively to each subclass S of C in which these properties have not been redefined.

For example, if the default value of the attribute Weight of the class Vehicle is changed to 2000, the change is reflected in all subclasses of Vehicle. However, if the default value of Weight in the class MotorizedVehicle (which is a subclass of Vehicle) had been changed to 1000, the change will not replace the default value in the class MotorizedVehicle and any of its subclasses.

The propagation of a name change in an attribute or a method, or a newly added attribute or method in a class may introduce a new name conflict in the subclasses. The following rule is used to reject such a change in any subclass (and all its subclasses) in which the change will give rise to a new name conflict.

Rule 5: A change in the name of an attribute or a method, or a newly added attribute or method in a class C is propagated recursively to a subclass S of C, only if the change does not cause a new name conflict in S.

The following rule governs the change to the domain of an attribute. It allows the domain of an attribute to be generalized, as long as it does not violate the domain invariant.

Domain Rule

The domain of an inherited attribute can be specialized at the time of inheritance, but the domain of an attribute of a class, whether it is inherited or locally defined, can only be generalized, if instances of the class have already been created. The reason is that specializing the domain of an attribute will invalidate the values of the attribute in existing instances. For example, suppose that the class VehicleCompany is a subclass of the class Company, and the domain of the Manufacturer attribute of the class is Company. Now, if the domain of the Manufacturer attribute of Vehicle is changed to VehicleCompany, all instances of the class Vehicle whose Manufacturer are instances of the class Company will become invalid.

Rule 6: The domain of an inherited attribute may be specialized at the time of inheritance. However, the domain of an attribute of a class, regardless of whether the attribute is inherited or locally defined, can only be generalized, once instances of the class have been created. Further, the domain of an inherited attribute in a class cannot be more general than the domain of the attribute in the superclass of the class in which the attribute was defined.

For example, if the domain of the attribute Manufacturer in the Vehicle class is the Company class, the domain of Manufacturer in the MotorizedVehicle class, a subclass of Vehicle, can be Company or a subclass of Company, say, MotorizedVehicleCompany. Further, the domain of Manufacturer in the class MotorizedVehicle can be generalized from MotorizedVehicleCompany to Company (which is the domain of Manufacturer in the class Vehicle), but not to a superclass of Company.

Class-Hierarchy Rules

There are three situations which can violate the class-hierarchy invariant by causing the class hierarchy to be disconnected. First is when a new class being added has no superclass. Second is when a class A is the only superclass of another class B, and A is removed from the list of superclasses of B. Third is when a class which is the only superclass of another class is dropped. The following rules govern the connectedness of the class hierarchy.

Rule 7: If no superclasses are specified for a newly added class, the root class CLASS is the default superclass of the new class.

Rule 8: If class A is the only superclass of class B, and A is removed from the superclass list of B, then B is made a direct subclass of each of A's superclasses.

The ordering of these new superclasses of B is the same as the ordering of the superclasses of A.

The following rule helps the system to avoid unnecessarily drastic changes to the database when a class A is made a new superclass of another class B by simply requiring the new superclass to be the last superclass in the superclass list of B. The rationale for this rule is that if A is made the new first superclass of B, the conflict-resolution rules that favor the first superclass may trigger new conflicts.

Rule 9: If a class A is made a superclass of a class B, then A becomes the last superclass of B. Thus, any name conflicts that may be triggered by the addition of this superclass can be ignored. However, if a newly inherited attribute causes an origin conflict, Rule 3 must be applied to resolve it.

The following rule also helps the system to avoid needless and expensive changes to the database by specifying the order in which the deletion of a class should be carried out.

Rule 10: The deletion of a node A is a three-step operation: first, all edges from A to its subclasses are removed; next, all edges directed into A from its superclasses are removed; and then node A itself is deleted.

5.3 Semantics

The semantics of each of the schema changes included in the schema-modification taxonomy are defined on the basis of the invariants and rules for schema modification that we have described. In this section we will examine the semantics of some of the schema changes in the taxonomy; we leave it to the reader to define the semantics of the rest of the operations.

5.3.1 Soft Changes

(1.1.1) add a new attribute V to a class C
If the new attribute V causes no new conflicts in the class C or any of its subclasses, the full-inheritance invariant tells us that V must be inherited into all subclasses of C.

If the new attribute conflicts with an inherited attribute, Rule 1 causes the new attribute to override the inherited attribute. If the old attribute was also locally defined in C, the new definition is rejected. If the new attribute is selected, by the full-inheritance invariant it is propagated to all subclasses of C. If there is a name conflict in a subclass during propagation, Rule 5 prevents further propagation. Once the new attribute V is added to C or any of its subclasses, existing instances of the class receive the user-specified default value, if there is one, or the null value.

(1.1.2) drop an attribute V from a class C
It is not possible to drop an inherited attribute. If V is dropped from C, the full-inheritance invariant and Rule 4 ensure that it is dropped recursively from the subclasses that inherited it but did not redefine it. Further, existing instances of these classes lose their values for V. However, if C or any of its subclasses has other superclasses that have attributes of the same name as that of V, it inherits one of those attributes; Rules 2 and 3 are used to determine which new attribute to inherit.

(2.1) make a class S a superclass of a class C
The addition of a new edge from S to C must not introduce a cycle in the class hierarchy; if it does, the operation would violate the class-hierarchy invariant. Operations 1.1.1 and 1.2.1 are applied, respectively, to add attributes and methods of S to C. By Rule 8, S becomes the last superclass of C. Rule 3 is used to resolve any origin conflicts during the propagation of attributes to the subclasses of C.

(2.2) remove a class S from the superclass list of a class C
The deletion of an edge from S to C must not cause the class hierarchy to become disconnected. If S is the only superclass of C, Rule 8 is used to ensure that C loses only those attributes and methods that were defined in S, but not any attributes or methods that were inherited from the superclasses of S. Operations 1.1.2 and 1.2.2 are applied, respectively, for each attribute and method to be dropped from C.

(2.4) add a new class C
If no superclasses of C are specified, by Rule 7 the class CLASS becomes the superclass of C. If multiple superclasses are specified, the full-inheritance invariant requires all attributes and methods from all superclasses of C to be inherited. Rules 2, and 3 are used to resolve any name or origin conflicts.

(2.5) drop an existing class C
By Rule 10, this operation proceeds in three steps. First, operation 2.2 is used to drop all edges from C to its subclasses. Second, all edges from the superclasses of C into C are removed. Third, the definition of C is dropped, and C is removed from the class hierarchy. However, all subclasses of C continue to exist. If the class C was the domain of an attribute V1 of a class C1, V1 is assigned a new domain; in accordance with Rule 8, the first superclass of C would become the new domain of V1.

(2.6) create a new class C as a generalized superclass of n existing classes
An object-oriented approach is biased towards a top-down design of software and databases. However, as experiences have shown in the past, it is often useful to allow a bottom-up design to augment a top-down design. In particular, to allow the integration of independently developed software or databases, it is important to be able to create a new class as a superclass of several existing classes by factoring out common attributes and methods from them.

Let us examine how a new direct superclass C is generated for existing classes C1, C2, ... , Cn. First, the new class C is created as a direct subclass of the closest common superclass of the classes C1, C2, ... , Cn. Next, all attributes common to the classes C1, C2, ... , Cn are factored out of the classes and placed in the new class C. There is no need to update any instance of any of the classes involved in this change. Figure 5.2 illustrates the process of creating a new superclass of existing classes. The classes D and E in Figure 5.2(a) are generalized into a new class X shown in Figure 5.2(b). The attribute X1, which is common to the classes D and E, is factored out of D and E, and becomes a part of the new direct superclass X. The closest common superclass of both D and E is the class A; thus the class X becomes a direct subclass of A.

5.3.2 Hard Changes

(2.7) partition a class C into n subclasses
In distributed relational databases, a relation may be partitioned in one of three ways:

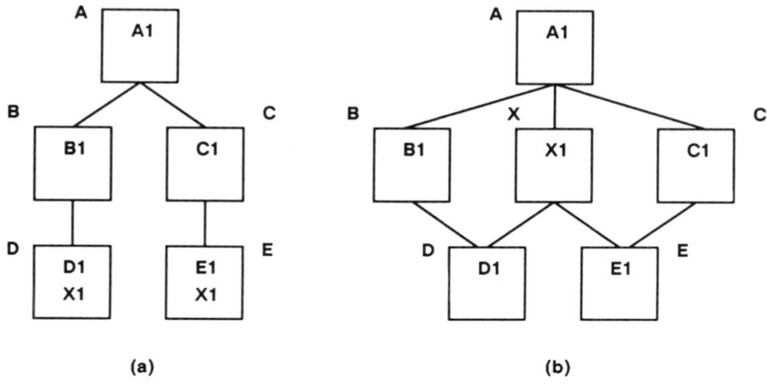

Figure 5.2
Generalization of Classes

horizontal, vertical, and mixed. A horizontal partition of a relation is obtained by applying selection predicates on attributes of the relation. A vertical partition of a relation is obtained by projecting a set of attributes of the relation. A mixed partition is obtained by applying the search predicates on the attributes of a relation and also projecting a set of attributes of the selected tuples of the relation.

A class may be similarly partitioned in object-oriented databases; for physical database reorganization, and, in the case of a distributed database, for database distribution. First, let us consider horizontal partitioning of a class C into subclasses C1, C2, ... , Cn. If any of the subclasses specified does not exist, it may be dynamically created. The partitioning conditions are evaluated against each instance of the class C. If an instance of C satisfies the partitioning conditions for a subclass Ci, the class of the instance is changed to Ci; otherwise, C continues to be the class of the instance.

If the class of an instance of C is changed to Ci, either the object identifier of the instance must be changed or the new class must be recorded in the instance, depending respectively on whether the class identifier is a part of the object identifier or not. Further, if the system maintains a policy of clustering instances of a class, an instance must also be physically moved from the cluster for its current class to that of the new class. Of course, all references to the instances of C that migrate to new classes become invalid.

Next, let us consider vertical partitioning of a class C into classes C1, C2, ... , Cn. The user will specify how the attributes and methods of the class C should be partitioned among the new classes. The classes specified are dynamically created, and populated with instances constructed from the existing instances of C. Afterwards, the class C is dropped, along with its instances. All existing references to the instances of C become invalid.

All superclasses of the class C become superclasses of each of the new classes. The class C shown in Figure 5.3(a) is vertically partitioned into two classes Cx and Cy in Figure 5.3(b). If the class C has subclasses, all subclasses of C become subclasses of each of the new classes, as shown in Figure 5.3; that is, each of the subclasses of C continues to inherit all attributes and methods of C.

C may have a method which references a set of attributes defined for C. The vertical partitioning of C may result in the distribution of these attributes to more than one new classes. Then the method cannot be placed in any of the new classes, since it can no longer access all the attributes it references. By default, the system will drop such methods.

5.4 Implementation

Some of the schema changes affect existing instances, that is, they require the values of existing instances to logically be deleted or null values to be inserted in newly added

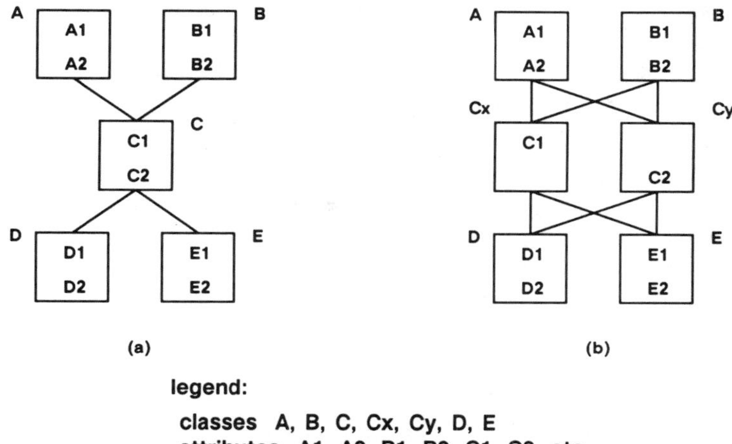

Figure 5.3
Vertical Partitioning of a Class

attributes in existing instances. These operations include dropping and adding new attributes, dropping a class, and changing the inheritance structure between a pair of classes. The following is a list of schema changes that logically affect the values of existing instances.

(1.1.1) add a new attribute V to a class C
(1.1.2) drop an attribute V from a class C
(2.1) make a class S a superclass of a class C
(2.2) remove a class S from the superclass list of a class C
(2.3) change the order of superclasses of a class C
(2.5) drop an existing class C

The operations 2.1, 2.2, 2.3, and 2.5 all involve operations 1.1.1 and/or 1.1.2. In particular, operation 2.1 requires adding attributes to class C; operation 2.2 requires dropping attributes from class C; operation 2.3 involves adding and/or dropping attributes from class C; and operation 2.5 requires, among other things, dropping attributes from all subclasses of C.

If a schema change does not affect the values of existing instances, only the schema information needs to be updated. There are basically two approaches to implement a schema change which affects the values of existing instances: immediate update and deferred update.

The *immediate-update* approach, adopted in GemStone, as the name suggests, immediately updates all affected instances. The drawback of this approach is that it makes a schema change potentially very time-consuming. However, after the update, the database does not contain obsolete information.

ORION uses the *deferred-update* approach, consistent with the approach used in schema changes in relational database systems, in particular, SQL/DS. In the deferred-update approach, if instances logically affected by a schema change are retrieved subsequent to the schema change, the system screens the obsolete information from them or inserts null values in them when the instances are presented to the user. For example, if the Weight attribute is dropped from the class Vehicle, the system removes the value of the attribute from any Vehicle instance that is retrieved after the attribute has been dropped. Further, if the Color attribute is newly added to the class Vehicle, the system inserts a null value in the Color attribute of any existing Vehicle instance that is subsequently retrieved.

The deferred-update approach requires the obsolete information to be cleaned out at some later time so that the database can be compacted for retrieval efficiency. The deferred-update guarantees that a schema change complete quickly; however, it has the disadvantage that obsolete information remains in the database until it is cleaned out. Further, for some of the meaningful schema operations, a deferred update is not possible. Such operations include merging more than one existing class into a single class; here, all instances of the classes will belong to a new class, and as such the class identifier in them must all be updated.

As we will discuss further in Chapter 16, views will make it possible to simulate some of the schema changes without actually causing the changes to be permanently reflected in the database. For example, a view of the schema may be defined in which an attribute of a class is omitted; this view will simulate the dropping of an attribute from a class.

5.5 Method Invalidation

A method can have references to other methods and attributes. A reference to a method or attribute embedded in a method presents a consistency problem when schema modification involves the referenced attribute or method.

There are two ways in which a method that contains a reference to an attribute or another method can become invalid. One is obviously when the referenced attribute or method is removed. For example, in Figure 5.4, if the attribute Vx is removed from class A, method Ma which references Vx will become invalid. This problem can be solved as follows. When a schema change causes a class and its subclasses to lose an attribute or a method, the list of parameters associated with each of the methods in the

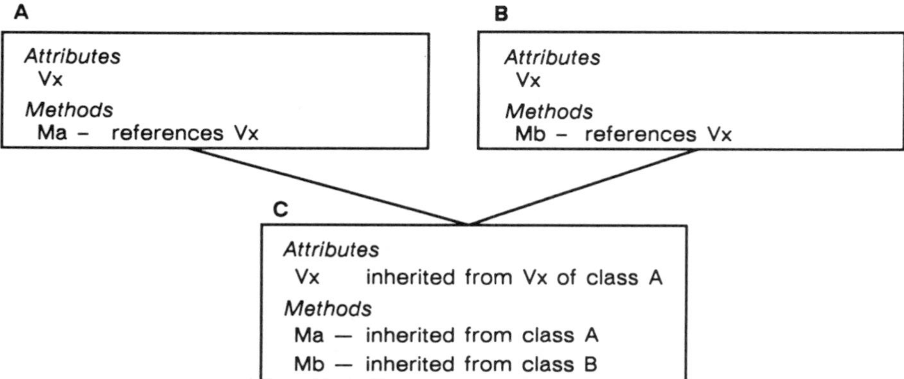

Figure 5.4
A Class Hierarchy with Name Conflicts

class and its subclasses may be examined to identify and invalidate affected methods. Invalidation of these methods can in turn cause other methods to be invalidated.

Another way is more subtle, and can happen only in systems that support multiple inheritance. Figure 5.4 illustrates the problem. The class C has two superclasses A and B. Class A has a locally defined attribute Vx, and a locally defined method Ma which references Vx. Similarly, class B has a locally defined attribute Vx and a locally defined method Mb which references Vx. Vx of A and Vx of B, although they have the same name, are different attributes. When class C is created, it inherits Ma and Mb; but C inherits Vx only from its first superclass A. Then Mb in C will reference Vx that C inherited from A!

This problem arises because a class inherits separately a method and an attribute that the method references. Therefore, one simple way to solve the problem is to require a method and an attribute it references to be inherited together, and make name changes to referenced attributes or methods that conflict. This means that, in the above example, C will inherit both Ma and Vx from A, and Mb and Vx from B. One way to resolve the conflict in the name of the attribute Vx is to inherit Vx from A as is, but inherit Vx from B by renaming Vx from B to, say, Vy; the reference to Vx in Mb in class C also needs to be changed to Vy.

5.6 Versions of Schema

There are two shortcomings to single-schema modification. One is that it does not allow the history of modification of objects to be preserved. For example, if an attribute of a class is dropped, the values of the attribute in existing instances are irreversibly lost; even if the attribute is later added, it will be treated as a different attribute, and the old values of the attribute cannot be seen. Another shortcoming is that, in a multi-user environment, it does not prevent a schema change by one user from impacting all other users' views of the database. For example, once any user deletes an attribute from a class, or changes the superclass/subclass relationship between a pair of classes, all other users will see the changes. This problem is by no means unique to object-oriented databases; the same problem exists for relational databases. The traditional solution to this problem has been to limit the privilege to make schema changes to database administrators or to support views over stored relations.

Schema versioning removes the shortcomings of single-schema modification. Just as an object may be versioned, the schema may be versioned. The system will manage more than one logical schema for one common database, and present different views of the database through different versions of the schema. For example, if a user wishes to drop an attribute from a class in one version of the schema, he may create a new version of the schema that will reflect the schema change. Under the new version of the schema, the user will of course not see the values of the attribute in existing instances of the class. However, if the user later chooses to access the class through the previous version of the schema, he will be able to see the values of the attribute in all instances of the class that existed before he created the new version of the schema.

No database system, object-oriented or otherwise, supports schema versioning today. In view of the fact that only a few database systems support even versions of objects today, schema versioning will be a very advanced feature in a database system.

Recommended Readings

The taxonomy of schema changes and the specification of their semantics given in this chapter are a modified and corrected version of those given in [BANE87]. [BANE87] and [PENN87] both discuss single-schema modification. They represent very different approaches. [BANE87] provides a model for multiple inheritance, while [PENN87] limits itself to single inheritance. Further, [BANE87] takes the deferred-update approach to propagating the impacts of schema changes to the existing instances; whereas [PENN87] resorts to the immediate-update approach.

However, neither [BANE87] nor [PENN87] addresses the problem of generalizing existing classes, that is, creating a new superclass for existing classes and factoring out attributes and methods common to the classes into the superclass. The approach suggested in [SCHR88] is a useful starting point for addressing this problem.

6 Model of Queries

One of the important areas of current research into object-oriented databases is the query model and query language. In some systems, the query model captured in the query language fails to take into account some of the fundamental object-oriented concepts. Some attempt to provide a new query language which is backward-compatible with a relational query language: SQL in the case of IRIS, and QUEL in the case of POSTGRES. Other systems, such as ORION and GemStone, support a new query language which is based more on the nested-relational model.

The query model recently proposed for ORION defines the semantics of object-oriented equivalent of the relational operations projection, selection, join, and set operations. The semantics are consistent with those of the core object-oriented concepts; further, they reflect the fact that the schema of an object-oriented database consists of a class hierarchy and class-composition hierarchies rooted at each of the classes on the class hierarchy.

In this chapter we will present this query model. In Section 6.1 we first define our model for a single-operand query, that is, a query whose target is only one class or a class hierarchy rooted at one class; the relevant operations are those comparable to relational restriction and projection. In Section 6.2, we will extend the model to account for a multiple-operand query, that is, a query which captures operations comparable to relational joins and set operations. In this chapter we will focus on describing our query model; a description of the query language corresponding to the model will be given in Chapter 7. As such, in the remainder of this chapter, we will use a rather intuitive syntax, without any detailed explanation, to illustrate the semantics of the queries we will use as examples.

6.1 Single-Operand Queries

6.1.1 Schema Graph

As we have seen, the definition of a nonprimitive class forms a two-dimensional directed graph of classes which we will call a *schema graph* for the class. Figure 6.1 is

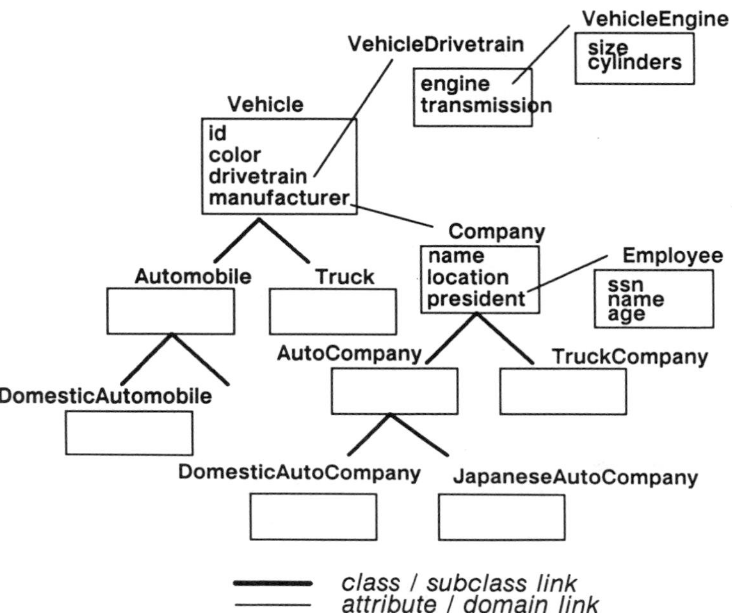

Figure 6.1
An Example Schema Graph

an example of a schema graph. The class Vehicle is the root of a class-composition hierarchy which includes the classes VehicleDrivetrain, VehicleEngine, Company, and Employee. The class Vehicle is also the root of a class hierarchy involving the classes Automobile, DomesticAutomobile, and Truck. The class Company is in turn the root of a class hierarchy with subclasses AutoCompany, JapaneseAutoCompany, DomesticAutoCompany, and TruckCompany. It is also the root of a class-composition hierarchy involving the class Employee.

The following is a more precise definition of the schema graph SG for a class C.

(1) SG is a rooted directed graph consisting of a set of classes N and a set of arcs E between pairs of classes. C is the root of SG, and is a nonprimitive class.

(2) E has two types of arcs. One is between a pair of classes C1 and C2, such that C2 is the domain of one of the attributes of C1. Another is between a pair of classes C1 and S1, such that S1 is an immediate subclass of C1. The direction of an arc is from a class to the domain of its attribute, and from a class to its subclass.

(3) An arc from an attribute of a class to the domain of the attribute may be either single-valued or set-valued. A single-valued arc means that the attribute can have only one value from its domain; while a set-valued arc means that the attribute has as its value a set of instances of its domain.

(4) The set of arcs from any class Ci on SG to the direct and indirect subclasses of Ci forms a directed acyclic graph; that is, the class hierarchy rooted at Ci on SG is a directed acyclic graph.

(5) The set of arcs from the root class C to the direct and indirect domains of the attributes of C forms a directed graph rooted at C; that is, the class-composition hierarchy of SG is a rooted directed graph which may be cyclic.

6.1.2 Query Graph

In relational databases, the schema graph for a relation is the relation itself. The selection operation on a relation, that is, a single-relation query on a relation with a Boolean combination of predicates on the attributes of the relation, identifies the tuples of the relation which satisfies all the predicates. In terms of the schema graph, the predicates apply on the lone node of the graph. To define the selection operation on a class in an object-oriented database, we extend this observation. The selection operation on a class C retrieves instances of the class C which satisfies a Boolean combination of predicates on a subgraph of the schema graph for C; we will call such a graph a *query graph.*

Let us consider an example query and its corresponding query graph. Using the schema for the class Vehicle shown in Figure 6.1, we may formulate a query to "find all blue vehicles manufactured by a company located in Detroit and whose president is under 50 years of age" as follows.

Q1: (**select** Vehicle (Color = "blue"
and Manufacturer Location = "Detroit"
and Manufacturer President Age < 50))

The query graph for this query on the class Vehicle is shown in Figure 6.2; it is a subgraph of the schema graph for the class Vehicle.

The query graph includes only those classes (and the class hierarchies rooted at them) on which the predicates of the query are specified (as we will show shortly, this is not completely accurate). A predicate may be one of two types: a simple predicate and a complex predicate. A *simple predicate* is of the form <attribute-name operator value>. The value may be an instance of a primitive class (string, integer, etc.) or an object identifier of an instance of some class. The latter is important, since it may be

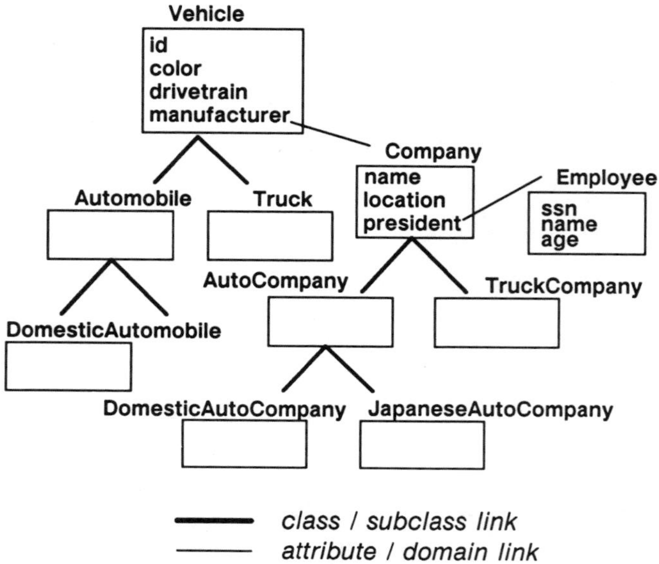

Figure 6.2
An Example Query Graph

used for testing the object equality, that is, equality of referenced objects. The predicate (Color = "blue") in the example query above is a simple predicate.

Another type of predicate is a *complex predicate*; this concept is also explored in the GEM language. A complex predicate is actually a predicate on a contiguous sequence of attributes along a branch of the class-composition hierarchy of a class. The predicate (Manufacturer Location = "Detroit") in the above example is a complex predicate. All classes (and the class hierarchies rooted at them) to which any of the attributes in the sequence of attributes specified in a complex predicate belong are included in the query graph.

So far we have assumed a predicate to simply be an expression of the form <attribute-name operator value>, without specifying what the operator is. In traditional database systems the operator is a scalar comparison operator (=, <, >, etc.) or a set comparison operator (contained-in, contains, set-equality, etc.). In object-oriented systems, the user may define methods on a class, a method may be used for any part of a predicate, that is, as the attribute-name, the operator, or the value. The use of a method in a predicate, as an attribute-name or as an operator, causes difficulties with query compilation and optimization.

Next, since any subclass of the domain of an attribute is also a valid domain of the attribute, it is certainly useful to be able to specify in a query a subclass of the domain of an attribute as the domain of the attribute. In other words, an arc in a schema graph from an attribute of a class to the domain of the attribute may be changed in the query graph to one from the attribute to any subclass of the domain. For example, it may be useful to be able to change the example query Q1 such that the domain of the attribute Manufacturer is the class DomesticAutoCompany, rather than the class Company as specified in the schema.

The following is a precise definition of a query graph QG for a single-operand query on a class C. The result of a single-operand query is a set of instances from the scope of the target class which satisfy the query predicates.

(1) QG is a connected subgraph of the schema graph SG for C. C is the root of QG; that is, QG for C and SG for C have the same root. C is a nonprimitive class.

(2) QG includes only those nodes of the corresponding SG on which at least one predicate of the query is specified.

(3) An arc from an attribute of a class to the domain in SG may be changed in QG to one from the attribute to a subclass of the domain. Then only the class hierarchy rooted at the new domain is included in QG.

(4) The set of arcs from the root class C to the direct and indirect domains of the attributes of C included in QG form a directed graph rooted at C; that is, the class-composition hierarchy of QG is a rooted directed graph, in which some branches contain cycles and others do not. (The nature of the cycles will be described further below.)

(5) The leaf node of an acyclic branch has only simple predicates on it. The interior nodes of any branch (cyclic or acyclic) may have both simple and complex predicates defined on them.

A single-operand query for object-oriented databases is significantly more powerful than a single-relation query for relational databases, because it implies joins of a number of classes along the class-composition hierarchy rooted at the target class, and the scope of its evaluation may also include class hierarchies rooted at the classes along the class-composition hierarchy. Further, as we will see shortly, a single-operand query for object-oriented databases may express recursion, which is not expressible in a relational query.

6.1.3 Cyclic Branch in a Class-Composition Hierarchy

Now we will characterize precisely the cyclic branch of the class-composition hierarchy (either in a query graph or in a schema graph). A branch of a class-composition hierarchy is cyclic, if it contains a class Ci and a class Cj on the branch, such that Cj is the (indirect) domain of an attribute of Ci, and Ci is the domain of an attribute of Cj; or Cj is the (indirect) domain of an attribute of Ci, and a superclass or a subclass of Ci is the domain of an attribute of Cj. This definition brings together four different types of cycle shown in Figure 6.3. Two of them, namely, type-ns and type-ss, may be regarded as quasi-cycles, since they are not cycles in conventional sense. They may be viewed as the type-n and type-s cycles, respectively, with additional conditions on the query result (we will illustrate this shortly). The following defines the four types of cycle for a branch of a class-composition hierarchy. We will assume that the branch has n nodes, such that each node may in turn be the root of a class hierarchy.

(1) A type-n cycle is a cycle formed by n > 1 nodes on the branch.

(2) A type-ns cycle is a quasi-cycle corresponding to a type-n cycle. It is formed by n > 0 nodes on the branch, and a superclass or a subclass of one of the n nodes.

(3) A type-s cycle is a cycle formed for a single node.

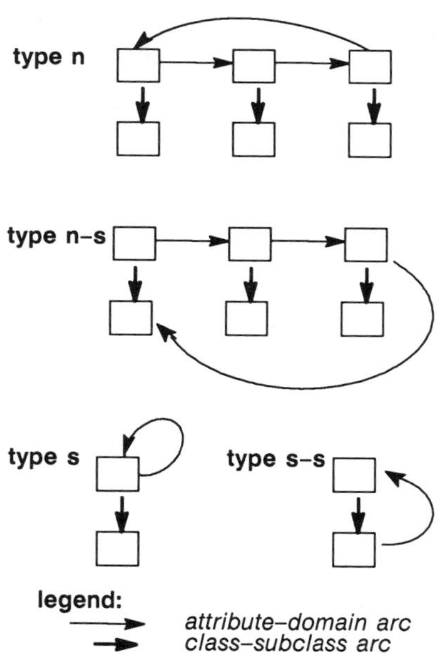

Figure 6.3
Cyclic Branches

(4) A type-ss cycle is a quasi cycle corresponding to a type-s cycle. It is formed by a class and its superclass or a subclass.

Assuming that the class Employee has an additional attribute Drives whose domain is the class Vehicle, a meaningful query is to "find all blue vehicles driven by the president of the company that manufactured them." This is an example of a query with a type-n cycle in its query graph. The following is an intuitive syntax for expressing the query. We leave it as a simple exercise for the reader to construct the query graphs for the following example queries.

Q-c1: (**select** (Vehicle :V) (Color = "blue"
and Manufacturer President Drives = V))

In this query, the variable :V is used for binding each instance of the class Vehicle, as the set of instances of Vehicle is scanned one at a time. The class Vehicle is the target class.

A query to "find all blue vehicles manufactured by a company whose president drives a Japanese automobile" is an example of a query with a type-ns cycle in the query graph. This query may be expressed as follows.

Q-c2: (**select** Vehicle (:J is-a JapaneseAutomobile) (Color = "blue"
and Manufacturer President Drives = J))

The expression (:J is-a JapaneseAutomobile) constrains the value the complex attribute (Manufacturer President Drives) may take to instances of the class JapaneseAutomobile. Note that the class Vehicle is still the target class.

For the next two examples, let us add the Manager attribute to the class Employee; the domain of Manager is the class Employee. The following is an example query with a type-s cycle. The query is to find "all managers of an employee named Johnson."

Q-c3: (**select** Employee (recurse Manager) (Name = "Johnson"))

The expression (recurse Manager) specifies that, once an instance of the class Employee is found which satisfies the predicate (Name = "Johnson"), the recursive values of the Manager attribute of the instance are retrieved.

For our final example, let us assume that the class Employee has a subclass FemaleEmployee. The following is an example query with a type-ss cycle, which finds "all female managers of an employee named Johnson."

Q-c4: (**select** Employee (recurse Manager :M (:M is-a FemaleEmployee))
(Name = "Johnson"))

The expression (:M is-a FemaleEmployee) restricts the result of the query to instances of the class FemaleEmployee.

6.1.4 Query Result

In relational databases, the result of a single-relation query is a subset of the tuples of the relation that satisfies the selection predicates. The concept of a class hierarchy in object-oriented databases captures the generalization abstraction, which means that a class, when used as a generalized concept, subsumes all its subclasses. This observation leads to two equally valid interpretations for the access scope of a query; the access scope of a query on a class C is either the set of instances of C, or the set of instances of the entire class hierarchy rooted at C. Therefore, the result of a single-operand query on a class C may be the set of instances of the class C or the set of instances of the entire class hierarchy rooted at C which satisfy the query predicates. For example, the access scope of a query against the class Vehicle may be restricted to the instances of Vehicle, or may be interpreted to also include the instances of all types of Vehicle, that is, all subclasses of Vehicle.

If a query involves a projection operation, only the desired attributes in the instances that satisfy the predicates will be returned, regardless of whether the access scope of the query is a single class or a class hierarchy. If the scope is a class hierarchy, we need to take into consideration the consequences of inheritance of attributes.

First, attributes may be renamed in classes which have inherited them, as observed in Chapter 5. For the purposes of queries, a renamed attribute should be regarded as the original attribute. For example, suppose that the attribute Color, defined in the class Vehicle, is renamed AutoColor in the class Automobile. Although the attribute has two different names, the distinction should be ignored in queries.

Second, in the case of multiple inheritance, a class may inherit an attribute from one of its superclasses. If the attributes in all superclasses are *identical*, that is, they have the same name and same domain, there is no problem. However, complications arise if the attributes are only *equivalent*, that is, they were all defined in the same class somewhere higher in the class hierarchy, but they have been renamed or their domains have been changed. Suppose that the superclasses Si and Sj of a class C have equivalent attributes Ai and Aj, and that C inherits only the attribute Ai of Si. Now consider a query on Sj whose scope of evaluation is the class hierarchy rooted at Sj, and the attribute Aj is to be output. Then the values of the attribute Ai inherited into the class C (and its subclasses) should also be output, since Ai and Aj are equivalent after all.

If the access scope of a query on a class C is the class hierarchy rooted at C, the result of the query is a heterogeneous set of instances, since the instances belong to a number of different classes with different numbers of attributes. The application (or the user) which issues the query must obviously be prepared to deal with this heterogeneous mix of instances. One approach is for the database system to return only a list of object identifiers (along with the class identifiers) of the instances in the query result, and have the application make explicit requests for all or some of the actual instances. This approach has been implemented in ORION; and it is in a sense similar to the cursor mechanism in SQL/DS or portals in POSTGRES. If the query involves a projection operation, the database system may return the set of object identifiers and the values of the projected attributes of the corresponding objects.

The projection operation entails the familiar problem of eliminating duplicates from the query result. For object-oriented databases, unlike relational databases, two different criteria exist for determining the uniqueness of an instance from a collection of instances. One criterion is the equality of the object identifiers, which may be called *object equality*; while another is the equality of the contents of the instances, which may be called *value equality*, that is, the values of the *user-defined* attributes in the instances. We note that an instance may contain a number of system-defined attributes, such as the version number, update timestamp, and so on, to support various functionality of the system, as we will see in Chapter 12. The values of system-defined attributes really should not be included in testing value equality of objects, since the users do not explicitly create their values. In relational databases, only value equality is used. For object-oriented databases, both may be useful; however, value equality requires some additional consideration. A class in general does not have the same set of attributes as its superclass, since a class inherits all attributes from its superclass and may have additional attributes defined on it. This means that value equality between classes with different sets of attributes need not be tested.

It is interesting to note that our type s and type s-s queries are recursive queries and that they are safe, that is, the result of such a query is a finite set of objects. This is because a primitive class is never the target of a query.

Throughout our discussion so far, we have assumed that the query result is simply returned to the application (or the user). Now we need to consider the problem of saving the result of a query. As we discussed earlier, an object belongs to a class, and a class has a position somewhere in the class hierarchy. These simple principles impose some difficult constraints on the query model for object-oriented databases. In relational databases, the result of a query is itself a relation, and it may simply be saved as a new relation. In object-oriented databases, the result of a query is a set of objects belonging to a class or a class hierarchy rooted at some class. Let us consider a query on a class C whose scope of access is the class hierarchy rooted at C. The result of the query will in general be a heterogeneous set of instances that form a separate class hierarchy each of whose classes is derived from a corresponding class in the original class hierarchy; let us denote the root of the new class subhierarchy by C-new. The instances in the newly created classes must all have different object identifiers from those in the corresponding instances of the original classes.

A difficult question is where we should place the class C-new in the class hierarchy for the entire database. Intuitively, there are two options to consider. One is to place C-new as a new subclass of the superclasses of the class C; and the other is to treat C-new as an immediate subclass of the class CLASS, which is the root of the class hierarchy for the entire database. These options are shown in Figure 6.4, where the class AutoCompany-new is the root of a new class hierarchy which is created to save the result of a query on the class hierarchy rooted at the class AutoCompany.

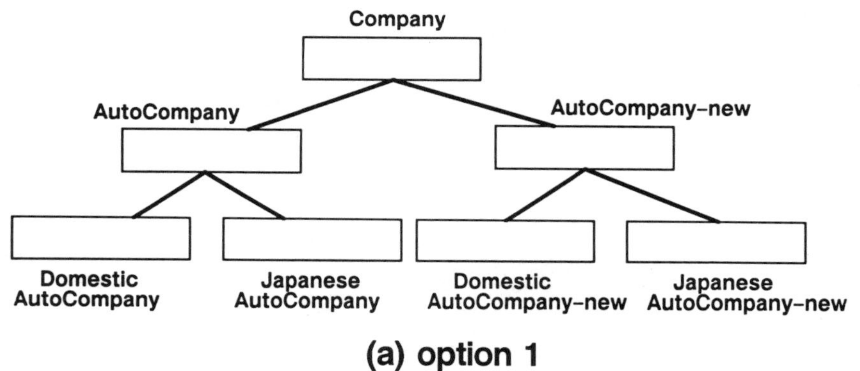

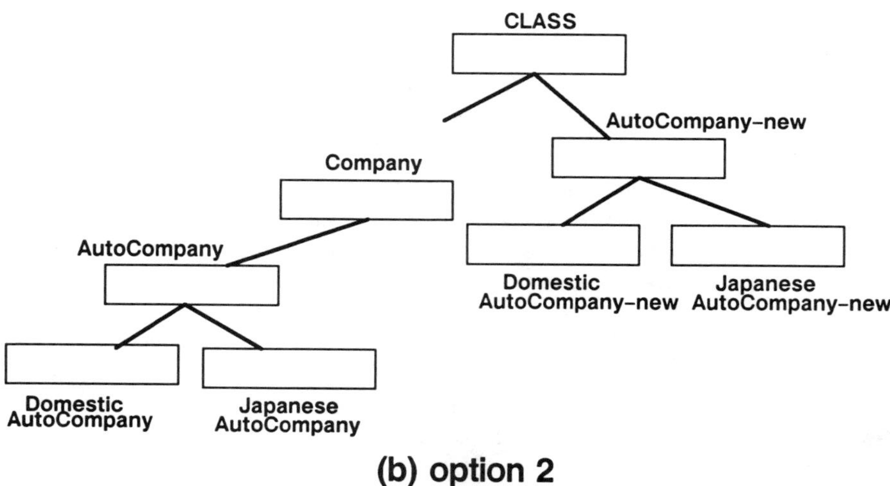

Figure 6.4
Disposition of the Query Result

Let us consider option-1, where C-new is made a subclass of the superclasses of the class C. If the query involves a projection operation, this solution would result in a subclass with fewer attributes than its superclass, thereby violating the *full-inheritance invariant* in schema evolution as observed in Chapter 5. In particular, if any attribute which C inherited from its superclasses is dropped from the query result, C-new will have fewer attributes than the superclasses of C; for example, in Figure 6.4, the class AutoCompany-New may have fewer attributes than the class Company. This suggests that C-new with fewer attributes than C should perhaps be made a superclass (rather than a subclass) of a superclass of C. However, this fix does not work either, if C-new contains any attribute which was defined in C (rather than inherited into C). C-new will then end up with an attribute which its subclass does not have.

There is another problem with option-1, regardless of whether the query involves a projection operation. If C-new is placed on the class hierarchy, it becomes subject to schema evolution on its superclasses. In other words, changes to the definition of any of its new superclasses propagate down to C-new, again in accordance with the full-inheritance invariant. For example, if an attribute is dropped from the class Company, the same attribute must be dropped from the class AutoCompany-New. This defeats the purpose of saving the result of a query.

Let us now consider option-2, where C-new is made an immediate subclass of the system-defined class CLASS. One drawback of this solution is that all attributes and methods inherited into C-new must now be explicitly replicated in C-new. This requires extra storage; however, it does not appear to be a serious drawback. Option-2 is our choice.

6.2 Multiple-Operand Queries

6.2.1 Join

A relational database consists of a number of relations. Join is used to correlate n different relations (n > 1) on the basis of the values in attributes common to the relations. It is important to realize that join is a crucial operation in relational databases largely because of the limitations of the relational model of data. In particular, the relational model of data restricts the attribute of a relation to a single primitive value; that is, an attribute may have only one value, and the value must be of a primitive data type (integer, float, string, boolean). This makes it necessary for the user to explicitly join relations on the basis of primitive attribute values in order to find logically correlated information. These limitations have been removed in object-oriented and nested-relational models of data.

Implicit Joins in a Class-Composition Hierarchy

Let us consider the three classes Vehicle, Company, and Employee in Figure 6.1.

These classes may be defined as relations as follows.

Vehicle (ID, Color, DriveTrain, Manufacturer)
Company (CompanyName, Location, President)
Employee (SSN, EmployeeName, Age)

We note that the domain of any of the attributes in these relations may only be a primitive data type. To find all blue vehicles manufactured by a company located in Detroit and whose president is under 50 years of age (example query Q1), the query must be formulated as a join of the above three relations, and the user must explicitly specify the join attributes. As we have seen already, however, the same query may be formulated in object-oriented databases as a retrieval from a class-composition hierarchy in which joins between the classes are defined in the schema between an attribute of a class and the domain of the attribute.

A single-operand query in object-oriented databases is then one type of join; it is an implicit join of the classes on a class-composition hierarchy rooted at the target class of the query. However, it has a few important limitations relative to the relational join. One is that the output attributes are restricted to those in the target class; that is, it is not possible to output any attribute in any class which is not the root of the query graph for a query. This may be easily remedied. The query syntax needs to be augmented with some means of specifying the output attributes; the output attributes may be specified in a single list, or they may be specified in a separate list associated with each of the classes in the query.

Another, much more serious, limitation of the implicit join in a single-operand query is that the join is restricted to the attribute-domain relationship specified in the schema; that is, the implicit join is essentially the materialization of the values of an attribute. Consider a class Ci with an attribute A whose domain is the class Cj. The materialization of the instances of Ci is equivalent to a join of Ci and Cj, in which the attribute A of Ci and the object-identifier attribute of Cj are the join attributes. Below, we elaborate on the limitations of the implicit join, and propose solutions to overcome these limitations.

Explicit Joins of Classes

The limitation of a join implied in a single-operand query is essentially that it statically determines the classes to be joined, and the join ordering of the classes. Let us examine this in more detail. The implicit join statically determines the join ordering between a pair of classes Ci and Cj, where Cj is the domain of an attribute of Ci, such that Ci is always the 'outer class' and Cj the 'inner class' (analogous to the outer and inner relations in a join ordering for a pair of relations in relational databases). This means that it is not possible to formulate a query whose semantics require implicit reversal of an attribute-domain link specified in the schema. For example, the class Company is the domain of the attribute Manufacturer of the class Vehicle in Figure 6.1. It is possible to find all vehicles manufactured by certain companies. However, it is not possible to find all companies that manufacture certain vehicles; the class Company has no attribute, say, Manufactures, whose domain is the class Vehicle.

In relational databases, the existence of a common attribute in a pair of relations implies, correctly, the attribute-domain relationship in both directions between the relations. It is certainly useful to extend our model of single-operand queries by postulating, for any attribute of a class C whose domain is the class D, an implicit attribute of the class D whose domain is the class C; and by allowing implicit joins to be formulated along the attribute-domain links defined by the implicit attribute. For example, the attribute Manufacturer of the class Vehicle, and the class Company define an implicit attribute of the class Company whose domain is the class Vehicle. Then a single-operand query on the class Company may be formulated in which instances of the class Vehicle are materialized as values of the implicit attribute of the class Vehicle.

However, the implicit join also statically determines the classes which may be joined to those pairs of classes Ci and Cj such that Cj is the domain of an attribute of Ci. This means that it excludes joins between an arbitrary pair of classes with attributes which share a common domain. For example, suppose that, as shown in Figure 6.5, the class Employee has an additional attribute Residence, and that the domains of Residence and the attribute Location of the class Company are the same, say a class City. Then a meaningful query may be to find all employees who live in the city in which their companies are located. However, as long as there is no attribute-domain relationship

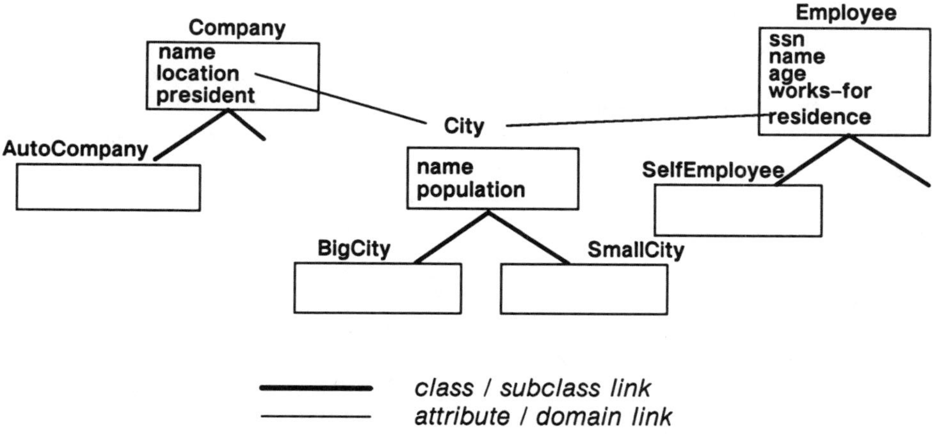

Figure 6.5
An Example Query Graph for a Join

between the attribute Residence and the class Company, or between the Location attribute and the class Employee, it is not possible to formulate this query.

We now extend our query model to admit joins of classes on user-specified arbitrary join attributes. Again, the extended model must be consistent with the object-oriented data model. To fully define the semantics of joins, we need to introduce the notion of attribute compatibility. Two attributes Ai and Aj are *compatible*, if the domain of Ai is identical to the domain of Aj, or is a superclass or a subclass of the domain of Aj. Unlike relational joins, in which the domains of the join attributes must be identical, we require the join attributes to only be compatible. For example, in Figure 6.5 the attributes Residence and Location are compatible, since they share the same domain. Suppose now that the domain of the Location attribute is the class BigCity, which is a subclass of City. The attributes Residence and Location are still compatible, since the domain of Location is a subclass of the domain of Residence.

Next, we must account for the class hierarchy in the scope of query evaluation. Each class to be joined is the root of a class hierarchy. The scope of query evaluation, for each class to be joined, may be either instances of the class alone or instances of the class hierarchy rooted at the class. The query syntax must allow the user to specify the scope for each class in a join, just as was the case for a single-operand query.

The result of a join is a set of instances formed by concatenating instances from different classes. This presents a problem for systems like ORION which first return the list of object identifiers and then return specific instances on demand; this problem does not arise in systems which directly return the actual set of concatenated instances. The problem is whether to return a set of n object identifiers (one for each class containing an output attribute from the join) for each concatenated instance or to return a new object identifier for the concatenated instance. If the system simply returns a set of n object identifiers for each concatenated instance, the user must in general send the entire list back to the system to request the retrieval of the actual concatenated instance. However, if the system must return a new object identifier for each concatenated instance, it must incur the overhead of generating the identifiers, and temporarily saving all the concatenated instances along with their identifiers. If the query result is not to be saved, this is a rather high overhead; therefore we adopt the first approach.

Just as is the case with a single-operand query, if the result of a join needs to be saved as a snapshot, the instances in the result must be given unique identifiers and assigned to a class. The same considerations we had for saving the result of a single-operand query apply here, and the result of a join is to be saved in a new class which is an immediate subclass of the class CLASS, the root of the class hierarchy for the entire database.

Figure 6.5 is the query graph for a query involving a join of two classes Company and Employee; the join attributes are Location and Residence. The following is a precise definition of the query graph for a join of a pair of classes Ci and Cj; it is straightforward to extend the definition for a join of more than two classes, and we leave it as an exercise to the reader. Let us denote by Si the domain of the join attribute in Ci, and by Sj the domain of the join attribute in Cj; let us assume that Si is a superclass of Sj or Si = Sj. The result of the join is a set of instances formed by concatenating the instances from the scope of query evaluation for Ci and Cj which satisfy the join predicate.

(1) Ci and Cj each is the root of a query graph corresponding to a single-operand query on Ci and Cj, respectively. That is, each query graph is the root of a class hierarchy and a class-composition hierarchy rooted at the class to be joined.

(2) The query graphs for Ci and Cj partially overlap, because of the compatibility of the join attributes. Si and Sj each is the root of a class-composition hierarchy, each of whose nodes is in turn the root of a class hierarchy. If Si = Sj, the entire class-composition hierarchy is shared by Ci and Cj via their respective join attributes. If Si is a superclass of Sj, the class-composition hierarchy rooted at Si is the domain of the join attribute of Ci; while the domain of the join attribute in Cj is the class-composition hierarchy rooted at Sj.

6.2.2 Set Operations

The set operations for object-oriented databases also require some extensions to the corresponding operations for relational databases. As in relational databases, these operations are useful largely for further manipulating the results of queries, that is, when the operands are queries.

The operand is a set of instances; more specifically, it may be the set of instances of a class defined in the database, or it may be a set of instances obtained as the result of a query. On the surface, the semantics of the set operations for object-oriented databases are identical to those for relational databases. Actually, however, they differ in three interesting ways.

First, for object-oriented databases, the operand, and the result of the operation, may be a heterogeneous set of instances; that is, the instances of the operand may not all belong to the same class. In relational databases, the operand is a homogeneous set of tuples.

Second, as we have seen already, for object-oriented databases, two different criteria exist for determining the uniqueness of an instance from a collection of instances, namely, object equality and value equality.

Third, as usual, the scope of evaluation for an operand may be instances of a class or the instances of a class hierarchy rooted at the class. The user may specify the scope for each class in the operation.

6.3 Other Query Models

There are three common, and major, differences between our query model and other query models, including those for hierarchical, relational, and nested relational data models. First, our query model reflects the semantics of the class hierarchy. The concept of a class hierarchy is not a part of a non-object-oriented data model, and therefore, of a query model derived from it. Unhappily, even the few query models proposed for object-oriented database systems neglect to account for the impacts of the class hierarchy on queries.

Second, the record-type hierarchy in hierarchical databases and the nested relations in nested relational databases are similar to the class-composition hierarchy in an object-oriented data model. However, the record-type hierarchy and nested relations form a directed acyclic graph, unlike our class-composition hierarchy which may include cyclic branches. The query model based on the normalized relational model does not give rise to a nested structure of relations.

Third, other query models use only value equality, that is, equality testing between entities is done on the basis of the contents of the entities, rather than object equality based on object identifiers. This difference is significant in the definition of a predicate and the definition of the semantics of the set operations.

One major difference between our query model and other models proposed for object-oriented databases is the treatment of a snapshot, that is, the query result which is saved and becomes a part of the persistent database.

Recommended Readings

This chapter is largely reprinted from [KIM89e]. The query model presented in [KIM89e] is in turn based on [BANE88] and [KIMK89]. Research into nested relational databases or extended relational databases is relevant to understanding the impacts of a class-composition hierarchy on the query model for object-oriented databases. Interested readers may refer to [MAKI77, JAES82, ZANI83, ABIT84, IEEE88]. The notion of object identity has important consequences on the query model for object-oriented databases. [KHOS86] discusses the semantics of object identity.

One of the potentially interesting and useful approaches that have been proposed to bridge object-oriented databases and relational databases is to augment a relational data language to an object-oriented data language. A preliminary proposal to extend SQL to an object-oriented SQL is given in [BEEC88]; and QUEL, the language for INGRES, to an object-oriented QUEL is presented in [ROWE87].

7 Query Language

In this chapter, we will present a proposal for a query language for object-oriented databases. The language is designed to make concrete the query model presented in Chapter 6. After a brief overview of the query language, we will describe the query language in two steps: first for a single-operand query, and then for an n-operand query. We will in turn describe the language for a single-operand query in two steps: first for an acyclic query, and then for a cyclic query.

7.1 Overview of the Language

Basics

A query in its simplest form is specified as follows. A more complex query may be formulated by combining more than one simple query with set operations, as we will discuss later.

SimpleQuery ::=
select TargetClause |
select TargetClause **from** RangeClause |
select TargetClause **where** QualificationClause |
select TargetClause **from** RangeClause **where** QualificationClause

The syntax of a query consists of three main clauses, as in relational query languages: target, range, and qualification clause. The target clause is the specification of the attributes to be output; the range clause indicates the binding of variables, called object variables, to corresponding sets of instances of classes; the qualification clause, also called the where clause, specifies the qualification conditions as a Boolean combination of predicates.

The range clause contains the declaration of the object variables as a sequence of pairs (range_set object_variable). In general, the range set is a class. The range clause may be omitted; then, a default object variable with the same name is assumed for each class referenced in the target clause or in the where clause.

Let us consider an example query. Using the schema for the class Vehicle in Figure 7.1, we may formulate a query to "find all blue vehicles manufactured by a company located in Detroit and whose president is under 50 years of age" as follows.

```
Q1:     select :V from Vehicle :V
               where :V color = "blue"
                  and :V manufacturer location = "Detroit"
                  and :V manufacturer president age < 50.
```

Query Q1 can be more concisely formulated as follows:

```
Q1':    select Vehicle
               where color = "blue"
                  and manufacturer location = "Detroit"
                  and manufacturer president age < 50.
```

Note that in the qualification clause the object variable has been omitted. This can be done if there are no ambiguities in the specification of the attributes on which the predicates apply.

Although the query structure is similar to the structure of relational queries, there are a number of important differences. These differences will become clearer as we proceed.

Object Identity

One important element of a query language is the facility to express equality of two objects. This facility is necessary for example when eliminating duplicates from the query results or when executing set operations. In relational databases, only value equality is supported. As we discussed in Chapter 6, two different criteria exist for determining the uniqueness of an instance from a collection of instances in an object-oriented database: object equality and value equality.

Therefore, our query language needs to support both types of equality. In particular, the comparator for object equality is denoted by =, while for value-based equality it is denoted by ==. Further, as we will see later, the language supports two forms of the set operations, depending on whether the uniqueness test must be based on object equality or value equality.

7.2 Single-Operand Queries

A single-operand query in object-oriented databases retrieves objects from only one target class. However, because of the two-dimensional nature of the schema graph for any given class, a single-operand query is actually evaluated against other classes related to the target class of the query.

7.2.1 Acyclic Queries

Class-Composition Hierarchy

Because of the nested definitions of objects arising from the class-composition hierarchy, the query language must easily allow the specification of predicates on a nested sequence of attributes. Therefore, the notion of path has been introduced in the query language. A path denotes a nested sequence of attributes of an object. We note that the path notation does not increase the expressive power of the language. However, it is a convenient and natural way to express queries along the class-composition hierarchy. In particular, it obviates the need to introduce additional object variables in the range clause and join predicates in the qualification clause.

An object variable can be used to specify a path, composed of a sequence of attribute names, in a complex object (e.g., manufacturer location, in example Q1). We call a path specification in a complex object a *path variable.* If all the attributes included in a path variable are scalar attributes, the path variable is a *scalar variable* (e.g., manufacturer name, in Q1). A path variable may also include set attributes. In this case, we may associate, with each set attribute, one of the keywords *each, exists,* or *set-of.* The keywords *each* and *exists* correspond to the universal and existential quantifier used in the predicate calculus. The keyword *each* (or *exists*) preceding the set attribute A indicates that the predicate must hold for each object (or for at least one object in the case of *exists*) in the set specified by A in the complex object. If either *each* or *exists* is associated with each set attribute in a path variable, the path variable is a scalar variable. If no keyword or the keyword *set-of* is specified for at least one set attribute in a path variable, the variable is a *set variable*; and a set variable denotes a set to which only set predicates can be applied.

A scalar path variable is specified as follows:

```
ScalarVariable ::= ObjectVariable  ScalarPath |
                   ScalarPath
```

Note that the object variable at the beginning of the path may be omitted if there are no ambiguities. A scalar path is a sequence of attribute names such that each attribute is single-valued or, if it is multi-valued, has a quantifier associated with it.

ScalarPath ::= ScalarPathElement |
ScalarPathElement ScalarPath.

A scalar path element defines an element in a path. A partial definition of a path element is the following. We will show later that there are additional ways to specify a path element.

ScalarPathElement ::= *ScalarAttributeName* /
Quantifier *SetAttributeName*

where the quantifier is either **each** or **exists**.

The definition of a set path variable is similar, except that at least one of the path elements must be a multi-valued attribute with no quantifier associated with it.

A *non-terminal path variable* is a path variable terminating on a non-primitive class (e.g., manufacturer president). A *terminal path variable* is a path variable terminating on a primitive class (e.g., manufacturer name).

We may use a *scalar comparator* (=, *equal*, *string-equal*, *string*=, >, etc.) between a scalar path variable and a scalar constant (e.g., a number, a string, etc.) or between two scalar path variables. Only the comparators = and == can be used between non-terminal path variables.

In the next example, we show a query where a scalar comparator (*string-equal*) is used between two terminal path variables; we compare the values (of type string) of the scalar attributes, and so any scalar comparator can be used. The example also shows a path containing a universal quantifier. The query retrieves all companies which have all their divisions located in the same city where the company headquarters is located.

Q-a1: **select** Company
where each divisions location **string-equal** location.

In query Q-a1 a scalar path variable is used. The path '**each** divisions location' consists of two path elements. The first is '**each** divisions' and contains a quantifier, since the attribute 'divisions' of the class Company is multi-valued. The second is 'location' and contains no quantifier, since the attribute is single-valued. A similar query to retrieve all companies which have at least one division located in the same city as the company headquarters is formulated by using the existential quantifier.

Q-a2: **select** Company
where exists divisions location **string-equal** location.

There may be a *set comparator* (*has-subset*, *is-subset* , *is-equal*, etc.) between a set path variable and a set constant (e.g., a list of numbers, a list of strings, etc.) or between two set path variables. There may be a *set-to-scalar* comparator (*has-element*, ¬:*has-element*) between a set path variable and a scalar constant, or between a set path variable and a scalar path variable. Similarly, there may be a *scalar-to-set* comparator (*is-in*, ¬:*is-in*).

Example Q-a3 shows how the same query can be expressed in two different forms. In the first form, the set path variable 'divisions function' is compared with a set constant. In the second form, since the quantifier *each* is used on the set attribute 'divisions', the path variable becomes scalar and its membership in the given set value is tested. The query retrieves all companies whose divisions are either automobile factories or truck factories.

Q-a3: **select** Company
  where divisions function **is-subset** '("Automobile Factory"
    "Motorbike Factory")

Q-a3': **select** Company
  where each divisions function **is-in** '("Automobile Factory"
    "Motorbike Factory") .

It is possible to bind a variable to a set of objects which are the values of an attribute of another object. This is accomplished by using a set membership predicate in the range clause. It is also possible to define *reference variables.* A reference variable can be used as a shorthand to avoid repeating a long path variable in the body of a query, especially when several predicates are issued against the path variable. As an example, let us consider a query which retrieves 'all companies that have at least one division which has at least one employee whose residence is in Rome and drives a Ferrari'. Without using a set membership predicate in the range clause, this query is expressed as follows:

Q-a4: **select** :C **from** Company :C, Division :D, Employee :E
  where :D **is-in** :C divisions **and** :E **is-in** :D staff **and**
  :E drives manufacturer name = "Ferrari" **and** :E residence = "Rome".

Query Q-a4 requires two set membership predicates that are used to connect the class Company with instances of the class Employee. The query is not a single-operand query. Using a set membership predicate in the range clause, the query is simplified as follows.

Q-a4': **select** :C **from** Company :C, :E **is-in** :C divisions staff
where :E drives manufacturer name = "Ferrari" **and** :E residence = "Rome".

In query Q-a4', each time the variable :C is instantiated by taking an instance of the class Company as value, a set for the variable :E is defined. This set, called a range set, is defined as the union of instances of the class Employee that are the values of the attribute 'staff' of all the 'divisions' of the given instance of Company. An instance of Company satisfies the query, if there exists at least one element in this set that satisfies the predicates in the qualification clause of the query. In this case, the properties of the objects represented by the variable :E are implicitly defined by the class which is the domain of the last element in the path ':C divisions staff'.

A query may contain variables that are bound by both a membership predicate and reference variables. For example, a query which retrieves 'all companies that have at least one division which has at least one employee whose residence is in Rome and who drives a blue car whose manufacturer is located in Milan' is formulated as follows.

Q-a5: **select** :C **from** Company :C, :E **is-in** :C divisions staff, :D **is** :E drives
where :E residence = "Rome" **and**
:D color = "blue" **and** :D manufacturer location "Milan".

In this query, the variable :E is bound by a set-membership predicate. The expression ':D **is** :E drives' specifies that :D is a reference variable equivalent of the path ':E drives'.

The definition of the range clause is expanded as follows:

RangeClause ::= RangeElement |
RangeElement, RangeClause

The range element is defined as follows:

RangeElement ::= ClassExpression ObjectVariable |
ObjectVariable **is-in** RangeSet |
ReferenceVariable

ObjectVariable ::= *VariableName*

RangeSet ::= *ObjectVariable SimpleSetPath*

ReferenceVariable ::= *ObjectVariable* **is** ObjectVariable ScalarPath |
ObjectVariable **is** ObjectVariable SetPath

A simple set path is a path which has no quantifiers and in which at least one attribute is multi-valued. A class expression consists of a class name in the simplest case.

A reference variable may also define a set. In this case, only set predicates may be applied to the reference variable in the qualification clause. As an example, let us consider a query that retrieves all companies all of whose employees drive cars either in the set (Fiat, Ferrari) or in the set (Ford, Chevrolet, Nissan). This is expressed as follows:

Q-a6: **select** :C **from** Company :C, :S **is** :C divisions staff drives
where :S **is-subset** '("Fiat", "Ferrari") **or**
:S **is-subset** '("Ford", "Chevrolet", "Nissan").

Class Hierarchy

The user must be able to specify whether the target of a query is a single class or the class hierarchy rooted at the class. If the name of the user-specified class is followed by the operator '*' (*hierarchy operator*), the query applies to all classes in the hierarchy rooted at the class.

A meaningful query is to retrieve a subset of the classes on a class hierarchy. Let us consider the class hierarchy rooted at the class Company, and suppose that a user is interested in retrieving 'all companies except truck companies'. We note that the user may tediously formulate this as a set of queries, one for each of the classes Company, AutoCompany, DomesticAutoCompany, JapaneseAutoCompany; the user then may perform the union of the results of these queries.

Our query language allows the user to specify a subset of the classes in a class hierarchy by binding an object variable not only to a class or a class hierarchy, but also to a union of the classes or the difference between a class hierarchy and a class (or class hierarchy). We can now generalize the class expression as follows.

ClassExpression ::=(ClassExpression) |
(ClassExpression **union** ClassExpression) |
(ClassHierarchy **difference** ClassExpression) |
Class |
ClassHierarchy

Class ::= *ClassName*

ClassHierarchy ::= *ClassName* *

Let us examine some examples of the class expression. The following query retrieves 'all instances of the class Company or any of its subclasses that have at least one division in Rome'.

Q-h1: **select** Company *
    where exists divisions location = "Rome".

A similar query, but which excludes truck companies, is expressed as follows.

Q-h2: **select** Company * **difference** TruckCompany
    where exists divisions location = "Rome".

The following query shows the use of union. The query retrieves 'domestic or Japanese automobile companies which have at least one division in Rome'.

Q-h3: **select** DomesticAutoCompany **union** JapaneseAutoCompany
    where exists divisions location = "Rome".

Note the use of the existential quantifier in the above examples. The quantifier applied to the multi-valued attribute "divisions" defines a scalar variable.

The domain of an attribute A of a class C is in turn a class D. This means that an instance of C can receive as the value of the attribute A any instance of class D or of any subclass of D. Therefore, a given path expression, such as :X A where :X is bound to the class C, denotes an object that belongs to D or to any subclass. Sometimes, however, we may only be interested in the values of attribute A that belong to a particular subclass of D.

For example, the following query retrieves 'all employees who drive a car with a turbo engine of more than 100HP'.

Q-h4: **select** :E **from** Employee * :E, Automobile * :A, TurboEngine * :T
    where :A **is-in** :E drives **and** :A drivetrain engine = :T **and**
    :T hppower > 100.

Note that we cannot express this query using the path expressions discussed earlier, and also that the query is not a single-operand query. In fact, the path expression ':E drives drivetrain engine' would return a set of all engines (of any type) that belong to vehicles (of any type) driven by a given employee. In order to constrain the domain of attribute values in a path expression, we allow the specification of the class expression in a path. With this extension, query Q-h4 can be expressed as follows:

Q-h4': **select** :E **from** Employee :E
    where :P **exists** drives **class** Automobile * engine **class**
        TurboEngine * hppower > 100.

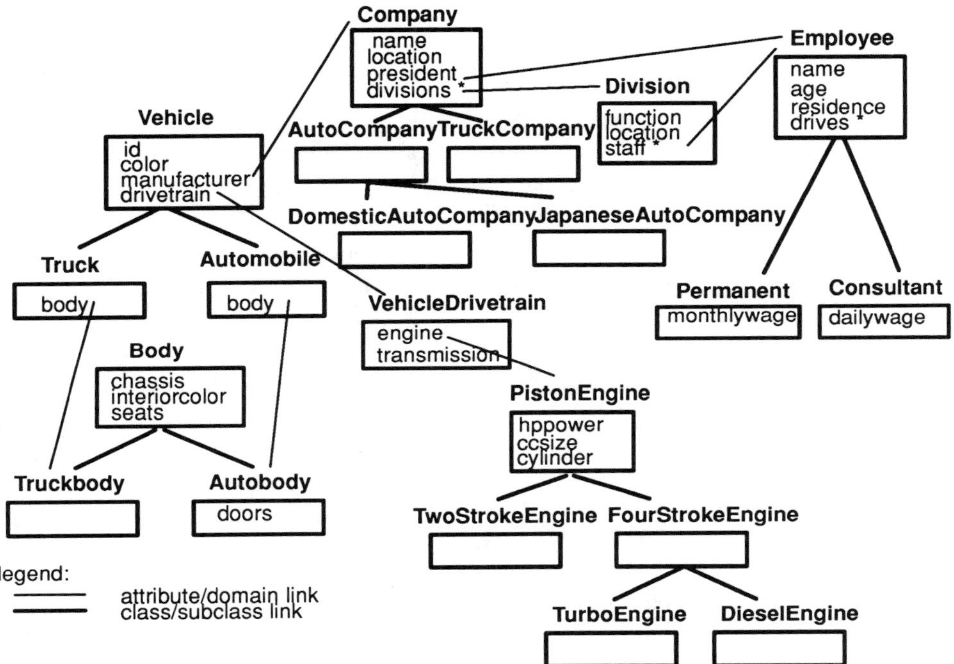

Figure 7.1
Definition of Classes of Person and Vehicle

In this query, the clause **class** Automobile * which follows the attribute 'drives' is used to denote the objects that are the values of this attribute and that belong to the class Automobile or any of its subclasses.

Let us now consider a query which retrieves 'all employees who live in Rome whose monthly wage is greater than 5,000 as permanent employees or dailywage greater than 1,000 as consultants'. This query can easily be expressed in our language as follows:

Q-h5: **select** :E **from** Employee * :E, Permanent :P, Consultant :C
where :E residence = "Rome" **and**
((:P montlywage > 5000 **and** :E=:P) **or**
(:C dailywage > 1000 **and** :E=:C)).

Note that a path variable of the form :E montlywage would be incorrect, because not all instances in the class hierarchy rooted at the class Employee have the attribute 'monthlywage'.

Using a path expression with the **class** clause, query Q-h5 can be more concisely expressed as follows:

Q-h5': **select** :E **from** Employee * :E
where :E residence = "Rome" **and**
(:E **class** Permanent montlywage > 5000 **or**
:E **class** Consultant dailywage > 1000).

A predicate applied to a path expression containing a **class** clause is false for all instances that do not belong to the class (or set of classes) specified in the **class** clause.

Let us now discuss the issue of compatibility among the attributes of the classes that appear in a class expression. One case is where the classes have an attribute with the same name and different domains. In this case the attributes are considered compatible with respect to a query Q if the domains belong to the same class hierarchy, and the path expressions used in Q are defined on the common attributes and methods of the class hierarchy. As an example, let us consider the following query:

Q-h6: **select** :X **from** Automobile **union** Truck
where :X color = "black" **and**
:X body doors = 2.

Query Q-h6 is incorrect, since the path expression ':X body doors' is not defined on the common attributes of the hierarchy to which the domains of the attribute 'body' (i.e., Truckbody and Autobody) belong. In fact, 'doors' is not an attribute of the class Body. The following however is a correct query.

Q-h7: **select** :X **from** Automobile **union** Truck
where :X color = "black" **and**
where :X body interiorcolor = "red".

Another case is where the classes have an attribute with equivalent semantics but different names. This case can easily be handled by using the alternative predicates previously described. To illustrate this, let us assume that an attribute called doors# is added to the class Truck. A query like Q-h6 may be formulated as follows:

Q-h8: **select** :X **from** Automobile **union** Truck
where :X color = "black" **and**
(:X **class** Automobile body doors = 2 **or**
:X **class** Truck doors# = 2).

7.2.2 Cyclic Queries

A class-composition hierarchy rooted at a particular class may contain one or more cycles. Some types of cycle may result from the interaction between the class-composition hierarchy and the class hierarchy, and from the fact that classes may have cyclic definitions. Let us now examine the syntax for the four types of cyclic queries defined in Chapter 6.

A meaningful query is to 'find all blue vehicles driven by the president of the company that manufactured them'. This is an example of a query with a type-n cycle in its query graph. This query is expressed as follows.

Q-c1: **select** :V **from** Vehicle :V
where color = "blue" **and** manufacturer president drives = :V.

In this query, the variable :V is used for binding each instance of the class Vehicle, as the set of instances of Vehicle is scanned one at a time. The class Vehicle is the target class.

A query to 'find all blue vehicles manufactured by a company whose president drives a Japanese automobile' is an example of a query with a type-ns cycle in the query graph. This query is expressed as follows.

Q-c2: **select** :V **from** Vehicle :V, JapaneseAutomobile :J
where :V color = "blue" **and** manufacturer president drives = :J.

The binding :J **in** JapaneseAutomobile constrains the value the nested sequence of attributes (manufacturer president drives) may take on to instances of the class JapaneseAutomobile. Note that the class Vehicle is still the target class.

For the next two examples, let us add the Manager attribute to the class Employee; the domain of Manager is the class Employee. The following is an example query with a type-s cycle. The query is to find "all managers of an employee named Johnson."

Q-c3: **select** Employee (**recurse** manager) **where** name = "Johnson".

The expression (recurse manager) specifies that, once an instance of the class Employee is found which satisfies the predicate (name = "Johnson"), the recursive values of the Manager attribute of the instance are retrieved. This example briefly shows how recursion is possible in the query language. We will provide a more extensive discussion of recursion shortly.

For our final example of a cyclic query, let us assume that the class Employee has a subclass FemaleEmployee. The following is an example query with a type-ss cycle, which finds "all female managers of an employee named Johnson."

Q-c4: **select** :F **from** FemaleEmployee :F, Employee :E
where :F **is-in** :E (**recurse** manager) **and** :E name = "Johnson".

This example shows that a set can be obtained by applying the recursion operator to an object attribute. In particular, the expression (recurse Manager) applied to the object variable :E defines a set containing all (direct or indirect) managers of an employee. Then the comparator is-in is used to test whether the retrieved female employee belongs to the set of managers of the selected employee (i.e., with :E name = "Johnson").

Recursive Queries

We now describe the language syntax for cyclic queries in greater detail. Consider the database schema in Figure 7.2 which contains two cycles. One is a type-s cycle on the class Device, and the other is a type-n cycle which involves the classes Device and Interface. For this database, the following recursive queries may be useful:

Q-r1: Find all electronic components of cars that recursively contain the electronic component EM-12 (i.e., ElectronicDevice of name "EM-12").

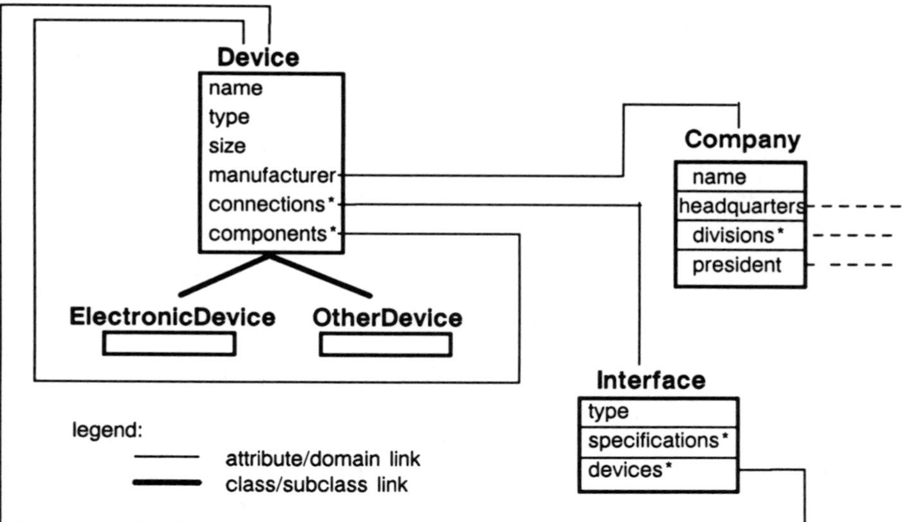

Figure 7.2
Example Schema with Cycles

Q-r2: Find all electronic components (i.e., ElectronicDevice) which can be recursively interfaced with bus FR-34 (i.e., device of type "bus" and name "FR-34").

These recursive queries can be expressed as follows:

Q-r1: **select** :X **from** ElectronicDevice :X, ElectronicDevice :Y
where :Y name = "EM-12" **and** :Y **is-in** :X (**recurse** components).

Q3: **select** :X **from** ElectronicDevice :X, :Y **in** ElectronicDevice :Y
where :Y type = "bus" **and** :Y name = "FR-34"
and Y **is-in** :X (**recurse** connections components *).

We allow the definition of a segment in the path specification of a path variable which can be repeated zero or more times. A recursive path segment is indicated by the keyword *recurse* followed by one or more attributes which constitute the repeating pattern.

The semantics of the recursive definition of a path segment in a query expression is defined as follows. The predicate

(<path-1> (*recurse* <segment>) <path-2>) <comparator> <value-or-variable>

is semantically equivalent to the following Boolean subexpression:

((<path-1> <path-2>) <comparator> <value-or-variable>) or
((<path-1> <segment> <path-2>) <comparator> <value-or-variable>) or
((<path-1> <segment> <segment> <path-2>) <comparator> <value-or-variable>) or
...
((<path-1> <segment> ... <segment> <path-2>) <comparator> <value-or-variable>)

where the number of predicates in logical OR, and therefore the number of repetitions of <segment> in the last predicate in the Boolean subexpression, is limited by the maximum length of the path <path-1> <segment> ... <segment> <path-2>, in all complex objects addressed by the query.

The termination condition is that the last attribute in the path variable is either a primitive class or has as value the object identifier of an object already present as value of a nested sequence of attributes in the same path variable. Given the termination condition and the fact that primitive classes (with infinite sets of instances) are not allowed as the target of a query, the recursive queries expressible in our query language are safe.

The recursive queries discussed here are limited to linear recursion. There is the widespread belief that most 'real life' recursive rules are indeed linear. Further, efficient algorithms have been developed to handle efficiently the linear recursion. There is a major difference between the recursive queries expressible in our language and those of logic-based languages. In our language, we require an explicit specification of the rules to apply, and their order, in defining the query (only the number of recursions is left unspecified); while in logic-based languages the system tries all possible rules for evaluating the goal of a query.

7.2.3 Methods

In terms of the role a method may play in a query, we distinguish two types of method: *derived-attribute method* and *predicate method.* A derived-attribute method has a function comparable to that of an attribute and returns objects (i.e., primitive values or object identifiers). Unlike an attribute, which holds a value, a derived-attribute method is a program which computes a value from the attribute values of the object or some other objects in the database. A predicate method is used as a predicate and returns the logical constants True or False. The value returned by the predicate method can then participate in the evaluation of the Boolean expression in a query.

The following example illustrates a query which contains the invocation of a derived-attribute method. Let us suppose that a method named Value is defined on the class Automobile, and that the method computes the value of an automobile from its components, such as the 'drivetrain' and the 'engine'. The query retrieves the persons who own at least one automobile of value greater than $10,000.

Q-m1: **select** Person
    where exists ownedvehicles **class** Automobile value > 10,000.

The next example illustrates a query which contains a predicate method. Let us suppose that a method named CompanyEarning is defined on the class Company. The method computes the earnings performance of a company and returns True if the result of the computation corresponds to the argument specified in the method invocation (e.g., "increasing"); and returns False otherwise. The method may access other objects in the database (e.g., financial information) and invoke additional methods. The query retrieves the companies that are located in Texas and have all their divisions in Texas and all of whose earnings are increasing.

Q-m2: **select** Company
    where location = "Texas" **and each** divisions location = "Texas"
    and companyearning ("increasing").

The examples used thus far returned only primitive values. Methods can also return complex objects to which other methods may be applied. Let us further extend the definition of the class Division by assuming that each division has an attribute named 'autopool' that represents a set of automobiles available to the staff of the division for business trips. Let us also assume that the class Employee has a method named 'availableauto' that receives as input the destination of a trip and returns a set of object identifiers of automobiles which can be used for the trip. This method determines available automobiles on the basis of the employee job category, the trip distance, and other considerations. A query to retrieve 'the names of the employees who may use an automobile manufactured by Cadillac to go to Rome' is expressed as follows:

Q-m3: **select** Employee name
  where exists availableauto ("Rome") manufacturer name = "Cadillac".

Note that since the method 'availableauto' returns a set of objects, the existential quantifier has been used. Now, we consider a query similar to Q-m3 which shows the use of path variables as input parameters for a method. Let us consider a query which retrieves 'the names of employees who may use an automobile manufactured by Cadillac to visit a factory division'.

Q-m4: **select** :E name **from** Employee :E, Divisions :D
  where :E **exists** availableauto (:D location) manufacturer name =
    "Cadillac" **and**
    :D function ="factory".

Note that it is possible to check the type correctness of a query which contains a method invocation against the database schema only if the class of the result is specified in the method definition. If the class of the result is not specified, the type correctness of a query cannot be determined before the query is executed. A method can also be used to generate an attribute name. In this case, the value returned from the method invocation is a string which is interpreted as an attribute name on which a given predicate must be applied. In this case, however, the type correctness of the query cannot be verified even if the method definition specifies the type of the result.

We can now extend the definition of ScalarPathElement as follows:

ScalarPathElement ::= *ScalarAttributeName* |
  ScalarMethodName MethodArguments |
  Quantifier *SetAttributeName* |
  Quantifier *SetMethodName* MethodArguments

Methods used in queries can cause side effects. This problem arises because sometimes the result of a query depends on the evaluation order of the predicates in the query; that is, different evaluation orders may yield different results for the same query. There is no satisfactory formal understanding of this problem at this time, and thus it will not be treated here.

7.2.4 Query Results

The projection operation in a query applies to both primitive and nested sequence of attributes of objects. Projections on a nested sequence of attributes are specified by using simple path expressions, that is, path expressions that do not contain quantifiers and class expressions. The following is an example.

Q-p1: **select** Vehicle color, manufacturer location
where manufacturer president age < 50.

Path expressions used in projections can return a set of objects. As an example, the following query retrieves 'the names and divisions of companies located in Rome'.

Q-p2: **select** Company name, divisions
where location = "Rome".

Note that a projection does not necessarily return only primitive objects. In fact, the projection on 'divisions' would return for each selected company a set of identifiers of complex objects. Our query language allows the use of methods in path expressions in the target clause. This is particularly useful in computing and outputting derived attributes. As an example, suppose that the class Permanent has a method that computes the bonus that each employee receives. A query to retrieve 'the names and bonuses of all employees who earn a monthly wage greater than 5000' is expressed as follows.

Q-p3: **select** Permanent name, bonus
where monthlywage > 5000.

The projection operation entails the familiar problem of eliminating duplicates from the query result. As we discussed earlier, the test can be based on object equality or value equality. Object equality is our default. However, the user may force the testing of value equality by using the key word UNIQUE VALUE. As an example, let us suppose that the class Vehicle has a composite attribute (defined in Chapter 2) 'drivetrain' whose domain is VehicleDriveTrain. Further, suppose that the class VehicleDrivetrain in turn has a composite attribute 'engine', whose domain is the class VehicleEngine. Two vehicles cannot reference the same instance of VehicleDrivetrain.

Therefore, if two vehicles have the same type of drivetrain, they reference two objects with different object identifiers but the same values for all user-defined attributes. Similarly, let us suppose that two drivetrains cannot have the same instance of the class VehicleEngine. Let us consider a query which retrieves 'all different types of engines used in cars manufactured by Ford'.

Q-p4: **select unique value** Vehicle drivetrain engine
where manufacturer name = "Ford".

This query returns, for each type of engine, the object identifier of one of the instances of the class VehicleEngine of that type.

7.3 Multiple-Operand Queries

7.3.1 Join

To admit joins of classes on user-specified join attributes, we must account for the class hierarchy in the scope of query evaluation. Each class to be joined is the root of a class hierarchy. The scope of query evaluation, for each class to be joined, may be either instances of the class alone or instances of the class hierarchy rooted at the class. The query syntax must allow the user to specify the scope for each class in a join, just as was the case for a single-operand query.

Join predicates are specified as follows:

ScalarVariable ScalarComparator ScalarVariable |
SetVariable SetComparator SetVariable |
ScalarVariable ScalarSetComparator SetVariable |
SetVariable SetScalarComparator ScalarVariable.

The first type of join predicate is similar to the relational join predicate. However, the join attribute is not just a primitive attribute; it may be a nested sequence of attributes. The second type of predicate allows the join of classes on multi-valued attributes; this is not supported in relational databases, since relational databases do not support multi-valued attributes. The third and fourth types of predicates allow the join of classes on a mixture of a scalar attribute and a multi-valued attribute. In this case the comparators that can be used are those defined for comparing a scalar value against a set, or vice versa.

Referring to the schema of Figure 7.3 (which is an extension of Figure 7.1), let us consider a query which finds 'all employees of the Ford company who live in a city where a factory belonging to an automobile manufacturing company is located'.

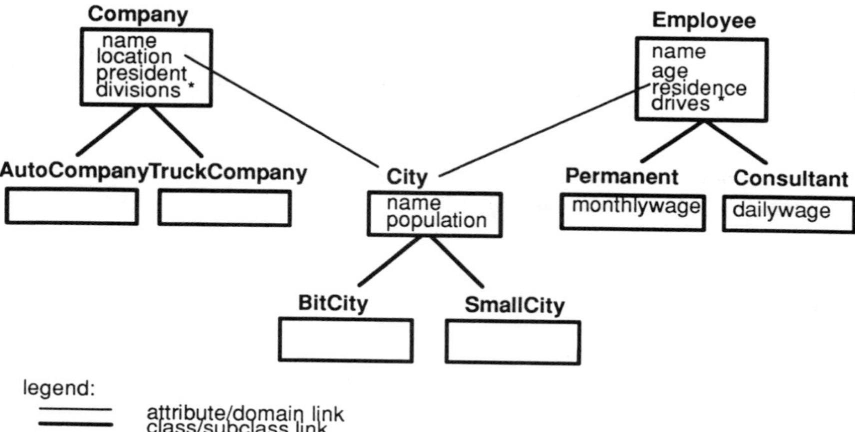

Figure 7.3
Example Schema for a Join

Q-j1: **select** :E **from** Employee :E, Company :C, Automobile :A,
:D **is-in** :A manufacturer divisions
where :E **is-in** :C divisions staff **and** :C name = "Ford" **and**
:E residence = :D location **and** :D function = "factory".

Q-j1 contains two join predicates. The first predicate is ':E **is-in** :C divisions staff'; it compares a scalar variable against a set by using a set membership predicate. The second predicate is ':E residence = :D location'; it compares two scalar variables. Since the scalar variable denotes two primitive attributes of the classes Employee and Division, this join predicate corresponds to the join predicate in relational queries.

Let us suppose that the domains of Residence attribute of the class Employee and the attribute Location of the class Company are the same, say a class City. Then a meaningful query may be to find 'all employees who live in the city in which their companies are located'. This query is formulated as follows

Q-j2: **select** :E **from** Employee :E, Company :C
where :E residence city = :C location city.

This query contains a join predicate that compares two scalar variables. The scalar variables denote two nested sequences of attributes of the classes Employee and Company.

7.4 Set Operations

Once the set operations are taken into account, the query is completely defined as follows:

Query ::= (Query) |
Query Union Query |
Query Intersection Query |
Query Difference Query |
SimpleQuery.

The operand of a set operation is a set of instances; more specifically, it may be the set of instances of a class defined in the database, or it may be a set of instances obtained as the result of a query. As we have seen already, for object-oriented databases, two different criteria exist for determining the uniqueness of an instance from a collection of instances, namely, object equality and value equality. Therefore, our language includes two forms for each set operation. As an example, Q1 **union** Q2 is a query where the union of the results is obtained by eliminating duplicates using object equality. Q1 **value-union** Q2 is a query where duplicates are eliminated using value equality.

Recommended Readings

Most of the materials in this chapter are taken from [KIM90a]. The query language specification for the O2 system is given in [BANC89]. [COPE84] presents a preliminary syntax for the query language of GemStone. [ZANI83] provides a good description of the GEM extended relational language from which some of the ideas were borrowed for the query language presented in this chapter.

8 Authorization

In a multi-user environment with a large shared database, it is necessary to restrict access rights (authorizations) to different parts of the database to different users. In database systems, an authorization is a specification of an authorization type (read, write, create) on a database entity (the entire database, a relation, a tuple) for a user. Most commercial database systems provide an authorization mechanism to allow the specification and enforcement of authorization. The current theory of authorization was developed in the mid-seventies in the context of research into consequences of the relational model of data on the database system architecture. The research during that period resulted in such (then) novel concepts as specifying individual columns (attributes) of a relation or a relational view as a unit of authorization, recursive granting and revoking of authorizations, and distribution of authorization-checking overhead to compile time and run-time.

An object-oriented data model is semantically richer than the relational model, and requires significant extensions to the current theory and implementation of authorization. In particular, such notions as methods and class hierarchy necessitate introduction of new authorization types, in addition to those traditionally provided. Further, in object-oriented systems, an object is a unit of access, and as such an object should be a unit of authorization; this is especially meaningful in systems of large objects, such as documents, images, audio passages, and so on. Relational database systems do not support tuple-level authorizations. The theory of authorization thus extended to address the additional data-modeling dimensions in the core object-oriented model needs further extensions when the core model is augmented with such semantic modeling concepts as composite objects and versions. The additional extensions are necessary largely to allow a set of objects related through the part-of relationships or version-of relationships into a single abstract object which may be used as a unit of authorization.

In this chapter, we will first review the current theory of authorization, and then present an extended model of authorization which is based on the core object-oriented data model. The extensions necessitated by the introduction of composite objects and versions will be discussed in Chapter 12. Relational database systems support views to support content-based authorization. A view is a subset of the database which satisfies an arbitrary user-specified conditions, and it is used as a unit of authorization. A user who is authorized to access the database through a view is allowed to access an arbitrary subset of the database which satisfies the user-specified conditions. A theory of views for object-oriented databases is yet to emerge, as we will discuss in Chapter 16; and impacts of object-oriented concepts on such issues as mandatory and discretionary authorizations and authorizations based on context of the database and access requests, as well as database contents, are only beginning to be explored at this point. Therefore, we will not deal with these issues in this chapter.

8.1 Authorization Model for Relational Databases

The basis of access to a relational database is a query. The user formulates a query against one or more relations, and specifies a Boolean combination of search conditions to restrict the query result. For example, an SQL query expression has the SELECT, FROM, and WHERE clauses: the list of attributes whose values are to be output is specified in the SELECT clause; the list of relations against whom the query is formulated is given in the FROM clause; and the WHERE clause consists of a Boolean combination of predicates. In other words, a relation and its attributes are the fundamental units of access in relational databases, and, as such, a relation or an attribute of a relation is the unit of access authorization. We emphasize that a query is never formulated against a tuple (i.e., the user cannot specify a list of tuples in the FROM clause of an SQL query), and thus a tuple is not a unit of authorization.

In relational databases, a user may read or update the tuples of a relation; or, more finely, the values of an attribute of a relation. The creator of a relation has full access privileges to the relation. The creator may grant some or all of his access privileges to the relation to any number of other users; and may later revoke some or all of the privileges from the other users. Further, the user may grant to other users the privilege to grant the access privileges to yet other users.

In relational systems which support pre-compilation of queries, authorizations on the relations (and their attributes) involved in a query are checked at pre-compile time, so that the authorization-check overhead will not degrade the run-time performance of the query. Further, if the compiled queries are stored in the database for repeated execution, as in SQL/DS, a compiled and stored query is invalidated if authorizations on any of the relations involved in the query are revoked; the query is then re-compiled from the source statement of the query stored along with the compiled query.

8.2 Impacts of Object-Oriented Concepts

An object-oriented data model has three concepts which require extensions to the conventional models of authorization: objects, methods, and class hierarchy. In this section, we discuss the impacts of these concepts on the authorization model. A model of authorization which accounts for these impacts will be presented in the next sections.

In object-oriented systems, every object is assigned a unique object identifier, and the user (application) is allowed to use the identifier as an explicit handle for an object. In other words, the assignment of a unique object identifier to every object makes an object a unit of access. Since an object is a unit of access, it must also be a unit of authorization; that is, in object-oriented databases, it makes sense to support object-level authorization. In contrast, in relational databases, the smallest unit of access is the relation; a query is the only means of accessing a database, and a query is always formulated against one or more relations.

If the application interactively manipulates many small objects, object-level authorization can cause a serious performance problem. If authorizations on the objects can be checked at compile time, the problem is not as serious. Regardless of when and how authorizations are checked, object-level authorization is both necessary and practical in an important class of object-oriented applications, namely, multimedia information management systems, such as a graphics system, a document-editing system, and so on. A common characteristic of multimedia information management systems is that the objects they deal with can be very large. The authorization-check overhead is negligible compared with the cost of retrieving and manipulating very large objects.

Next, the definition of a class in object-oriented systems includes attributes and methods. In contrast, the specification of a relation in relational databases includes only attributes. Attributes and methods are both properties of a class. An authorization on an attribute of a relation in relational databases restricts access privileges to the values of the attribute in tuples of the relation. A method, since it is a code, is used much differently from an attribute. A method may be either invoked; or the code or the name of the method may be changed. Therefore, we may define two types of authorization on methods: one for invoking them, and one for changing them.

Now let us examine authorization issues which arise from the concept of inheritance on a class hierarchy. The fact that subclasses inherit attributes and methods from superclasses, and the fact that the access scope of a class may include all instances of that class and instances of all its subclasses, raise a few questions about authorization on a class hierarchy. One question is whether the creator of a class should be prevented from changing the definition of the class, once any other user derived a subclass from the class. This question is motivated by the fact, as discussed in Chapter 5, that a change in the definition of a class is propagated to all direct and indirect subclasses of the class. It may be useful to the creator of a class to prevent the creator of a superclass of the class from changing the definition of the superclass. However, it is unreasonable to take away any authorization on a class from the creator of the class, especially when all he has done is to allow other users to derive new classes and inherit attributes and methods from the class.

Another question is whether the creator of a class should be given access privileges to all direct and indirect subclasses of the class. There are two positions which can be taken concerning authorization on the instances of a subclass. The first position is that the creator of a class should have no implicit authorizations on the instances of a subclass derived from the class. Therefore, the creator of the class Vehicle should not be able to update or read instances of the class Automobile unless explicitly given that authorization by the creator of the class Automobile (or other authorized grantor). This position encourages reuse of existing classes without diminishing privacy. However, a query whose scope of access is a class and its subclasses will only be evaluated against those classes for which the issuer of the query has a read authorization. The second position is that the creator of a class should have implicit authorizations on instances of a subclass. This means that the creator of the class Vehicle should be able to update and read instances of the class Automobile. This means that a query whose scope of access is a class and a class hierarchy rooted at the class will be evaluated against the class and all its subclasses. A reasonable approach is to adopt the first position as the default, and the second as a user option. An explicit authorization is necessary on a class to create subclasses of the class. Further, an authorization is necessary to control the access to instances of a subclass by the creator of a class.

An authorization issue related to a class hierarchy is the creation of indexes called class-hierarchy indexes. A class-hierarchy index is an index on an attribute (or a combination of attributes) shared by a class and all its subclasses; we will discuss class-hierarchy indexes in detail in Chapter 9. One question is whether a user should be able to create a class-hierarchy index rooted at a particular class, if he does not have authorizations on all subclasses of the class. It is reasonable to allow the user to create the index, but restrict access to only those subclasses on which he has authorizations.

8.3 A Basic Model of Authorization

The need for object-level authorization provides a strong motivation for the notion of implicit authorization. For example, a database may be organized as a hierarchy, called an authorization-object hierarchy, of successively smaller granules with which authorizations may be associated; each node in an authorization-object hierarchy is called an authorization object. If a user has an authorization on an authorization object, he has implicit authorizations on all authorization objects logically subsumed by the object. For example, if a user is authorized to read a set of instances, he need not be explicitly authorized to read each individual instance. The notion of implicit authorizations facilitates authorization control, especially if object-level authorization must be supported. Further, it helps to keep storage requirements manageable to maintain authorization information. Implicit authorizations incur a compute overhead to determine whether a particular authorization is implied by an explicitly stored authorization. This compute overhead must be carefully weighed against the space advantages that implicit authorizations offer.

An authorization is expressed as "a user having a certain access privilege to an object created by some user." From this, we can see that an authorization specification consists of three elements: the user, the object, and the access type In other words, an authorization model has three dimensions (domains). The notion of implicit authorizations models each of the three domains of an authorization model in terms of a hierarchy such that an authorization associated with a node implies the same authorization on all direct and indirect descendants of the node. For example, a manager should be able to access any information which the employees of the manager may access; if a user has the delete authorization on a class, then he should have the same authorization on any instance of the class; and if a user has the write authorization on an object, he should also have the read authorization on the object.

The notion of implicit authorizations necessitates the concept of weak authorizations, and the concept of weak authorizations in turn necessitate the concept of negative authorizations. A *weak authorization* is an authorization on a node of one of the three authorization hierarchies which may be overridden at a lower level of the hierarchy. An authorization in existing models is a *strong authorization*, in the sense that it cannot be overridden.

A *negative authorization* is an explicit specification of exceptions to an authorization on each of the three domains of authorization. Conventional authorization mechanisms do not provide authorization primitives that can be used to specify exceptions to a group of authorized users (e.g., authorize all but Smith), exceptions to a set of objects (e.g., authorize access to all classes but the class Confidential-Documents), and exceptions to a set of access types (e.g., all authorization types except Generate-Class). They assume that the default authorization, when nothing is specified, is null. This means that an authorization is inherently positive and the fact that a user has no access to a specific object is described only by the absence of authorization.

The combination of the concepts of positive/negative authorizations and strong/weak authorization allows a more concise and flexible representation of diverse authorization requirements. It helps to alleviate the storage requirements. Further, combining one weak negative authorization with a few strong positive authorizations has the effect of allowing a few exceptional positive authorizations to override a negative authorization at a higher level. Similarly, combining one weak positive authorization with a few strong negative authorizations allows singling out a few exceptional negative authorizations from a positive authorization at a higher level. This is illustrated in the following example.

Suppose that the class Automobile has 1000 instances, and that we wish to grant a read authorization to user John on all instances of the class except one instance, say instance[2]. The conventional approach would require us to specify a read authorization on 999 individual instances of the class, except instance[2]. With a combination of one weak positive authorization and one strong negative authorization, we can accomplish the same operation simply. We specify a weak read authorization on the class Automobile for John, and grant to John a negative strong read authorization on instance[2].

In the remainder of this section, we will describe a model of authorization which incorporates all the concepts motivated above. In Section 8.4 we will show how the model may be extended to account for methods and class hierarchy.

8.3.1 Authorization Subject Hierarchy

An authorization subject is one or more users who share the same access privileges on the same set of objects. One or more users form an authorization subject, and one user may belong to more than one subject. The authorization subjects are organized as a rooted directed acyclic graph, which we will call an *authorization-subject hierarchy*. A node of the graph represents a subject, and a directed arc from node A to node B indicates that authorizations for subject A include authorizations for subject B. A subject can have multiple child subjects, subsuming all authorizations of all the child subjects. Further, a subject can have multiple parent subjects, so that all users who belong to the ancestors of a subject share all the authorizations of that subject. The subject hierarchy has a single root, the super-user subject.

An example authorization-subject hierarchy is shown in Figure 8.1. In the figure, if object A is accessible to the subject mgr and user-1 belongs to the subject mgr, then user-1 can access object A. Further, if user-2 belongs to the subject accounts-recv-mgr, user-2 can also access object A.

8.3.2 Authorization Type Hierarchy

We assume a *partial ordering* of all authorization types; that is, the authorization types are arranged in an *authorization-type hierarchy*, a rooted directed acyclic graph. An arc from node A to node B indicates that authorization type A implies authorization type B.

To be concrete, let us consider the authorization types: R (Read), W (Write), G (Generate), and RD (Read Definition). Figure 8.2 is the corresponding authorization-type hierarchy. The figure shows that W implies R and G, and R and G each implies

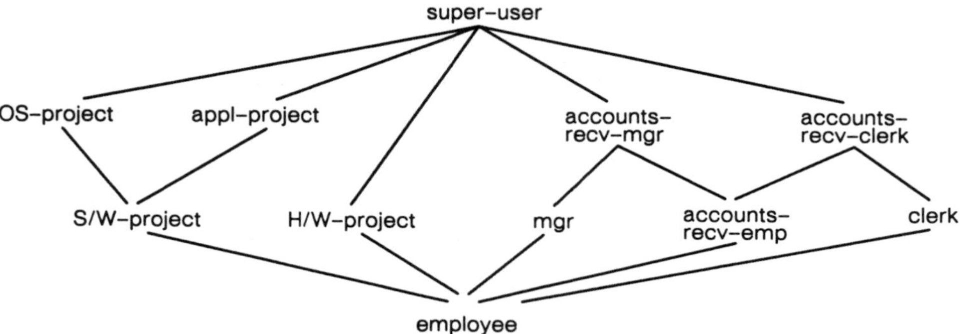

Figure 8.1
Example Authorization-Subject Hierarchy

RD. Note that a generate authorization on a class implies a read definition authorization on the same class, since a user must be able to read the class definition in order to create instances of that class. However, a generate authorization on a class does not imply a write (or read) authorization on instances of that class. This is reasonable since the fact that a subject can create instances of a class does imply that the subject can modify or read all instances of that class. A subject can only modify or read the instances that he has created or on which an authorization has been granted.

8.3.3 Implicit Authorizations for Authorization Objects

Implicit authorizations for the set O of authorization objects have greater impacts on performance and functionality of a database system than those for authorization types and authorization subjects. The reason is that the number of objects in a database is in general much larger than the number of subjects or authorization types. For the authorization objects we need to exploit as much as possible the fact that an authorization can be deduced from another authorization and so need not be explicitly stored.

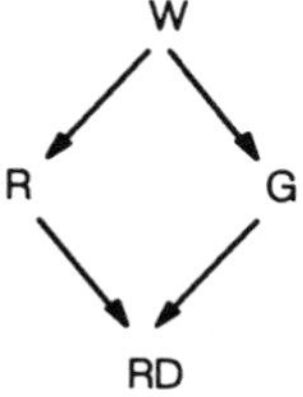

Figure 8.2
Example Authorization-Type Hierarchy

The objects which may be used as a unit of authorization are called authorization objects. Authorization objects are organized in a hierarchy called an authorization-object hierarchy (*AOH*). As shown in Figure 8.3, an *AOH* is a rooted directed acyclic graph where each node is an authorization object, and each directed arc is an *implication link* which defines an implicit authorization relationship between two nodes. An arc from node A to node B indicates that an authorization on node A implies an authorization on node B.

Each node in an *AOH* belongs to one, and only one, *authorization object category.* The authorization object categories collectively constitute the schema for the authorization objects: we call this schema the *authorization object schema (AOS).* Figure 8.4 shows a diagram which represents the schema for the authorization objects of Figure 8.3. Each node in an *AOS* is an authorization object category and a directed arc represents an implication link between authorization objects of two categories.

We note that authorization objects are not in one-to-one correspondence with database objects. That is, there is an important difference between an authorization-object hierarchy and a database-granularity hierarchy, such as the one represented in Figure 8.5. In a database-granularity hierarchy, we can see that each node represents at least two types of information: about the node itself and about the set of nodes at the next lower level. For example, operations on a class in Figure 8.5 may be on the class object or on the set of instances of the class. Therefore, it makes sense to define explicitly two different authorization objects to represent the class: a class authorization object

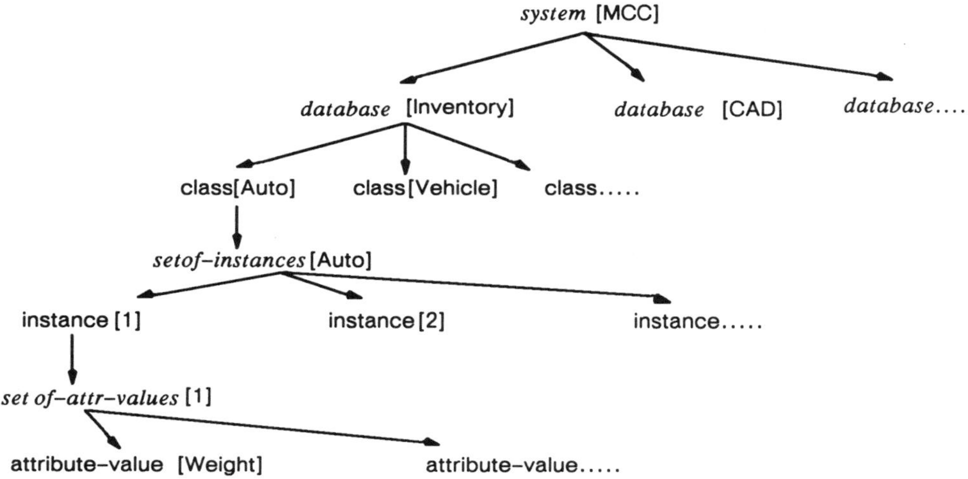

Figure 8.3
Example Authorization-Object Hierarchy

Figure 8.4
Authorization-Object Schema

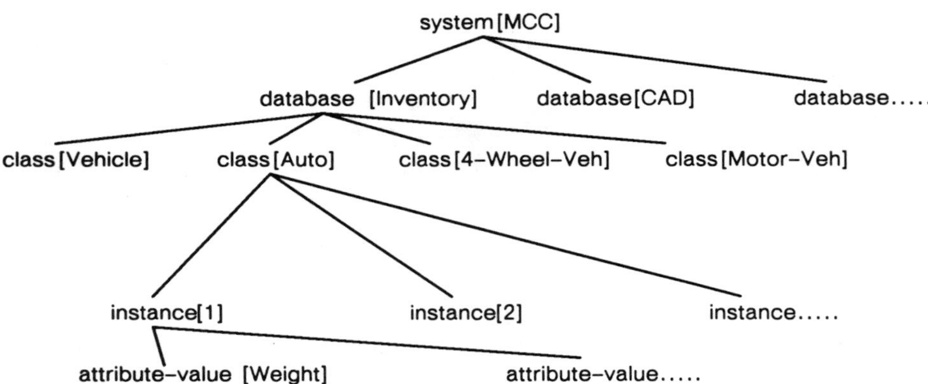

Figure 8.5
Example Database-Granularity Hierarchy

and a *setof-instances* authorization object. A write authorization on the class[Auto] authorization object means that the class definition can be updated. A write authorization on the *setof-instances*[Auto] authorization object means that all of the instances can be updated.

The nodes shown in *italics* in Figure 8.3 are authorization objects which may have implication links to a set of authorization objects at the next lower level. For example, the *setof-instances*[Auto] authorization object may have implication links to all instance authorization objects of the class[Auto]. The nodes shown in non-italics in Figure 8.3 are restricted to one implication link to the node at the next lower level. For example, the class[Auto] authorization object has an implication link to only one *setof-instances* authorization object.

The use of an authorization-object hierarchy makes it unnecessary to double the set of authorization types we have defined: that is, we can use them with the *same partial ordering* among them, for most of the authorization objects in O. Without this, we would have to double the set of authorization types: one for an authorization object, and another for the set of next lower-level authorization objects. For example, if we did not split the class node into two authorization objects, we would need four authorization types for the class node: write class object, read class object, write all instances of the class, and read all instances of the class.

8.3.4 Operations

Authorizations are stored in authorization catalogs. There are two types of authorization catalogs: one for strong authorizations and one for weak authorizations. As in conventional model of authorization, basic authorization operations include checking, granting and revoking authorizations. Checking an authorization involves determining if the authorization is explicitly stored or is implied by stored authorizations. Grating an authorization causes the authorization to be stored in the authorization catalogs; and revoking an authorization causes the authorization to be deleted from the authorization catalogs.

- **Check Authorization**. To check an authorization, first the strong authorization catalogs are looked up. If the authorization is not stored or deducible from any stored authorization in the strong authorization catalogs, the weak authorization catalogs are looked up.
- **Grant Authorization**. Granting a strong (weak) authorization means inserting it into the strong (weak) authorization catalogs, if the authorization is not alredy stored or implied. An authorization may be granted with or without the GRANT option, to allow the grantee to grant it to other authorization subjects.
- **Revoke Authorization**. Revoking a strong (weak) authorization means deleting it from the strong (weak) authorization catalogs.

8.4 Extensions to the Basic Model

In this section, we will describe how the basic model of authorization may be extended to account for two object-oriented concepts, namely, properties of classes and class hierarchy. The extensions manifest themselves as additional authorization object categories in the *AOS*. Figure 8.6 is the extended *AOS*. These new authorization objects are connected through the implication links defined in Section 8.3. The set of authorization types for the new objects is W, R, and G.

We first describe how authorizations on various properties that apply to classes are modeled by introducing new authorization objects. Then, we present authorization for the class hierarchy.

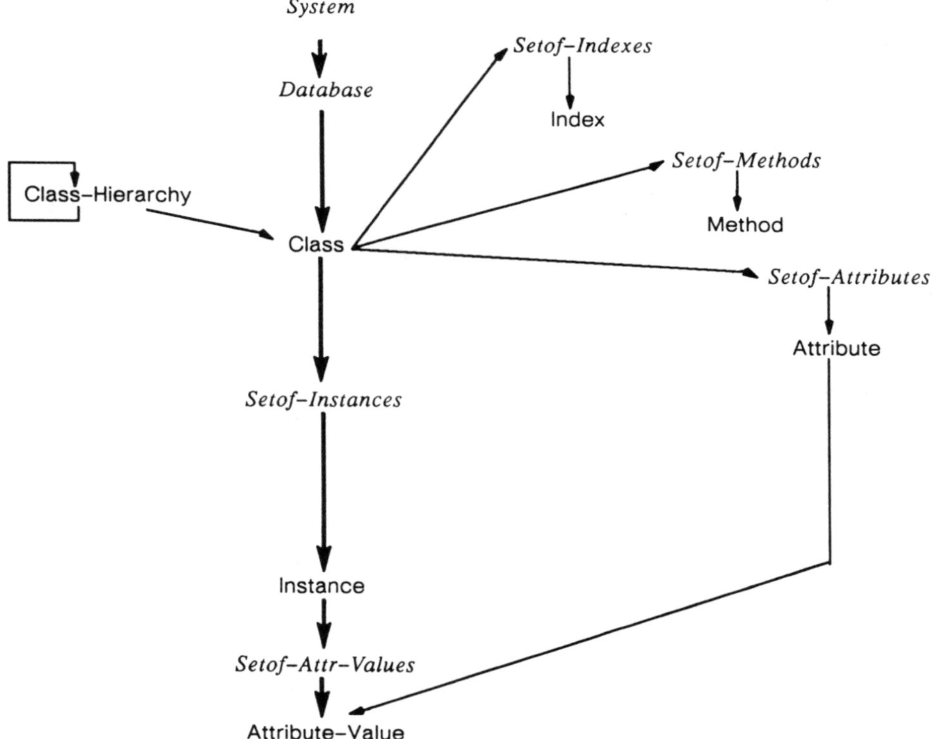

Figure 8.6
Extended Authorization-Object Schema

8.4.1 Authorization Objects for Class Related Authorizations

To describe any specific authorization on the attributes of a class, we introduce the authorization objects *Setof-Attributes* and Attribute (see Figure 8.6). A W (or R) authorization on a particular attribute means that the subject can update (or read) the values of this attribute in all instances of the class. The implicit authorization on the corresponding attribute values of all instances is reflected in the implication link from node Attribute to the node Attribute-Value in the *AOS*. We note that this implication link does not exist for class attributes.

Similarly, we model authorizations on methods by introducing the authorization objects *Setof-Methods* and Method. Since most object-oriented systems do not allow methods to be specified for instances, there is no implication link from the node Method to the instance node. We assume that an R authorization on Method means authorization to invoke the corresponding method. However, all the operations which are performed during the execution of the method must be further checked by the authorization mechanism. If during the execution of a method invoked by subject s, an attempt is made to update a particular attribute value of an instance, the authorization for s to update the attribute value is checked by the authorization mechanism.

The authorizations on attributes and methods are restricted to the extensional aspects of a class, that is, values of attributes in instances or invocation of methods on instances. They do not affect the intensional aspects of a class, that is definition of attributes and methods; these are controlled by a W authorization on the node Class (i.e. an authorization to change the class definition).

Authorizations on indexes are modeled by the authorization objects *Setof-Indexes* (e.g., to drop all indexes) and Index (e.g., to drop a particular index). It does not seem useful, although it is possible, to control the use of indexes in query processing by individual users using the R authorization on Index. In fact, an index is a resource which may speed up the database access but does not give more information on the database contents. A *G* authorization on the category *Setof-Indexes* is used for the authorization to create an index on a class.

8.4.2 Class Hierarchy

Figure 8.6 illustrates the new authorization object Class-Hierarchy which we introduce to support authorizations on a class hierarchy. We can use the authorization mechanism to control the creation of subclasses of a class. For this reason, we have introduced in the set A the authorization type G for the authorization object Class. A G authorization on a class is an authorization to create subclasses of the class, and inherit properties of the class. Note that a W authorization on a Class implies a G authorization on the Class. However the G authorization on a class does not imply a G authorization on the *setof-instances* of that class. We have also introduced the authorization object

Class-Hierarchy to control the access to instances of a subclass by the creator of a class.

Figure 8.7 shows an example of a portion of a class hierarchy. The class Auto is a subclass of both the class 4-Wheel-Vehicle and the class Motor-Vehicle, which are both subclasses of the class Vehicle. The class Auto inherits attributes and methods from both of its superclasses. Let us suppose that a subject *S* wishes to create a new class Auto, which would inherit properties from both 4-Wheel-Vehicle and Motor-Vehicle. Of course, *S* needs a G authorization on *database*[Inventory] to create the class Auto. *S* also needs to have a G authorization on class[4-Wheel-Vehicle] and class[Motor-Vehicle]. *S* will then have a W authorization on class[Auto], and hence an implicit G authorization on class[Auto]. Therefore, *S* may now create new subclasses of Auto. This cascading of G authorization on a chain of subclasses is similar to that of a G authorization on the database granularity hierarchy.

Figure 8.8 illustrates an *AOH* for an example database where the class Pickup has been created as a subclass of the class Auto. When a subject, say S1, requested to create the class Auto, S1 was required to have an explicit or implicit G authorization on *database*[Inventory]. S1 will then have a W authorization on class[Auto] and class-hierarchy[Auto]. This gives S1 the authorization to read and update all instances of the class Auto and the instances of any subclasses of Auto which may later be created by S1.

If a different subject, S2, is to create the class Pickup as a subclass of the class Auto, S2 needs a G authorization on *database*[Inventory] and class[Auto]. S2 will then have a W authorization on class[Pickup] and class-hierarchy[Pickup]. At that point, the system gives S2 the option of allowing S1, the creator of class [Auto], to read or update instances of class [Pickup]. If, for example, S2 chooses not to allow S1 to update instances of the class[Pickup], the system will grant a negative W authorization to S1 on *setof-instances*[Pickup]. The system will also change the strong W authorization which S1 has on the class-hierarchy[Auto] node to a weak W authorization. Note that

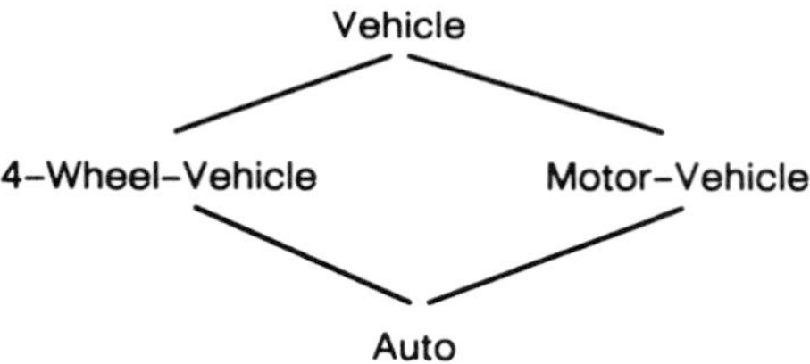

Figure 8.7
Example Class Hierarchy

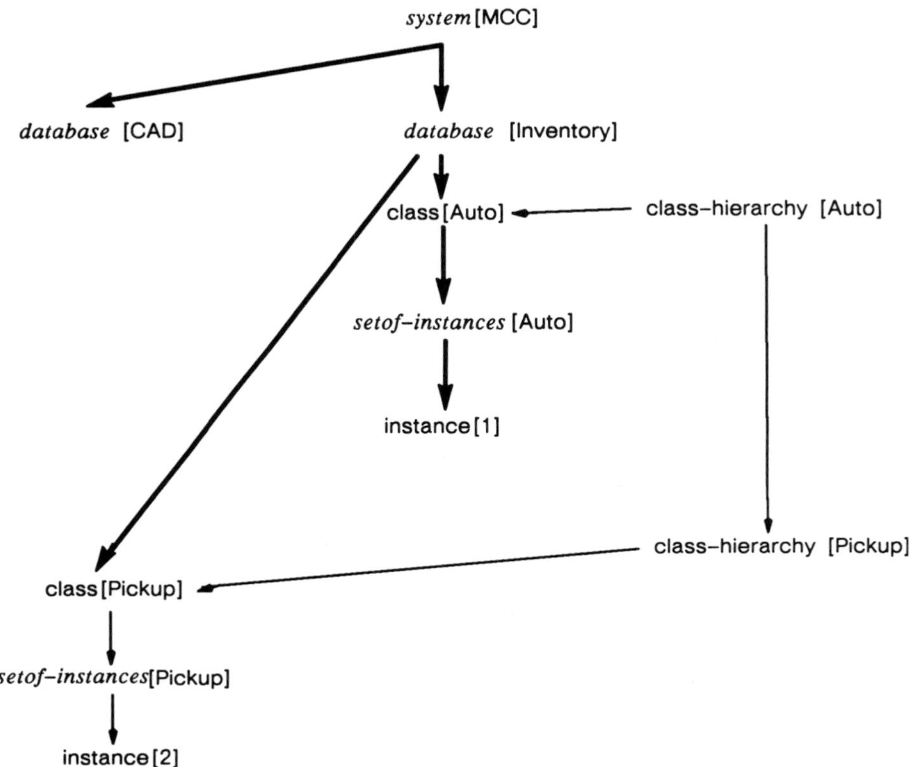

Figure 8.8
Extended Authorization-Object Hierarchy

S2 would not normally have the authorization to change the strong W authorization on class-hierarchy[Auto] to a weak W authorization. However, in this case the system makes this change so that the creator of the subclass can protect instances of the subclass.

8.5 Authorization Catalogs

In this section we discuss the data structures needed to implement the authorization subject hierarchy and the authorization objects.

8.5.1 Authorization Subject Hierarchy

Two data structures are needed to implement the authorization subject hierarchy. One maintains the authorization subject hierarchy. For each node in the hierarchy, the list of its children and parents is recorded. This data structure is defined as a class as follows, using the syntax provided in Chapter 3.

```
(Subject
    :attributes ((Subject        : domain String)
                 (Children       : domain (set-of Subject))
                 (Parents        : domain (set-of Subject)))
    :methods    ((RetrieveDescendants (set-of Subject)))
                 ((RetrieveAncestors  (set-of Subject))))
```

The class Subject has two methods. Given a subject *S.i*, the method RetrieveDescendants determines all subjects *S.j* that are direct and indirect descendants of subject *S.i*; the method is used when checking positive authorizations. The method RetrieveAncestors determines, for a subject *S.i*, all subjects *S.j* that are direct and indirect ancestors of subject *S.i*; the method is invoked when checking negative authorizations.

A second data structure associates users with their subjects. A user *U* may belong to more than one subject. This data structure is specified as the following class:

```
(UserSubject
    :attributes (UserName       : domain String)
                (Subject        : domain (set-of Subject)))
```

8.5.2 Authorization Objects

Authorizations are stored in several system catalogs. Each of the catalogs maintains authorizations on objects of a particular authorization object type. Maintaining several catalogs allows efficient authorization checking for authorization objects belonging to higher levels (close to the root) in the *AOS*, even when the granularity of authorization is very small. For example, allowing object-level authorizations does not impact the time needed to check authorizations at the database level, since authorizations on databases and those on instances are stored in separate catalogs. Further, this approach is cleaner and allows the authorization mechanism to be more easily modified and extended. Figure 8.9 shows the catalogs used for the authorization object types in our authorization model. As an example, we represent the catalog ClassAuth as a system-defined class as follows (the others can be defined in a similar way):

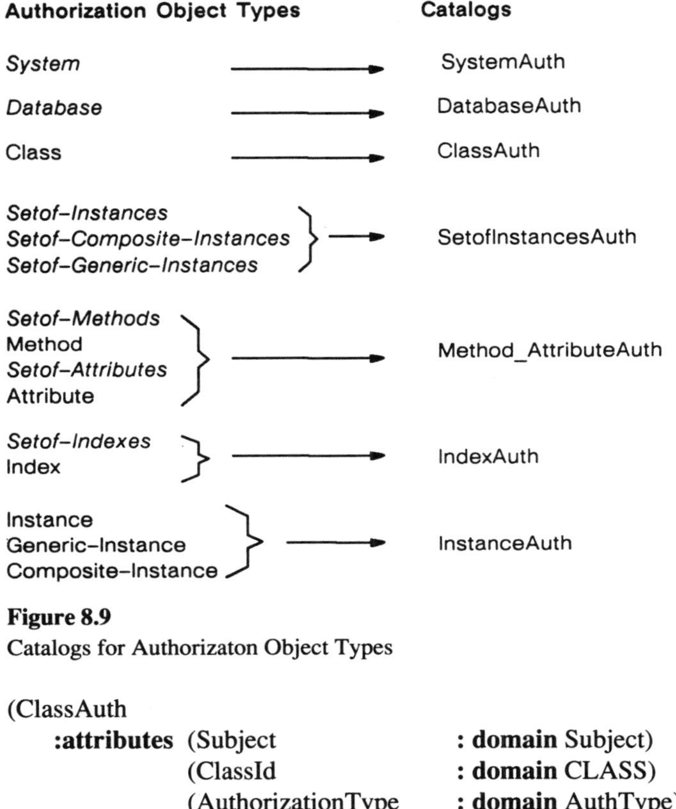

Figure 8.9
Catalogs for Authorizaton Object Types

```
(ClassAuth
    :attributes (Subject              : domain Subject)
                (ClassId              : domain CLASS)
                (AuthorizationType    : domain AuthType)).
```

The authorization catalogs are used to store both strong and weak authorizations. One issue concerning weak authorizations is the computation of implicit authorizations. In particular, exceptions to a given weak authorization may occur on objects at several levels down in the *AOS* from the object on which the weak authorization holds. For example, a subject may have a positive weak R authorization on a database and a negative R authorization on a composite instance. In order to make it efficient to compute the scope of weak authorizations, we associate an *exception flag* with each weak authorization. If the flag is on, additional accesses to other catalogs may be needed.

Figure 8.10 summarizes the catalog access strategies for each authorization category. In the figure the arrow from one catalog to another indicates that the latter

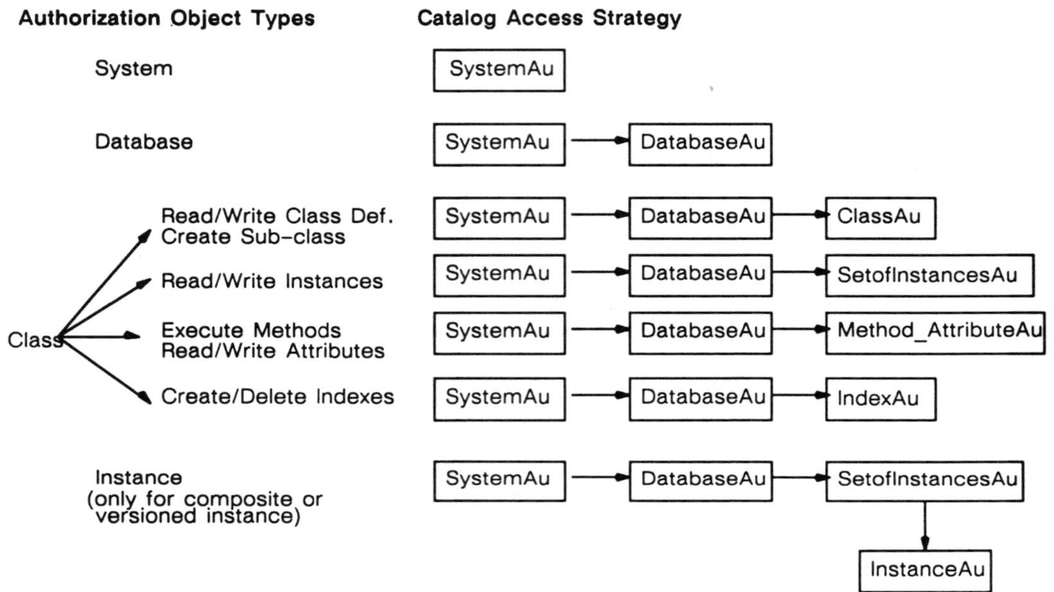

Figure 8.10
Authorization Catalog Access Strategies

catalog must be accessed if the authorization is not found or a weak authorization with exceptions is found in the first catalog.

Recommended Readings

The authorization model for object-oriented databses that we presented in this chapter is largely based on [RABI89]. The model of authorization presented in this chapter does not include considerations of more general authorization issues, such as mandatory and discretionary authorizations, content and context-based authorizations. [THUR89] is perhaps the first paper which extends some of these issues to object-oriented databases. [DATE84] and[GRIF76] provide detailed descriptions of authorization mechanisms supported in relational database systems DB2 and SQL/DS, respectively.

9 Storage Structures

The richness of an object-oriented data model requires a reexamination of storage structures for a database. The predominant pattern of object access in today's object-oriented applications is the direct access to single objects using the object identifiers as handles. The integration of object-oriented programming systems with database systems is expected to influence future applications to use declarative queries to extract sets of objects. Thus storage structures for object-oriented database systems must support efficient access to single objects given their object identifiers, and to sets of objects belonging to one or more class given queries with arbitrarily complex search conditions. Further, a significant subset of the applications for object-oriented database systems is expected to be, as it is today, compute-intensive; which means that object-oriented database systems must support storage structures to efficiently manage objects in memory once they have been fetched from the database. In other words, object-oriented database systems require two types of storage structures: one for managing persistent objects in the database, and one for managing objects accumulated in memory.

In this chapter, we will focus on storage structures for managing persistent objects on the basis of those used in ORION. In particular, we will describe the storage structures for individual instances, classes, and the database schema. Next we will discuss access methods necessary to support efficient access to the database, including physical clustering of instances, hashing, and indexing. We will discuss the storage structures for managing in-memory objects, including storage structures necessary to support message passing, in Chapter 14.

9.1 Structure for Instances

One way to store individual instances in the database is shown in Figure 9.1. The UID is the globally unique identifier of an object. The OBJECT-LENGTH and ATTRIBUTE-COUNT record the total length of the object and the number of attributes stored in the disk format. The ATTRIBUTE-VECTOR consists of the identifiers

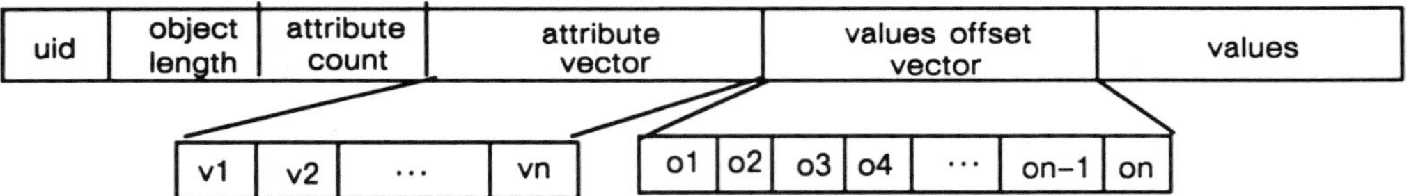

Figure 9.1
Storage Format for Instances

Vi of all attributes for which the object has explicitly specified values. An attribute may be user-defined, or system-defined. System-defined attributes include, for example, the version number and update timestamp for versioned objects and objects whose update must be notified (we will discuss these in detail in Chapter 12). An attribute is itself an instance of the system class Attribute, as we will show shortly, and, as such, has a unique identifier.)

The VALUES-OFFSET VECTOR consists of the offsets Oi, in the VALUES part of the object storage format, of the values of the attributes Vi. A value can be a primitive value or a reference to another instance, namely, the UID of the referenced object. If an object has a default value or a shared value for an attribute, that attribute does not appear in the storage format. The shared value and the default value of shared-value and default-value attributes are stored in the system class Attribute in which information about all attributes in the database is maintained.

Object Identifier

One of the distinguishing characteristics of object-oriented systems is that each object has a system-generated unique identifier. The identifier of an object may be constructed in a few different ways: each has different advantages and disadvantages. In one approach, used in ORION, an object identifier consists of a <class identifier, instance identifier> pair, where the class identifier is the identifier of the class to which the object belongs, and the instance identifier is the identifier of the instance either within the class or within the entire database. In a distributed system, the identifier needs to be further augmented with a site identifier; however, for simplicity, we will assume a centralized database for now. The class object maintains the specification of the attributes and methods for all instances of the class.

One advantage of this approach is that, when a message is sent to an object, the system can extract the class identifier of the object from the object identifier specified, without first having to fetch the object. The system must look up the class object to determine if the message is valid, and, if the message is valid, it will proceed to fetch the object and dispatch the corresponding method. Class objects may be cached to optimize system performance. One disadvantage of the approach, however, is that it makes it very expensive to migrate objects from one class to another class. If an object migrates from one class to another, its class identifier must be updated; that is, the object must be updated. Further, an object may reference any number of other objects, and an object may be referenced by any number of other objects. This means that, if the class identifier of an object is changed, all objects which contain references to the object will wind up with invalid references. It is of course very expensive to be able to identify such objects and update their references to the new identifier.

In another approach, used in Smalltalk, an object identifier consists only of an instance identifier. This approach still requires the class identifier of an object to be maintained; however, it is stored in a separate system-defined attribute of an object.

This approach has a few shortcomings. First, it makes message processing somewhat inefficient by causing needless fetching of objects for invalid messages. When a message is sent to an object, the system must first fetch the object, examine the class identifier in the object, and then look up the methods stored in the class object. Second, this approach makes type checking expensive, since the types (domains) of the objects referenced in an object can only be determined by actually fetching the objects and examining the class identifiers stored in them. One advantage of this approach is that it alleviates to a good extent the problems of migrating objects between classes. It still requires the class identifier to be updated in objects that migrate from one class to another. However, even if an object migrates, all references to the object from other objects remain valid, since the references do not contain the class identifier.

9.2 Structure for Class Objects

A class object maintains two types of information. One is the specification of the attributes and methods shared by all instances of the class, regardless of whether they are user-defined or system-defined. A class object in essence factors out the specification of attributes and methods that are common to all instances of the class; the names and properties of the attributes, and the names and codes of the methods are applicable equally to each instance. This type of attribute and method is sometimes called an instance attribute and an instance method, respectively. The class object contains references to instances of the system-defined classes Attribute and Method, respectively, as we will see shortly.

Another type of information maintained in a class object is the specification of the attributes and methods which apply to the class object itself. This type of attribute and method is sometimes called a class attribute and a class method, respectively; and applies to either all instances of the class or to any aggregate property of all instances of the class. An example of a class attribute is a default attribute: the value, as well as the name and the property, of the attribute is shared by all instances of the class for which the attribute value is not explicitly provided. Another example is a class attribute which represents some aggregate property of all instances of the class, such as the average age, total salary, and so on; the values of such attributes are shared by each instance of the class.

9.3 Structure for Database Schema

The schema of a relational database is represented as a set of system-defined relations, including a relation which describes all relations in the database, a relation which describes all attributes in all relations, and so on. Of course, there are additional system-defined relations to maintain information about access authorizations on relations, statistics about the database which the query optimizer utilizes, and so forth. It is natural to represent the schema of an object-oriented database as a set of system-defined classes. This set of system-defined classes must not only maintain information about all classes in the database, and attributes and methods defined for each class, but also capture the aggregation relationships between a class and its attributes, and the generalization relationships between a class and its subclasses, as we discussed in Chapter 2. Three of the system-defined classes which represent the schema of an object-oriented database are shown, in a simplified form, in Figure 9.2. For each class, attribute, or method defined in the database, there is a corresponding instance in one of these system-defined classes.

The class Class contains attributes ClassName, Attributes, Superclasses, Subclasses, and Methods. ClassName is the name of the class. Attributes is the set of all attributes defined for or inherited into the class. The attributes Superclasses and Subclasses are sets of superclasses and subclasses of the class, respectively. Methods is a set of methods defined for or inherited into the class. For simplicity, we do not differentiate between instance attributes (methods) and class attributes (methods).

The class Attribute (Method) has an instance for every attribute (method) defined for or inherited into each class. The class Attribute has attributes Class, Domain, and InheritedFrom. The attribute Class references the class to which the attribute belongs. Domain specifies the class to which the value of the attribute is bound. InheritedFrom

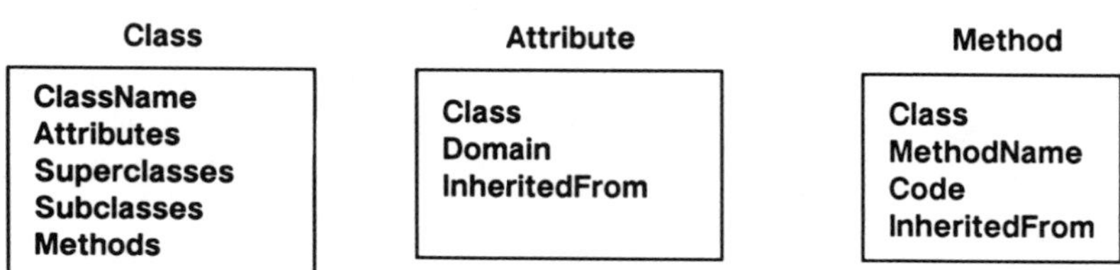

Figure 9.2
Classes for the Schema

refers to an instance of the class Attribute, and it indicates the attribute of the superclass from which the attribute is inherited.

We note that the Attributes and Methods attributes for a class hold values for not only the attributes and methods defined for the class, but also those inherited from all superclasses. This technique is known as 'flattening' of the class hierarchy, and is used often to speed up access to the schema. If the class hierarchy is maintained in the system such that each class represents only the attributes defined for it, processing a message sent to an object will require a search up the class hierarchy to identify the superclass from which the class of the object inherited the attribute or method in question.

9.4 Disk and Page Layout

The disk and page layout is pretty much the standard layout used in conventional database systems. A raw disk may be divided into a set of partitions (analogous to cylinder groups in file systems). Each partition consists of a number of segments; and each segment in turn consists of a number of blocks or pages. Figure 9.3 illustrates this. The disk header contains information such as the number of partitions, the address and size of each partition and the recovery log file. Segments in a partition are described by a segment table in which the addresses and sizes of the page tables for the segments are stored. Each page table in a segment records information about the size of each page in number of blocks.

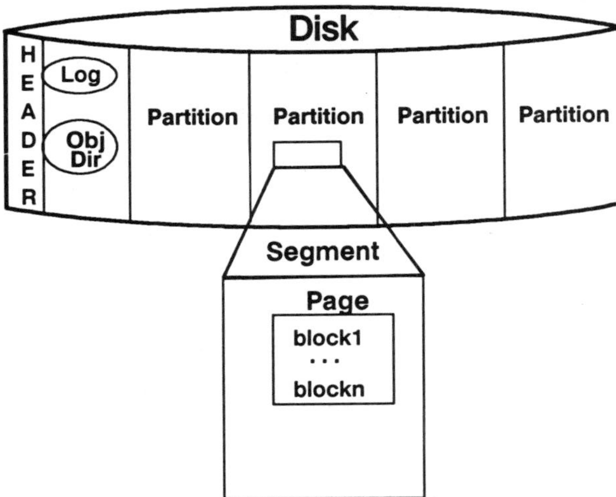

Figure 9.3
Organization of a Raw Disk

Figure 9.4 illustrates the format of an object page. Every page contains a header, objects, and an indirect pointer array. The header provides information about the page, such as number of objects, total free space, contiguous free space, offset to free space, etc. When an object is stored in the page, an index into the indirect pointer array is assigned to the object. The slot value of the indirect pointer array is a page offset to the page location where the object is placed. The offset location of an object may change when the object grows or when the page is compacted (e.g., to accommodate new objects).The page In Figure 9.4 contains four objects Z, A, F, and B and some holes for deleted or moved objects. (The formats of index pages and multimedia pages are similar and are not described in this chapter.)

The physical storage address (i.e., page number and slot number) of an object is recorded in an object directory as we will see later in this chapter.

9.5 Clustering

Clustering is a database-design technique used to store a group of objects physical close together so that they may be retrieved efficiently. There are two basic alternatives for clustering in relational databases. One is to store tuples of only one relation in the same segment of disk pages, on the basis of the values of an attribute (or a combination of attributes) of the relation; for example, assuming a Vehicle relation corresponding to our Vehicle class, tuples of the Vehicle relation which share the same value in the Color attribute may be clustered. Another is to store tuples of more than one relation in the same segment of pages, on the basis of the relationship between the values of the attributes of the relations; for example, tuples of the Vehicle relation whose Manufacturer attribute shares the same value with the Manufacturer-Name attribute of the Manufacturer relation may be clustered to facilitate joining of the two relations.

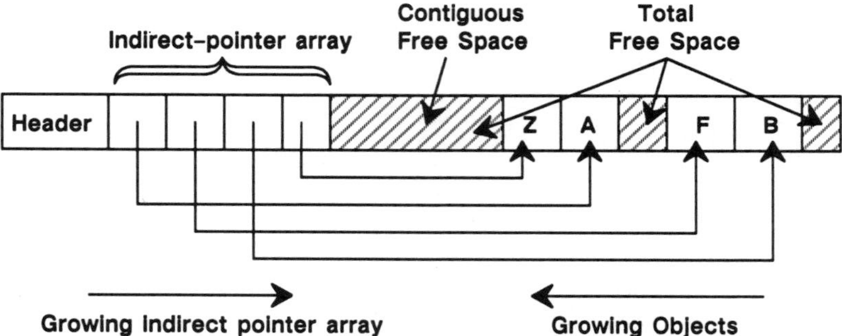

Figure 9.4
A Page Format

In object-oriented databases, clustering is also an important technique to improve system performance; there are five basic alternatives for clustering. The two basic clustering alternatives for relational databases apply to object-oriented databases. The third alternative is to cluster instances of the class along a class-composition hierarchy; this may be regarded as a variation of the second alternative, namely, clustering tuples from more than one relation in the same physical segment. Since a class-composition hierarchy is equivalent to the specification of joins of the classes on the hierarchy, it may seem like a good idea to cluster instances of all classes on a class-composition hierarchy, for example, the class-composition hierarchy rooted at the class Vehicle in Figure 9.5, or a particular branch of the hierarchy. However, not all constituents of a nested object are equally likely to be of interest to any given application; for example, it may be useful to store physical components of a Vehicle object in the same segment, but not the company object for the Manufacturer attribute of the vehicle object. In general, it is necessary to cluster some, but not all, constituent objects of a nested object; that is, clustering is an orthogonal concept to the joins of classes implied by the class-composition hierarchy. Further, since the same object may be shared by more

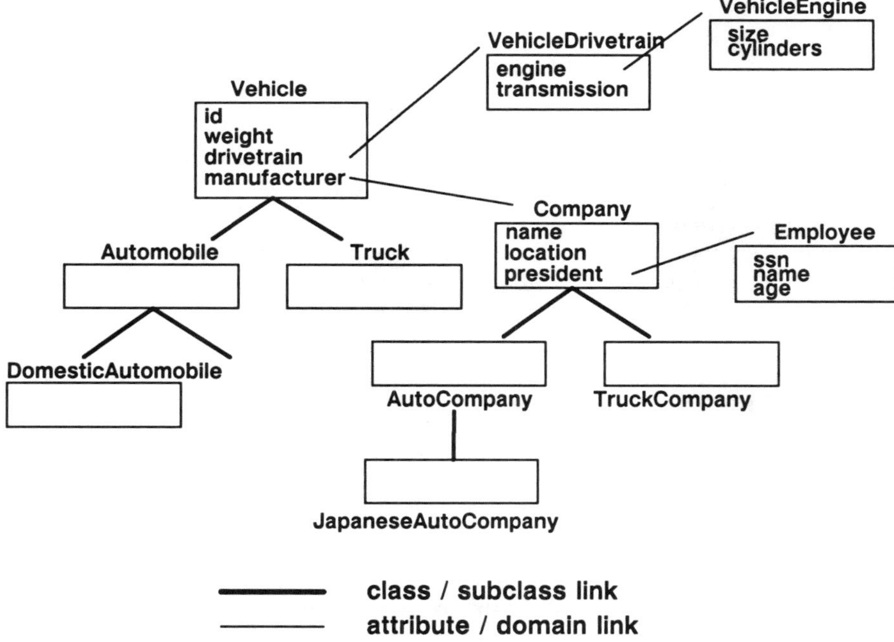

Figure 9.5
Class Hierarchy and Class-Composition Hierarchy

than one nested object, and an object can participate in only one clustering, at most one composition hierarchy can be chosen as the basis for clustering.

The class hierarchy gives rise to the fourth alternative for clustering instances from more than one class. It may be desirable to cluster all instances of a class hierarchy rooted at some user-specified class, for example, the class hierarchy rooted at the class Vehicle in Figure 9.5.

Naturally, the fifth alternative is to cluster instances from any connected subgraph of the schema graph; namely a class hierarchy rooted at some class, and some of the class-composition hierarchies rooted at any of the classes on the selected class hierarchy. An example is to cluster instances of a subgraph of the schema graph of Figure 9.5 defined as follows: the class hierarchy rooted at the class Vehicle; the class-composition hierarchy which is rooted at the class Vehicle and which has the class Employee and the class VehicleDrivetrain as the leaf nodes; and the class hierarchies rooted at VehicleDrivetrain.

As in relational systems, the users must specify the scope of the classes to be included in a cluster, namely, the root of a desired class hierarchy, the root of a class-composition hierarchy, and the leaves of the class hierarchies.

9.6 Instance Access Methods

9.6.1 Hashing

Object-oriented applications to a large extent access objects through their object identifiers. If the objects happen to be in memory, the database system can bind the application to the desired object using storage structures we will describe in Chapter 14. If the objects are not memory-resident, they must be fetched from the database, that is, secondary storage. If the database is very large, extendible hashing may be used to quickly map the object identifiers of objects to their physical addresses. The physical address of an object is usually a concatenation of the page that holds the object and the byte offset within the page, if the object fits in one page; if the object is too large to fit in one page, usually the pages are chained together. If the database is not very large, a B+-tree index may be used instead; as long as the root page of a B+-tree index is cached in memory, the performance of a B+-tree is at least as good as that of extendible hashing.

9.6.2 Indexing

Relational database systems often allow the users to create a secondary index on an attribute (or a combination of attributes) of a relation for use in evaluating queries against the relation. The data structure most often used for an index is a B+ tree. It costs only O(log N) index-page fetches to identify a set of tuples that satisfy a search condition involving the indexed attribute, where N is the total number of index pages. Indexing is also an important technique for expediting query evaluation in object-oriented databases. However, the richness of the data model introduces at least three new types of index: a class-hierarchy index, a nested-attribute index, and a two-dimensional index. A class-hierarchy index is maintained on an attribute of classes on a class hierarchy, while a nested-attribute index is maintained on a class-composition hierarchy. A two-dimensional index is a nested-attribute index augmented with a class-hierarchy index for each class in the sequence of classes between the indexed class and the class to which the indexed attribute actually belongs. Let us examine class-hierarchy indexing and nested-attribute indexing in some detail. We invite the reader to figure out the properties of two-dimensional indexing on the basis of the discussions in this section; to the best of our knowledge, there is no published account of two-dimensional indexing.

Class-Hierarchy Indexing

A *class-hierarchy index* on an attribute A of a class C is a single index on the attribute A of all classes on the class hierarchy rooted at the class. An *indexed attribute* is the attribute on which an index is maintained, while an *indexed class* is the root of the class hierarchy of classes on whose attribute an index is maintained. For example, a class-hierarchy index may be created on the Weight attribute of the class Vehicle and all its subclasses. Weight is the indexed attribute of the index, and Vehicle is the indexed class.

In object-oriented systems, a class inherits attributes from its superclasses, all direct and indirect subclasses of a class share the same attributes; as such, it is meaningful to maintain a class-hierarchy index on a class hierarchy rooted at some class. A proposal similar to class-hierarchy indexing has also been made for relational databases to support an index on an attribute common to a number of relations. However, these relations are not semantically related (e.g., via the generalization relationships); they merely have a common attribute.

Let us consider a query against a class. There are two meaningful interpretations for the target of a query. One is obviously the class. The other is the class hierarchy rooted at the class, that is, the class and all its direct and indirect subclasses. For example, when a user issues a query against the class Vehicle, the intended result of the query may be a set of Vehicle instances, or may be a set of instances of all types of vehicle, that is, Vehicle and all its subclasses. This interpretation may also be extended to the domain of an attribute. When a user specifies a class D as the domain of an attribute of a class C, the attribute may take on as its values objects from the class D and any direct or indirect subclass of D.

To see how a class-hierarchy index can be used, let us consider the following query.

Find all blue vehicles manufactured by Ford Motor Company
select Vehicle
where color = "blue"
and manufacturer name = "Ford Motor Company"

One of the ways in which this query may be evaluated is as follows. All instances of Company are identified which have the string "Ford Motor Company" in the Name attribute. A class-hierarchy index on the Name attribute can be used to expedite the search of the class Company. The unique identifiers (UIDs) of these instances are then looked up in the Manufacturer attribute of the class Vehicle. The result of the query is the set of instances of Vehicle which has the string 'blue' in the Color attribute and which contain in the Manufacturer attribute a UID that is in the list of UIDs for Ford Motor Company instances.

If a class-hierarchy index is not available on a class hierarchy, a separate index must be maintained on the common attribute for each of the classes on the class hierarchy. Figure 9.6a shows a class-hierarchy index rooted at the class Company; while Figure 9.6b illustrates the corresponding set of single-class indexes, that is, indexes on a single

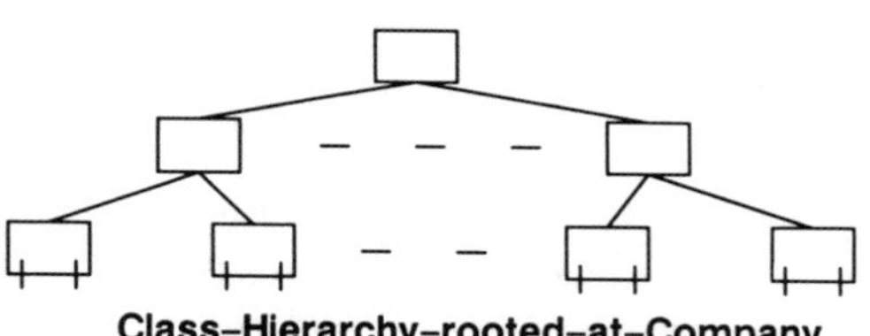

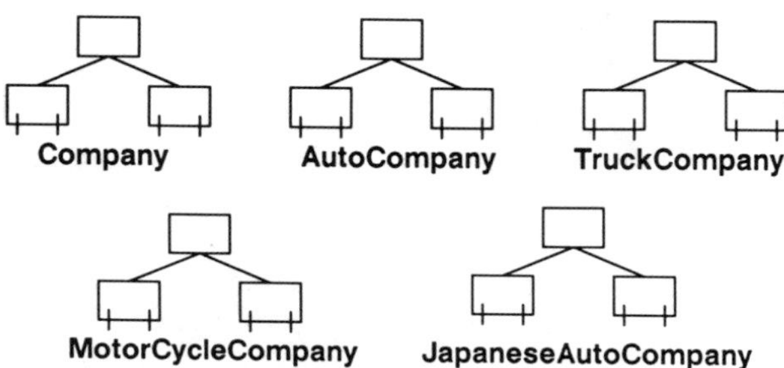

Figure 9.6a,b
A Class-Hierarchy Index and Single-Class Indexes

class, on the class hierarchy. The tradeoffs between these two indexing techniques in an object-oriented database can be quantified in terms of storage requirements and I/O performance in query evaluation. The storage requirements of a class-hierarchy index is the total number of index pages necessary to maintain the UIDs of all instances of all classes on the class hierarchy rooted at the indexed class; while the storage requirements of the corresponding set of indexes on each of the classes on the class hierarchy are the sum of the total number of index pages for each of the indexes. Similarly, the performance of a class-hierarchy index for a query involving a single equality predicate is simply the height of the index; while that for the corresponding set of indexes on each of the classes on the class hierarchy is the sum of the heights of each of the indexes. The number of index pages fetched with a class-hierarchy index is almost always more efficient than single-class indexes if the query requires access to at least two classes in a class hierarchy. Further, the size of a class-hierarchy index is often comparable or smaller than the sum of the sizes of the corresponding set of single-class indexes. A simple intuitive argument for the superiority of class-hierarchy indexing is as follows. The size and performance of a class-hierarchy index for N pages necessary to hold the UIDs of all instances belonging to the class hierarchy rooted at the indexed class is proportional to O(log N); while those of the corresponding set of single-class indexes is the *sum* of O(log n), where n is the average number of pages necessary to keep the UIDs of all instances of a single class on the hierarchy. O(log N) grows slowly relative to the sum of O(log n). For example, Figure 9.4 shows a class-hierarchy index of height 3 pages; the index takes the place of five single-class indexes, each with a height of 2 pages. The class-hierarchy index will cost at most 3 index-page fetches to find a key; while the use of single-class indexes will cost as much as 10 index page fetches.

Nested-Attribute Indexing

A nested-attribute index is obtained by generalizing the conventional index. A conventional index is created on an attribute of a class (relation); however, in a nested-attribute index on a class, the attribute indexed is an indirect, nested attribute of the class. In other words, in a conventional index, the indexed attribute is defined for the indexed class; while in a nested-attribute index, the indexed attribute need not be an attribute of the indexed class. More precisely, a nested-attribute index on a nested attribute A of a class C is a single index on the attribute A on a sequence of classes between the class C and the class for which the attribute A is defined. For example, as shown in Figure 9.5, the domain of the Manufacturer attribute of the class Vehicle is the class Company; and the class Company has the President attribute. Further, the domain of President is the class Employee which has the Age attribute. Then Age is a nested-attribute of the class Vehicle. In a nested-attribute index on a class, the index record associates the value of the indexed attribute with a list of UIDs of the instances of the indexed class. Figure 9.7 illustrates in a linear form a nested-attribute index on the Age nested-attribute of the class Vehicle. An index record associates a distinct key value of the Age attribute, say "55", with a list of UIDs of Vehicle whose Manufacturer is an instance of the class Company the Age of whose President is the key value (i.e., vehicle manufactured by a company whose president is 55 years old). Nested-attribute indexing makes it possible to evaluate a type of complex query by traversing a single index. The type of query for which nested-attribute indexing is ideally suited is one which contains a predicate on a deeply nested attribute of the indexed class; for example, the nested attribute Age of the class Vehicle in the query "find all vehicles manufactured by a company whose president is 55 years old" has nesting depth 2.

It is complex and expensive to update a nested-attribute index. A nested-attribute index on a class need potentially be updated upon insert, delete, and update of instances of any class in the sequence of classes between the indexed class and the class to which the indexed attribute actually belongs. For example, suppose that, as Figure 9.8 illustrates, the Vehicle instance whose UID is 125 currently references the Company instance whose UID is 500 through the Manufacturer attribute; and the Company instance in turn references the Employee instance whose UID is 1000 through the President Attribute; and the Age attribute of the Employee instance is 50. Now the Manufacturer attribute of the Vehicle instance is changed to reference a different Company instance, say, one whose UID is 550. The nested-attribute index on Age must be searched and the UID 125 must be deleted from the list of UIDs (for the key value 50); this is potentially a very expensive operation, since the index is keyed on the Age values, rather than the Vehicle UIDs. Further, the system must look up the Com-

Age key value	list of UIDs of Vehicle Instances
45	144 165 180
50	105 125 160 200
55	100 115 175 250
60	101 102 116 122 130 134 142 146 148 149 .....

Figure 9.7
Nested-Attribute Indexing

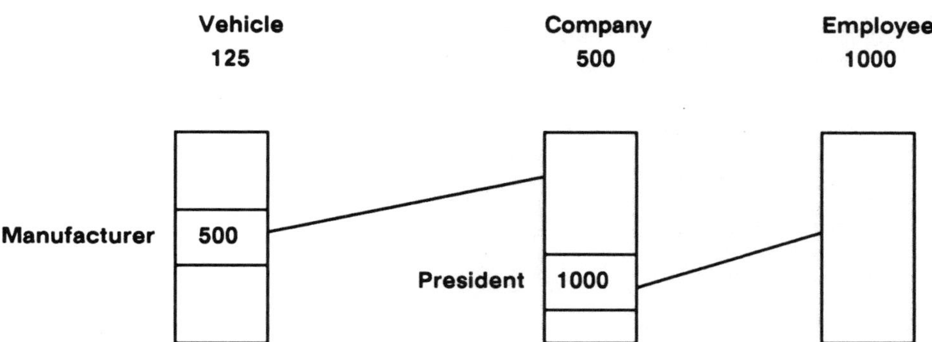

Figure 9.8
An Example Nested Object

pany instance 550, and the Employee UID stored in the President attribute of the Company instance; and then look up the referenced Employee instance and find the value of the Age attribute. Let us suppose that the Age value found is 55. Then the Vehicle UID 125 must be inserted into the list of UIDs associated with Age 55.

Just as relational systems support indexes on combinations of attributes, it is possible (at least theoretically) to create a nested-attribute index on a combination of attributes of an indexed class. For example, the Location attribute of the class Company is a nested attribute of the class Vehicle. Then a nested-attribute index may be maintained on a combination of the nested attributes Location and Age, and the nonnested attribute Weight. Obviously, a nested-attribute index on a combination of attributes complicates index maintenance significantly.

Recommended Readings

[KIM89b] presents a cost model for class-hierarchy indexing, and compares the performance and size of class-hierarchy indexes against corresponding sets of single-class indexes. [BERT89] extends this work by comparing the performance of class-hierarchy indexing, nested-attribute indexing, and single-class indexing not only for retrieval queries but also for updates.

10 Query Processing

Perhaps the most novel element of the relational database technology, as compared with the past-generation database technologies, is declarative queries and techniques supported to automate their evaluation. The evaluation of a relational query proceeds essentially in two phases in state-of-the-art relational database systems. The first is the query-optimization phase, and the second is the query-processing phase. During the query-optimization phase, the query optimizer automatically generates a set of reasonable plans for processing a given query, and selects one optimal plan on the basis of the expected cost of each of the plans generated. During the query-processing phase, the system executes the query using the optimal plan generated.

Query optimization and processing in object-oriented databases requires additional research; however, it is not the fertile ground for fundamental new research which it may appear to be. The reason is that query optimization and processing in object-oriented databases requires only relatively minor changes and augmentation of all the techniques which have been developed and successfully used for optimizing and processing queries in relational databases. The relatively minor changes are necessary to negotiate the semantic differences between relational and object-oriented queries. For simplicity, henceforth we will use the phrase object-oriented (relational) query to mean a query in object-oriented (relational) databases; and object-oriented (relational) query processing to mean query optimization and processing in object-oriented (relational) databases.

In this chapter, we will first establish the reason all essential techniques for relational query processing are directly applicable to object-oriented query processing. Then we will outline these techniques. Next, we will discuss changes to the techniques for relational query processing which are necessary for object-oriented query processing.

10.1 Structural Similarities between Object-Oriented and Relational Queries

The reason all the techniques for relational query processing are directly applicable to object-oriented query processing is that, if we ignore the class hierarchy, the structure of an object-oriented query is basically that of a relational query. Let us revisit an example query and its corresponding query graph which we examined in Chapter 6. Using the schema shown in Figure 10.1, a query to "find all blue vehicles manufactured by a company located in Detroit and whose president is under 50 years of age" may be formulated as follows.

Q1: **select** Vehicle **where** Color = "blue"
and manufacturer location = "Detroit"
and manufacturer president age < 50

The query graph for this query is shown in Figure 10.2. Figure 10.3 is a simplified query graph, in which only the classes along the composition hierarchy rooted at the target class of the query are retained from the full query graph of Figure 10.2; that is, the simplified query graph of Figure 10.3 is obtained by suppressing the class-hierarchy dimension in the full query graph of Figure 10.2.

The attribute/domain link between a pair of classes in Figure 10.3 in effect represents the join of the classes. For example, the attribute/domain link between

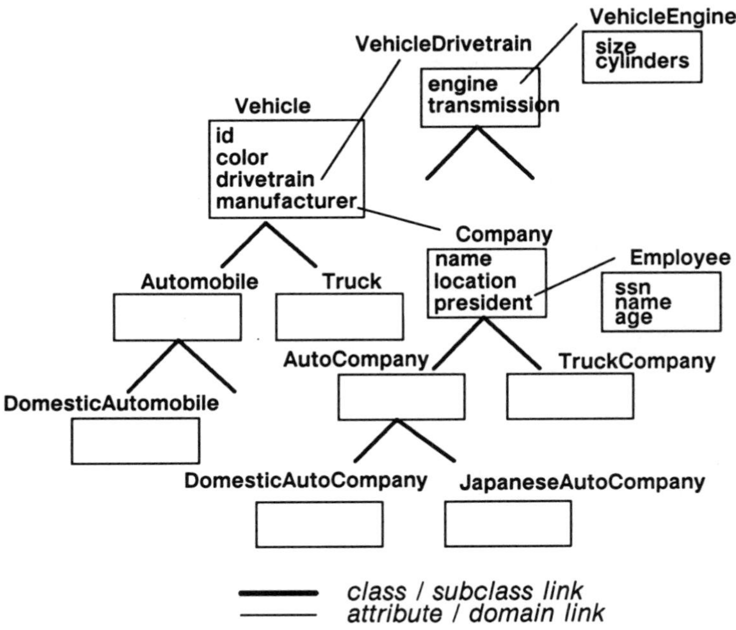

Figure 10.1
An Example Schema

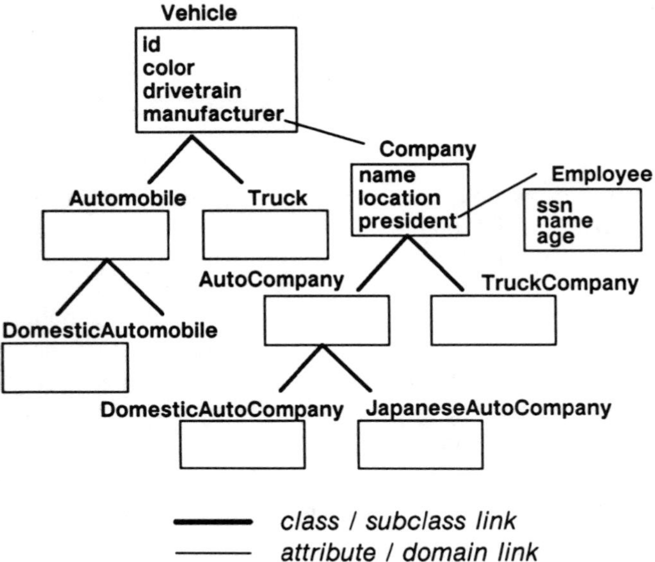

Figure 10.2
An Example Query Graph

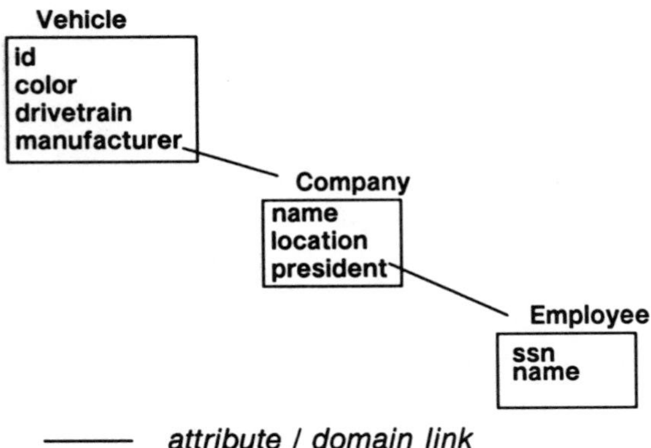

Figure 10.3
A Reduced Query Graph

Vehicle and Company joins the two classes; the join attributes are the attribute Manufacturer of the class Vehicle, and the system-defined unique identifier (UID) attribute of the class Company. In general, the attribute/domain link between a class C and the domain D of one of the attributes A of C joins the classes C and D, where the join attributes are the attribute A of the class C and the system-defined UID attribute of the class D.

On the basis of the above observation, we can see that a single-operand object-oriented query involving a total of N classes along the class-composition hierarchy rooted at the target class of the query is equivalent to a relational query which joins N relations corresponding to the N classes. This conclusion extends straightforwardly to a multiple-operand object-oriented query. Figure 10.4 illustrates the query graph for an object-oriented query involving two target classes, namely Company and Employee. If the class-hierarchy dimension in the query graph is suppressed, the resulting reduced query graph indicates join of the two target classes. The join attributes for each pair of the target classes in a multiple-operand object-oriented query are both user-specified attributes, whereas one of the join attributes for each pair of classes in a single-operand object-oriented query is the system-defined UID attribute of one of the two classes. In general, each of the target classes in a multiple-operand object-oriented query may be the root of a class-composition hierarchy.

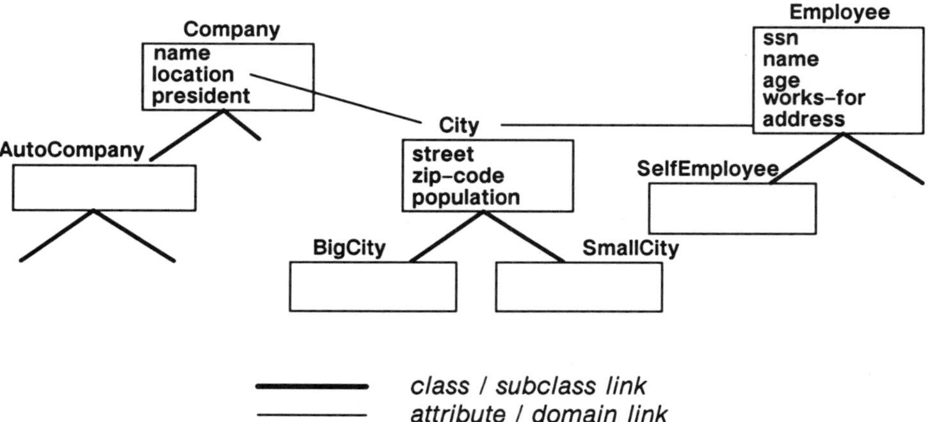

Figure 10.4
An Example Query Graph for a Join

10.2 Query Processing Techniques

Just as N relations may be joined in any one of N! permutations, N classes on the class-composition hierarchy rooted at the target class of a single-operand object-oriented query may be 'joined' in any one of N! permutations. For example, the 3 classes in the reduced query graph for our example query may in principle be evaluated in any one of 3! permutations of the 3 classes. Just as some permutations yield Cartesian product results and are omitted from the list of candidate plans for evaluating a relational query, permutations of the classes that result in a Cartesian product are omitted from consideration in object-oriented query processing. For example, of the 3! permutations for evaluating the 3 classes in our example, those permutations in which the classes Vehicle and Employee appear back to back need not be considered; there are no common join attributes that link these two classes.

The techniques which have been developed for relational query processing are the following. These techniques apply straightforwardly to object-oriented query processing because of the fundamental similarities between object-oriented queries and relational queries as discussed above.

(1) computation of all reasonable permutations of the relations in a query, except those that result in a Cartesian product of any pair of relations.

(2) generation of a query-execution plan for each permutation of relations obtained; a query execution plan specifies the access method to be used (index, hashing, etc.) to fetch tuples of each of the relations, and the method to be used (nested-loop, sort merge, etc.) to concatenate tuples of one relation with tuples of the next relation in a given permutation.

(3) estimation of the cost of each query-execution plan generated; cost formulas and database statistics are used to compute the expected number of tuples that satisfy search conditions on any relation or join conditions on a pair of relations.

(4) in the case of a distributed database, the generation of a global query plan as a collection of local query plans that are executed on each database site.

Let us examine in more detail the processes in which instances of a class are logically concatenated with instances of the next class in a given permutation of the classes in an object-oriented query. Given a pair of classes C and D, such that D is the domain of an attribute A of C, the values of the attribute A of the class C are the UIDs of instances of the class D. If the classes C and D appear in that order in a given permutation of classes, instances of C are joined with instances of D by iterating the following steps. An instance of C is retrieved. Next, the value of the attribute A is extracted from the instance. Then the instance of D whose UID is the value of the attribute A extracted is retrieved. Any predicate on D is evaluated against the instance retrieved.

If the permutation has the class D preceding the class C, the two classes are joined by iterating the following steps. An instance of D is retrieved. The UID of the instance is extracted. Next, an instance of C which has the UID extracted as the value of the attribute A is retrieved. Then any predicate on C is evaluated against the instance retrieved.

There are two basic algorithms for concatenating instances: nested loop and sort-merge. The nested-loop algorithm traces the reference path from an individual instance to the instances which are referenced directly or indirectly by this instance. In the sort-merge algorithm, the UIDs selected from a class in the query graph are sorted and passed to the next class in a given permutation of classes.

The drawback of the nested-loop algorithm is that for each instance of a class, pages containing instances referenced by the instance must be fetched; and the same pages may have to be fetched repeatedly. The problem with the sort-merge algorithm is the cost of sorting the list of UIDs extracted from a class, especially if the list is very long. As in relational query processing, the relative merit of the nested-loop and sort-merge algorithms depends on the characteristics of a given query, of the database, and the physical organization of the database. The sort-merge algorithm is more appropriate for distributed query processing, because the communication costs of the nested-loop algorithm can be prohibitive.

10.3 Changes to Techniques for Relational Query Processing

Although object-oriented queries are structurally similar to relational queries, as we discussed in Chapters 6 and 7, there are several important semantic differences. In particular, an object-oriented query requires access to a class hierarchy, as well as the class-composition hierarchy. An object-oriented query may cause methods to be invoked. Further, an attribute of a class in object-oriented databases may be scalar-valued or set-valued. Surprisingly, the impacts of the complicated semantics of an object-oriented query on query processing do not necessitate truly fundamental changes to the techniques used for relational query processing. Let us now examine these impacts.

Indexing

In Chapter 9, we showed how the class hierarchy and class-composition hierarchy in object-oriented databases give rise to the need for class-hierarchy indexes and nested-attribute indexes, respectively. The introduction of these new types of index affects query processing in object-oriented databases. The changes it necessitates are, however, confined to the cost-estimation aspect of query optimization.

Multi-Valued Attribute

As we showed in Chapters 2, 6, and 7, an attribute of a class may be a single primitive value, a single object, or a set of objects. Therefore, as we saw in Chapter 7, the existential quantifiers *each* and *exists* may be associated with a set attribute, that is, an attribute whose value is a set of instances of its domain. Obviously, object-oriented query processing must account for these set-attribute quantifiers. Again, extensions to relational query processing that are necessary are largely related to the cost-estimation aspect associated with the evaluation of these quantifiers on the intermediate results of a query.

Methods

As we discussed in Chapters 6 and 7, a method may be used in a query as a derived attribute or as a predicate. The use of a method in search conditions in a query makes it very difficult, if not impossible, for the query to be compiled or evaluated using such standard access methods as B-tree indexes and hashing. Optimization and processing of queries involving methods needs additional research.

Database Statistics

In a relational query, statistics are needed about individual relations, such as the number of tuples in a relation and the number of distinct values in individual attributes. In an object-oriented database, the statistics need to be augmented to reflect the class hierarchy, that is, they need to contain information such as the number of instances of all classes on a class hierarchy, and the number of disk pages that hold these instances. ORION maintains such statistics.

As in relational databases, statistics are best updated upon request by the user. Immediate updates to the statistics upon each database update incur excessive performance overhead; besides, up-to-date statistics do not significantly improve accuracy of the query optimizer compared with somewhat outdated statistics.

Recommended Readings

No operational object-oriented database system presently supports the full model of queries we developed in Chapter 6. Preliminary results on supporting object-oriented queries involving a single target class have been reported in [KIMK88, KIMK89]. Techniques for supporting cyclic queries and queries involving more than one target class require additional research. [SELI79] provides perhaps rather comprehensive discussions of issues and solutions to the optimization and processing of relational queries.

11 Transaction Management

A transaction is a sequence of reads and writes against a database. A transaction as used in conventional applications has two properties: atomicity and serializability. The atomicity property means that the sequence of reads and writes in a transaction is regarded as a single atomic action against the database. It ensures that if a transaction cannot complete, the system backs out all writes which may have been recorded in the database; that if a transaction successfully completes, the system guarantees that all writes are recorded in the database. The serializability property means that the effect of concurrent execution of more than one transaction is the same as that of executing the same set of transactions one at a time. It ensures that a transaction is completely shielded from the effects of any other concurrently executing transactions.

The objective of transaction management is to ensure the atomicity and serializability properties of transactions. Transaction management consists of two components: concurrency control and recovery. Concurrency control refers to automatic control of simultaneous accesses to a common part of the database by more than one transaction. Recovery refers to the ability to restore the database to a state which existed at some point before the failure of any transaction. Most commercial database systems use a locking protocol to implement concurrency control, and logging protocol to implement recovery.

The atomicity and serializability properties of transactions have been highly useful for conventional business data processing applications. However, they have highly undesirable consequences for long-duration transactions, that is, transactions whose duration is much longer than that of conventional transactions. The atomicity property means that if a long-duration transaction cannot complete, all the work that has been done must be backed out. The serializability property means that if a long-duration transaction holds a lock on an object, any other long-duration transaction that must access the same object in a conflicting mode must be blocked until the first long-duration transaction completes.

A long-duration transaction is often defined as a set of conventional short-duration transactions. The atomicity and serializability properties continue to apply to the short transactions which comprise long-duration transactions. Beyond this, however, there is still no clear-cut consensus about the semantics of long-duration transactions. Insofar as a transaction is in essence a framework for enforcing database consistency, the difficulty with long-duration transactions lies in defining a practical notion of database consistency for interactive and cooperative application environments.

In this chapter we will discuss first how conventional transaction management is extended for object-oriented databases. This discussion will be based on transaction management supported in ORION. Then we will discuss long-duration transaction management.

11.1 Conventional Transaction Management

The ORION transaction subsystem provides mechanisms to protect database integrity while allowing the interleaved execution of multiple concurrent transactions. The transaction subsystem consists of a number of major modules shown in Figure 11.1. The lock manager is responsible for maintaining the lock table, which indicates the locks each active transaction holds or is waiting for. The storage subsystem interacts with the lock manager to set locks on objects before retrieving or updating the objects. All locks (logical locks) acquired by a transaction are released when the transaction terminates (either commits or aborts). The deadlock manager is responsible for deadlock detection and resolution; ORION uses a simple technique based on the use of timeouts. Each lock request is given a time limit for lock wait, and, if the request times out, the deadlock manager proceeds to abort the transaction. The log manager accumulates the log of changes to objects (update, create, delete) within a transaction. The log is used to back out a transaction, or to recover from system crashes in the middle of a transaction which leaves the database in an inconsistent state.

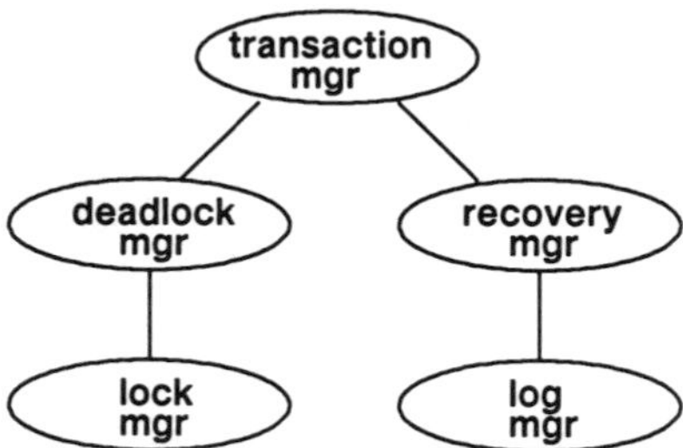

Figure 11.1
ORION Transaction Subsystem

11.1.1 Concurrency Control

In this section we first summarize the impacts of object-oriented concepts on concurrency control requirements in a database system. Then we will describe specific solutions incorporated in the implementation of concurrency control in ORION.

11.1.1.1 Impacts of Object-Oriented Concepts

Object-Level Concurrency Control

Object-oriented databases necessitate three types of change to conventional locking techniques. First, object-oriented databases present a strong case for locking at the object level (equivalent to the record level in conventional databases). The smallest unit of access to a relational database is a relation; the only way a relational database is accessed is through a query against one or more relations. The result of a query is zero or more tuples of a relation. The case for setting locks at the tuple level becomes strong only if queries return only small subsets of the database. However, object-oriented systems use object identifiers as keys to access objects; that is, the smallest logical unit of access to an object-oriented database is an object rather than a class. This means that it is logical to set locks at the object level in object-oriented databases. Figure 11.2 compares the units of locking in relational databases and object-oriented databases.

Class Object

Next, the notion of a class in object-oriented databases is similar to the notion of a relation in relational databases, but a class is used to hold more information than a relation. This means that richer semantics are needed for locking a class object than for locking a relation. In relational databases, a relation is simply a set of tuples. In object-oriented databases, however, a class is not only a set of instances, but also a repository for information about all its instances, in particular, various aggregate properties of the instances. For example, the average weight and default color of Vehicles may be maintained in the class object for the class Vehicle. This means that for the purposes of

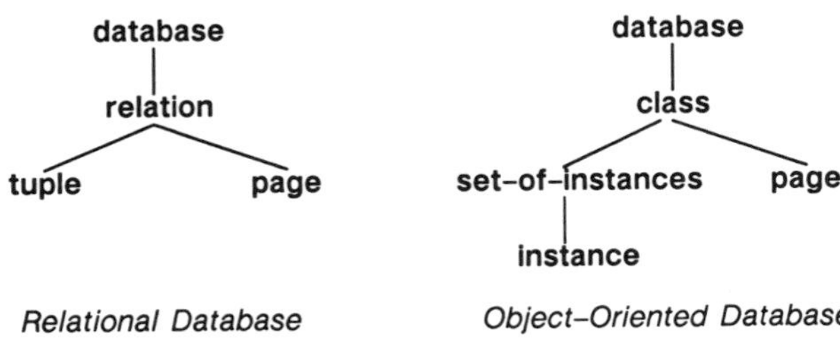

Figure 11.2
Units of Locking

locking, a class object should be split into two virtual objects: a set-of-instances object, and an aggregate-of-instances object. The database system should set a lock on one or both of these objects, depending on the nature of the access being requested by the user.

Class Hierarchy and Class-Composition Hierarchy

The notion of a class hierarchy necessitates another type of change to locking. In object-oriented systems, a class inherits attributes and methods from its superclasses; and, as we have seen already, if attributes or methods are deleted from or added to a class, they will also be deleted from or added to all its subclasses. This means that while a transaction accesses instances of a class, another transaction should not be able to modify the definition of the class or any of the superclasses of the class. Further, a query directed against a class in general requires evaluation against not only that class, but also all its subclasses. This means that while a transaction is evaluating a query, classes on a class hierarchy must not be modified by another transaction.

11.1.1.2 Concurrency Control in ORION

Transactions in ORION are *serializable*, which means that ORION completely isolates a transaction from the effects of all other concurrently executing transactions. A serializable transaction acquires a read lock before reading an object, and a write lock before updating an object. This corresponds to the notion of level-3 consistency in SQL/DS, and protects a transaction from such consistency anomalies as lost updates, dirty read, and unrepeatable read.

As in conventional commercial database systems, ORION supports both logical locking and physical locking. The lock manager sets a lock on a logical object, namely each node (lockable granule) on a granularity hierarchy, a class hierarchy, and a composite object. A physical lock is a lock on a physical page that contains logical objects, and must be acquired before logical locks are set on objects in the page. The lock manager holds logical locks until the end of the transaction which acquired them; however, it releases physical locks as soon as objects in the pages are accessed.

In this section, after a brief review of the current theory of locking for the granularity hierarchy, we will describe the issues of class-hierarchy locking that ORION addressed. There are proposals for increasing concurrency by exploiting the semantics of the contents of objects; for example, an insert into the tail of a FIFO queue by one transaction should not conflict with a read of the head of the same queue by another transaction. This semantics-based concurrency control is rather tangential to object-orientation, and is not treated here.

Review of Granularity Locking

The fundamental motivation of the granularity locking protocol is to minimize the number of locks to be set in accessing the database. For example, when most of the instances of a class are to be accessed, it makes sense to set one lock for the entire class, rather than one lock for each instance. A lock on a class will imply a lock on each instance of the class. However, when only a few instances of a class need to be accessed, it is better to lock the instances individually, so that other concurrent transactions may access any other instances.

A node of a granularity hierarchy may be locked in one of a number of lock modes. ORION supports the five lock modes, as in SQL/DS: IS, IX, S, SIX and X. Instance objects are locked only in S or X mode to indicate whether they are to be read or updated, respectively. However, class objects may be locked in any of the five modes. An IS (Intention Share) lock on a class means that instances of the class are to be explicitly locked in S mode as necessary. An IX (Intention Exclusive) lock on a class means instances of the class will be explicitly locked in S or X mode as necessary. An S (Shared) lock on a class means that the class definition is locked in S mode, and all instances of the class are implicitly locked in S mode, and thus are protected from any attempt to update them. An SIX (Shared Intention Exclusive) lock on a class implies that the class definition is locked in S mode, and all instances of the class are implicitly locked in S mode and instances to be updated (by the transaction holding the SIX lock) will be explicitly locked in X mode. An X (Exclusive) lock on a class means that the class definition and all instances of the class may be read or updated. As in SQL/DS, an IS, IX, S, or SIX lock on a class implicitly prevents the definition of the class from being updated.

In general, a directed acyclic graph (DAG), such as that shown in Figure 11.2, is needed to model the *lockable granules* in a database. The following summarizes a locking protocol on a DAG of lockable granules.

(1) To set an explicit S lock on a lockable granule, first set an IS lock on all direct ancestors, along *any one* ancestor chain, of the lockable granule on the DAG.

(2) To set an explicit X lock on a lockable granule, first set an IX or SIX lock on all direct ancestors, along *each* ancestor chain, of the lockable granule on the DAG.

(3) Set all locks in root-to-leaf order.

(4) Release all logical locks in any order at the end of a transaction, or in leaf-to-root order before the end of a transaction

The compatibility matrix of Figure 11.3 defines the semantics of the lock modes. A compatibility matrix indicates whether a lock of mode M2 may be granted to a transaction T2, when a lock of mode M1 is presently held by a transaction T1. For example,

	IS	IX	S	SIX	X
IS	√	√	√	√	No
IX	√	√	No	No	No
S	√	No	√	No	No
SIX	√	No	No	No	No
X	No	No	No	No	No

Figure 11.3
Compatibility Matrix for Granularity Locking

in Figure 11.3, we see that when a transaction T1 holds an X lock, no lock of any mode may be granted to any other transaction. However, when T1 holds an S lock, another transaction T2 may be granted an IS or S lock.

Class-Hierarchy Locking

A number of useful operations can be defined on a class hierarchy which involve a class and all its subclasses (and their subclasses). There are two types of operations on a class hierarchy: schema changes and queries.

As we saw in Chapter 6, the fact that an object-oriented database schema explicitly captures the IS-A relationship between a pair of classes has two major impacts on the semantics of queries. One is that the search space for a query against a class C may be only the instances of C, or it may encompass the instances of the class hierarchy rooted at C. Another major impact is that the domain D of an attribute of a class C is really the class D and all subclasses of D. This means that the search space for a query against a class includes class hierarchies rooted at the domain class of each of its attributes.

Two different approaches have been developed that satisfy the locking requirements on a class hierarchy. The approach selected for ORION is to apply the lock modes and locking protocol for a granularity hierarchy to a class hierarchy. This means that for a query involving a class C and all its descendants, and for a schema change operation on a class C, a lock is set not only on the class C, but also on each of its descendant classes on the class hierarchy. The following illustrates this simple protocol.

(1) Select all instances of vehicle and its subclasses such that ...
(a) lock vehicle class object and those of vehicle's subclasses in IS mode
(b) lock every selected instance in S mode

(2) Change the definition of the vehicle class
(a) lock vehicle class object and those of vehicle's subclasses in X mode

This approach is particularly appropriate when accessing a class near the leaf level of a deep class hierarchy. A potential disadvantage of this simple approach is the locking overhead for changes to the definition of a class or for a query against a class, when the class or the domains of the attributes of the class are close to the root of a deep class hierarchy.

However, a protocol that is efficient for accessing a class near the root of a deep class hierarchy is clearly useful for an application environment in which complex queries involving a domain class near the root are frequently used. The alternate protocol requires introduction of two new lock modes: read-hierarchy (R) and write-hierarchy (W). An R lock on a class C is in essence an explicit S lock on the class C, and implicit S locks on all subclasses of the class C. A W lock on a class is similarly an explicit X lock on the class, and an implicit X lock on each of the subclasses of the class. An X lock on a class allows updates to instances of the class, and it allows the definition of the class to be read but not updated. To update the definition of a class, a W lock must be set on the class. Since the R and W modes cause implicit locking of the subclasses of a class hierarchy, the superclasses of the class must be locked in intention modes IR and IW, respectively. Further, all of the lock modes discussed in the previous subsection will require the IR or IW intention-mode locking of the superclasses of a class being locked. This requirement for intention-mode locks is analogous to the intention-mode locks in granularity locking.

The above protocol is correct for a class hierarchy in which a class has only one superclass; but it does not work for a class hierarchy in which a class may have more than one superclass. Figure 11.4 provides an example class hierarchy in which a class E has two superclasses, C and G. Suppose a transaction T1 sets an IR lock on A and an R lock on C, implicitly locking subclasses D, E, and K in R mode. Suppose now

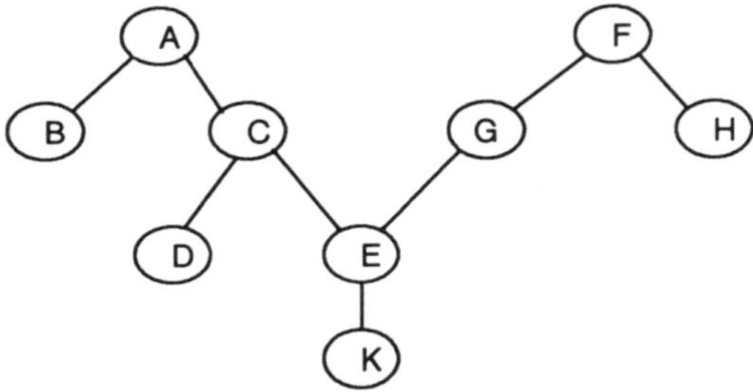

Figure 11.4
An Example Class Hierarchy

that a transaction T2 sets an IW lock on F, and a W lock on G. T2 will then implicitly lock the classes E and K in W mode. This means that setting intention-mode locks on superclasses of the class being locked is not sufficient to detect conflicting lock requests from different transactions. Before a W lock can be set on the class G, it must first be determined whether its subclasses E and K may have already been implicitly or explicitly locked by other transactions. To do this will require an upward traversal of the class hierarchy for each of the superclasses of each of the classes on the class hierarchy to be locked. This of course can be very expensive, if the class to be locked has many subclasses and many of the subclasses in turn have many superclasses.

One solution to limit the above overhead, when setting an explicit R or W lock on a class C, is to set explicit R or W locks, respectively, on those subclasses of C which have more than one superclass. Then only those subclasses need to be examined for conflict. In the current example, this means that when transaction T1 sets an R lock on C, an explicit R lock will also be set on the class E. Then transaction T2's request for a W lock on the class G can be rejected by simply determining that the class E, the only subclass of G with more than one superclass, is already locked in R mode by transaction T1.

One important point about this protocol is that to set an explicit R or W lock on a class C requires IR or IW locks, respectively, on only one superclass chain of the class C. Further, any superclass chain of the class C may be chosen for locking. For example, the class E in Figure 11.4 has two superclass chains, A-C and F-G. Only one of them needs to be selected, and the classes along the chain locked in IR or IW mode. The reason this is sufficient is that, unlike the conventional granularity locking protocol, the present protocol does not rely entirely on the intention locks on superclasses for lock conflict resolution. Lock conflict resolution in the protocol requires examination of the locking status of the subclasses of a class being locked. Since the protocol does not rely solely on intention locks for conflict resolution, the IR or IW intention locks need to be set only on the classes along one superclass chain of the class being locked.

The following illustrates the protocol.

(1) Select all instances of vehicle such that . . .
(a) lock vehicle class object in IS mode and those of vehicle's superclasses along any one superclass chain in IR mode
(b) lock each instance of vehicle in S mode

(2) Select all instances of vehicle and its subclasses
(a) lock vehicle class object in R mode and those of vehicle's superclasses along any one superclass chain in IR mode
(b) lock each subclass of vehicle with more than one superclass in R mode

(3) Select all instances of vehicle and its subclasses such that . . .
(a) lock vehicle class object in IS mode and those of vehicle's superclasses along any one superclass chain in IR mode
(b) lock each subclass of vehicle in IS mode
(c) lock each instance of vehicle or any subclass of vehicle in S mode

(4) Change the definition of the vehicle class
(a) lock vehicle class object in W mode, and those of vehicle's superclasses along one superclass chain in IW mode
(b) lock each subclass of vehicle with more than one superclass in W mode.

One potential disadvantage of this protocol is that, even for access requests involving only a single class, it requires intention locks on the superclasses along a superclass chain of the class. In other words, even when a class C is to be locked in IS, IX, S, or X mode, its superclasses along one superclass chain must be locked in IR or IW mode. This is especially undesirable, if the class C is close to the leaf level of a deep class hierarchy, and access to a single class is much more frequent than access involving a class hierarchy.

It is not known at this time which protocol is more appropriate in general, since schema evolution and queries are relatively new concepts to object-oriented systems and as such there is insufficient data about their usage. Further, it may be a worthwhile exercise to study applicability of the locking protocols for a class hierarchy to a class-composition hierarchy. Further, class-hierarchy locking may be combined with class-composition-hierarchy locking.

Index-Page Locking

ORION supports B+-tree indexing on attributes of a class that the user specifies to speed up associative searches of objects that satisfy an arbitrary combination of predicates. The locking technique used on index entries is summarized below for completeness.

(1) To fetch an index page for a read-only access to an index, acquire a page-lock in S mode on the index page.

(2) To insert, delete, or update any entries in an index page, acquire a page-lock in X mode on the page. An X lock on a non-leaf index page is released as soon as it is not needed.

(3) In the event of an index-page split during insertion of new entries, acquire an X lock on both the old index page and the newly allocated index page.

(4) In the case of page-merging during deletion of entries, set X locks on both the old index page that has become empty and the index page into which entries from the old page have been distributed.

All locks on index pages, except the X locks on the leaf pages of an index, should be released as soon as the pages are no longer needed. The X locks on the leaf pages must be held until the end of the transaction, when the transaction manager releases them, along with all other locks acquired during the transaction.

A deadlock may result if a transaction reads an index page P, releases the S lock on P (thereby allowing another transaction to lock the page), and then must acquire an X lock on P because of the split/merge of index pages at a lower level of the B+ tree that percolates upward to P. To prevent deadlocks due to such upward percolation of page split/merge, ORION uses a technique which changes the nature of a B+ tree somewhat. During insertion, while accessing an index page P (holding an X lock on it), the index manager must determine if the insertion will result in the split of Q, the next page to be accessed (a child page of P); if so, it will split Q, into Q and R, and insert an entry in P that will point to the newly allocated page R. Conversely, during deletion, while accessing an index page P (with an X lock on it), the index manager will determine if a pair of child pages of P (the next page to be accessed and one to its left or right) may be merged; if so, it moves entries from one to the other. In both cases, entries in the parent page that point to the child pages are updated while the parent page is locked in X mode. That is, the transaction does not attempt to reacquire the X lock on the parent page, after it has released a lock on it.

11.1.2 Recovery

Most commercial database systems support database recovery from soft crashes (which leave the contents of disk intact) and hard crashes (which destroy the contents of disk). ORION cut a lot of corners on recovery in order to simplify implementation. What conventional commercial database systems have done for recovery is much better. ORION supports transaction recovery only from soft crashes and user-initiated transaction abort. In other words, ORION does not support archival dumping of the database to recover from disk head crashes. There are three options in a log-based transaction recovery scheme: maintain only the UNDO log, only the REDO log, or both the UNDO and REDO logs. ORION uses the UNDO logging option, for implementation simplicity. This approach requires the pages containing updated objects to be forced to disk at the end of a transaction: this is necessary because if the updates only remain in the buffer pool and the system crashes, there is no way to redo them using the UNDO log.

The use of logging in ORION for multimedia data and index page recovery is somewhat interesting, and will be described in the remainder of this section.

Multimedia Data Logging

A naive use of the logging techniques can cause some serious problems for the long, multimedia data. A strict log-based recovery will keep UNDO and/or REDO logs of very long data. As shown in Figure 11.5, ORION distinguishes multimedia data from its descriptor. The descriptor references, via an object identifier, the multimedia data. The storage subsystem maintains a free list of storage blocks which may be allocated for storing multimedia data. The long data manager in the object subsystem logs the changes in the descriptors and the free list, but not the multimedia data. In this way, if a transaction that created multimedia data aborts, the descriptor will be returned to referencing nil, and the entry in the free list which points to the storage block allocated to the multimedia data will be reset as available for allocation. Similarly, if a transaction that deleted multimedia data aborts, the reference in the descriptor will be returned to its initial value and the free-list entry will be deleted.

Index Page Logging

In some commercial database systems, such as SQL/DS, updates to index pages are not logged. This is to reduce the logging overhead during normal transaction processing. However, it complicates the recovery manager, since the recovery manager must reconstruct the entries in the index pages from the log of updates to the data pages. This is the right approach; however, to simplify implementation, ORION logs updates to index entries. ORION implements the following protocol for index-page logging.

(1) In the case of an index-page split during insertion, it will distribute half of the entries in the current page to a new page. The entry in the parent page that points to the new page must be logged. Also, those entries that are deleted from the current index page must be logged; however, the entries that are copied into the new page need not be logged. In case of a crash, the entire new page is simply dropped.

(2) In the case of a index-page merge during deletion, entries in the current page are copied over to another page. The entry in the parent page that points to the current page must be logged. Further, the entries that are copied into the new page must be logged; however, the entries being deleted from the current page need not be logged. In case of a crash, the current page will be reclaimed, since a dropped page is not returned to a free-page list until the transaction commits.

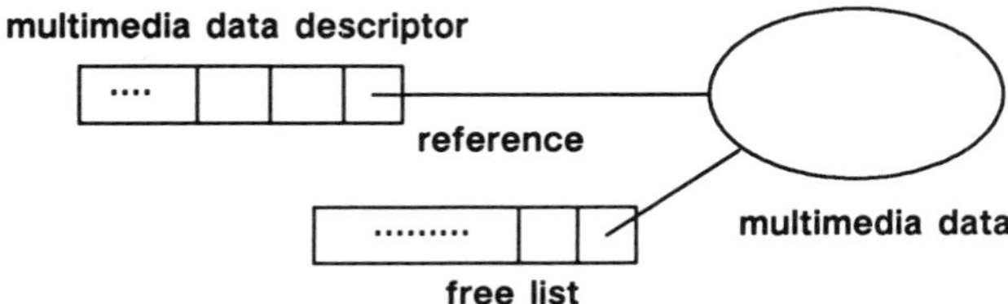

Figure 11.5
Logging of Multimedia Data

The index-page entries that are logged must be identifiable through the page identifier and an offset within the page. The operation code (insert or delete) and the length of the entry must be recorded as well.

11.1.3 Hypothetical Transactions

ORION supports two types of transactions: normal and hypothetical. A session may contain any sequence of normal and hypothetical transactions. When a normal transaction commits, all its updates are permanently recorded in the database; and when it aborts, all its changes are undone. A *hypothetical transaction*, in contrast, is a transaction that always aborts. No matter how such a transaction is ended, its changes are never reflected in the database. Thus, hypothetical transactions provide a mechanism for experimenting with the effects of 'what-if' changes to the database. Since the changes are never recorded permanently, the user has the freedom of examining the impacts of complex changes to the database, and yet does not have to worry that the database will become corrupted.

Of course, the conventional transaction mechanism, with its abort option, can be used to provide the desired effect of a hypothetical transaction. However, the conventional transaction mechanism incurs significant overhead to make it possible for a transaction to be recoverable and to shield a transaction from the effects of other concurrently executing transactions. Within a hypothetical transaction, the first time an object is updated, a copy of the object is made for all subsequent updates within the transaction. The initial object is never updated. The initial object is called the *shadow copy*, and the new copy that gets updated the *current copy*. The current copy is discarded when the transaction terminates, regardless of whether the transaction commits or aborts. Further, each hypothetical transaction has its own current copy of an object for updates, so that multiple hypothetical transactions may concurrently update the same object.

Since a hypothetical transaction makes updates only to the current copy of an object, and each hypothetical transaction has its own current copy of the object, only an S lock needs to be set on the single shadow copy of an object, both for read and update. An S lock is needed to prevent some concurrently executing non-hypothetical transaction from directly updating the shadow copy of the object, thereby causing the hypothetical transaction to read *dirty data,* data that is subject to a backout by the non-hypothetical transaction.

At a first glance, it seems obvious that the shadow/current copy approach for updates eliminates the need for logging the updates. However, it is somewhat difficult to avoid logging altogether. There is a situation which may require logging of updates of a hypothetical transaction. When the database buffer pool becomes full, some objects will have to be swapped out to make room for new objects that currently executing transactions need. The shadow copies of objects will be the first to be swapped out. After that, if still more space is needed in the buffer pool, some of the current copies will have to go. Then the current copies must be logged before getting swapped out and an X lock set on the shadow copy, so that the updates are backed out when the transaction terminates.

Logging may be avoided, if the transactions that require new objects are simply to be blocked. The blocked transactions may resume when some of the current transactions terminate, making it possible to swap out their objects. This approach will work, except in the pathological case where the buffer requirement of a single hypothetical transaction exceeds the size of the database buffer pool.

11.2 Long-Duration Transaction Management

The two primary deficiencies of the conventional model of transactions are long-duration waits in case of conflicts in database accesses, and the total backout of database updates. In this section, we outline our proposal for removing these deficiencies. We regard a long-duration transaction as a set of short-duration transactions. A short-duration transaction continues to be the unit of concurrency control and recovery. The user may optionally relax the serializability constraint of a short-duration transaction; further, the user may cause a partial backout of a long-duration transaction. We address the problem of long-duration waits by a combination of mechanisms, including versioning, group transactions, non-serializable transactions, soft locks, and change notification. We propose to address the recovery problem by allowing partial backouts of a long-duration transaction; a long-duration transaction may be backed out backward from the current short-duration transaction up to a specified committed short-duration transaction.

11.2.1 Long-Duration Waits

In this subsection we will describe several mechanisms which can be used to solve the problems of long-duration waits. These mechanisms include versioning of objects, versioning of the database schema, group transactions, and soft locks.

11.2.1.1 Versioning of Objects

In systems which support checkout and checkin of objects from a shared database (public database) to a private database, such as computer-aided design or software engineering systems, objects may be checked out in read or update mode. A read-mode checkout of an object means that a copy of the object is made available to the private database of the requesting user only for read purpose; the object cannot and need not be checked back into the shared database. An update-mode checkout of an object means that a copy of the object is made available to the private database of the requesting user, and may be updated and checked back into the shared database.

If an object is checked out which is not versionable, the checkin of an updated object means replacing the original object. In this case, a checkout of an object in update mode can cause long-duration waits for other transactions requesting access to the object in a conflicting mode. Mechanisms such as group transactions or soft locks are needed to alleviate this problem.

If an object is versionable, however, it is not always necessary to replace it with an updated copy when the latter is checked in; a versionable object may be checked out, updated, and checked back in as a new version. This means that the checkout of a versionable object need not require a long-duration lock; of course, the original object must be locked while it is copied.

Of course, versioning is a mechanism which allows the user to derive and experiment with several functionally equivalent objects and which manages the status and history of creation of such objects. As we will see in Chapter 12, versioning incurs both processing and storage overhead to maintain such information as version history. Therefore, it is not desirable to make every object in the database versionable, and additional mechanisms are needed to address the problem of long-duration waits.

11.2.1.2 Versioning of Schema

If a database system maintains only a single schema for the database, it can be disruptive if the users are permitted to make dynamic changes to the schema. In object-oriented systems, the effects of changes to the schema can be particularly disruptive to the users, because changes to the attributes or methods defined for a class must be propagated recursively to all subclasses of the class.

A solution to this problem is to version the schema; if a user wishes to update the schema, he may do so by deriving a new version of an existing version of the schema, and make the changes to the new version of the schema. The user may view a single database differently under different versions of the schema.

The schema is one of the hot spots in any database, since to access any part of the database the schema must be read or updated. Versioning of the schema alleviates the problem of long-duration waits primarily by dispersing the access contentions on the schema to more than one version of the schema.

11.2.1.3 Group Transactions

The transaction management subsystem in ORION allows a user to open several windows on the screen, and use different windows to issue reads and writes against the database within the same transaction. This is a primitive manifestation of the notion of a group transaction. A group transaction is in essence a group of transactions which are treated as a single transaction. The transactions in a group transaction may be issued by more than one user. Although a group transaction may conflict with some other group transaction, a transaction within a group transaction does not conflict with any other transaction in the same group transaction. A group transaction may be terminated by any user at any time.

The use of a group transaction makes it possible for a group of users closely collaborating on a project to work without being encumbered by concurrency control. We emphasize that the group of users must work as though they are one user, if they are to take advantage of the flexibility of a group transaction.

11.2.1.4 Change Notification

Change notification is a useful function in systems that manage a large number of interconnected objects. If an object A makes use of object B, by including a reference to it, the user of object A may optionally request to be notified of some types of changes to object B, for example, deletion, update, or creation of a new version of object B.

Change notification, as applied to a set of interconnected objects, is also a means of reducing the number of objects that must be locked in a transaction, regardless of the duration of the transaction. If a change-notification mechanism is not available, and the integrity of a set of interconnected objects must be protected within a transaction, the transaction must set a lock on every object in the set, thereby potentially holding up other transactions. In a cooperative group environment, a change-notification mechanism may allow the users to set locks on selected objects, and deal with the impacts of changes to related objects separately.

11.2.1.5 Non-Serializable Transactions

The designers of the System R relational database system introduced the concept of levels of consistency for transactions. In particular, System R supported three levels of consistency. At the beginning of a transaction, the user must declare the desired level of consistency for the transaction. All three levels of consistency require an update lock to be held until the end of a transaction; however, they differ in their treatment of read locks. Level-1 consistency does not require a lock for a read, that is, a request to read an object is accepted even if some other transaction already holds an update lock on the object. Level-1 consistency suffers from *dirty reads*, that is, reading of objects which are updated by some other transaction and which may later be backed out. Level-2 consistency is achieved if a read requires a read lock only for the duration of a read operation, but not for the duration of a transaction. The consequence of level-2 consistency is non-repeatable reads, that is, reads of the same object which return different results within the same transaction. Level-3 requires a read lock, as well as an update lock, to be held for the duration of a transaction. The designers of System R eventually abandoned level-2 consistency, because they recognized that it provides a lower degree of consistency at a system overhead comparable to level-3 consistency.

Level-1 and level-2 consistency does not ensure serializability. However, they can be useful in eliminating long-duration waits for read locks. Level-2 consistency, although it may incur a system overhead that is comparable to that of level-3 consistency, is useful for increasing concurrency by addressing the problem of long-duration waits.

11.2.1.6 Soft Locks

A soft lock is a lock which may be broken through negotiation between users. Soft locks violate serializability of transactions. Below we present our proposal for a locking protocol involving soft locks.

First, we distinguish *long-duration locks* and *short-duration locks*. A short-duration lock is automatically set by a database system; the system may hold it until the end of a read or write operation, or until the end of a transaction. A long-duration lock must be set by the user explicitly; it persists beyond the short-duration transaction in which it was set. A long-duration lock may be released explicitly within some short-duration transaction, or is released at the end of a long-duration transaction.

A short-duration lock is always a hard lock. However, it may be converted to a long-duration lock in one of two ways. The user may explicitly convert the lock duration. Further, the system may automatically convert the lock duration once a short-duration lock has been held beyond a prespecified lock duration. Similarly, the user may explicitly downgrade a long-duration lock to a short-duration lock; however, a long-duration lock is not automatically converted to a short-duration lock.

Second, a long-duration lock may be hard or soft. A long-duration lock is a hard lock by default, but the user may override it by specifying the lock to be soft. The user may explicitly attach or remove the soft-lock option to a long-duration lock.

When the lock-manager subsystem detects a conflict involving a soft lock, it will return an informational flag to the requesting transaction indicating that the lock is soft and therefore may be broken through negotiation with the holder of the lock. The user who holds a soft lock may explicitly release it.

This approach is satisfactory, except when the holder of a soft lock is unavailable for negotiation for a long time. There are two ways to address this problem. One is for the new user to receive a copy of the requested object, and attempt a negotiation later sometime before committing the transaction. This may be useful if the requested object has a soft share lock on it, and if the holder of the lock becomes available for negotiation before the new transaction must commit.

Another way to solve the problem is to provide a *notification option* to soft locks. The notification option may be exercised at the time a soft lock is set, or at any time afterwards. The notification option indicates that the soft lock may be broken in case of a conflict, but that the holder of the lock must be notified that the lock has been broken.

11.2.2 Recovery

The basic unit of recovery in a long-duration transaction is the most recent short-duration transaction. In case of a crash or user-initiated abort, the current short-duration transaction is backed out.

The soft-lock protocol gives rise to a problem with recovery. If a transaction being backed out had a soft update lock that was broken, the update that was performed under the soft lock really should not be backed out. It may not be possible to retake the lock; further, even if it may be possible to get the lock back, some other transactions may have updated the object, and the updates should not be backed out. The approach we propose is to back out the updates done under a soft lock only if no other transaction has updated it after the lock was relinquished; in other words, we need to avoid *cascaded backouts*. (We will discuss shortly a technique for avoiding cascaded backouts.)

It is sometimes desirable to be able to back out more than just the current short-duration transaction, that is, to back out a sequence of short-duration transactions beginning with the current transaction. In our model of long transactions, once a short-duration transaction commits, all short-duration locks it acquired are released. There are two problems in backing out these committed transactions. First, the locks necessary to back out the transactions may now be held by other transactions. Second, even if the locks may be acquired, other transactions may have committed updates using the locks; that is, these updates may be backed out. Again, we wish to avoid cascaded backouts.

One technique we can use to allow a database system to avoid cascaded backouts is to include a commit-timestamp in the commit-record in the log, and also in each object. The commit-timestamp indicates the time at which a short-duration transaction committed. During backout, the recovery manager compares the commit-timestamps in the commit-record of the committed transaction being backed out and the commit-timestamps in the objects referenced by the log records. If the recovery manager finds that a hard lock cannot be set on an object, the object is not considered for backout; this is because the object is being accessed by another transaction. Further, if a hard lock can be set, but the commit-timestamp in the object is more recent than that found in the commit-record, the object is not backed out; this is because the object had been updated by some other transaction after the transaction being backed out released the lock on it.

Now let us examine more closely the partial backout of a long-duration transaction. We take the view that the partial backout of a long-duration transaction proceeds backward from the current short-duration transaction to the beginning of some short-duration transaction. In other words, it is unreasonable to consider backing out a short-duration transaction T-i unless all short-duration transactions T-j that followed it are backed out first. The reason is that updates by a transaction is made on the basis of the database state left by earlier transactions; that is, backing out transactions committed earlier in a sense removes the basis on which later transactions can be executed. For example, let us consider a sequence of short-duration transactions T-1, T-2, and T3. T-1 creates an object X1 with value 3 and commits; T-2 creates an object X2 with value 3 and commits; and T3 creates an object X3 and computes its value by multiplying the values of X1 and X2. Now, suppose T-1 is backed out, destroying X1. Then T-3 has no basis for computing the value of X3.

Recommended Readings

A significant portion of the section on conventional transaction management in this chapter is taken from [GARZ88]. The reader should see [GRAY78, GRAY81] for general discussions of transaction management. [STON81] discusses the notion of hypothetical databases, which is related to hypothetical transactions. A hypothetical database is a database derived from a 'real' database, and persists across any number of 'normal' transactions.

The readers interested in long-duration transactions may start the literature search with [KIM84, KATZ84, BANC85, KORT88]. The notion of soft locks is also proposed in [HORN87]. A survey of semantics-based concurrency control can be found in [SKAR89].

12 Semantic Extensions

An object-oriented data model captures some important semantic relationships among objects, including the generalization relationship between a class and its subclasses, the instance-of relationship between an instance of a class and the class (as well as all superclasses of the class), and the aggregation relationship between a class and its attributes. The core object-oriented data model would be a subset of a semantic data model in terms of the modeling power, except for the fact that the semantic data model lacks the notion of methods. There are many semantic relationships which are not part of the core object-oriented data model. Perhaps the most important of these which are frequently useful in classes of data-intensive applications that are well-suited to an object-oriented design are the version-of and part-of relationships. An object-oriented data model, once augmented with these relationships, allows the user to deal with a collection of related objects as a single unit. In particular, a collection of objects related by the part-of relationship forms a composite object; and a composite object may be used as a unit of access in a query and as a unit of integrity. Further, a collection of objects related by the version-of relationship represents an abstract versioned object; a versioned object manages the history of evolution of versions.

In this chapter, we will describe the semantics and architectural impacts of versions and composite objects. In particular, we will discuss extensions to the database architectural concepts, such as schema evolution, authorization, and concurrency control, that the implementation of these concepts necessitates.

12.1 Versions

Many researchers have proposed plausible semantics for versions. However, at this time ORION and IRIS are the only object-oriented database systems that support versioning of objects. ORION and IRIS support very similar semantics of versions; and we will adopt the ORION semantics here.

12.1.1 Semantics

Whether or not an object may be versioned is one of the properties of the class to which the object belongs; that is, the user includes in the definition of a class whether instances of the class may be versioned. We will call an object that may be versioned a *versionable object*. A versionable object may have one or more versions. As we showed in Chapter 2, there are two relationships for versions. There exists a version-of relationship between each of the versions and the versionable object. Further, a new version may be derived from an existing version of a versionable object. Therefore, there exists a derived-from relationship between a pair of versions of a versionable object. Figure 12.1 illustrates these relationships.

Now let us examine the semantics of the derived-from relationship in more detail. When an instance of a class whose instances may be versioned is created, the first version of the versionable object is created.

Once the first version has been created, any number of versions v-i may be recursively derived from the first and any subsequent versions, giving rise to a *version hierarchy* for a given versionable object. We note that early version systems, such as SCCS, allowed only one new version to be derived from the most recent version,

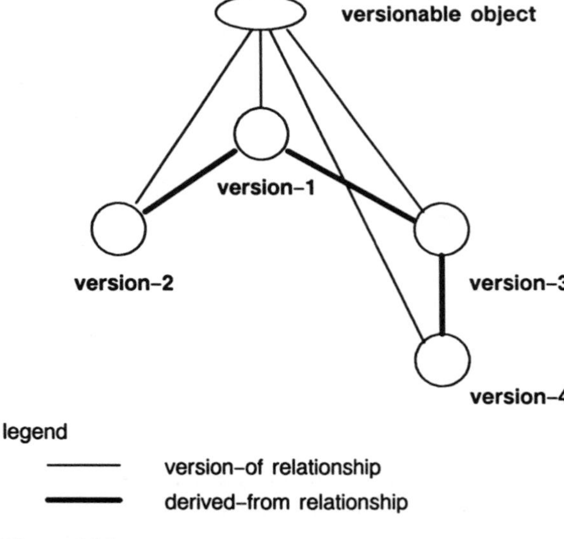

Figure 12.1
Version Relationships

reducing the version hierarchy to a *version chain*. The current literature suggests an increasing acceptance of the more flexible version hierarchy.

A version may be distinguished into a transient version, a working version and a released version, on the basis of its robustness. A *transient version* is essentially a temporary version which is expected to undergo a significant amount of updates before reaching a robust state; as such it may be updated or deleted at any time. A *working version* is a version which in the view of the user has reached a reasonable state of robustness that it may be shared and therefore cannot be updated; however, it may be deleted. A *released version* is a version which has reached the final state of robustness and therefore cannot be updated or deleted.

A new version, when it is created or derived from an existing version, starts out as a transient version. The user may later *promote* a transient version to a working version once it reaches a robust state, and a working version to a released version. Conversely, the user may *demote* a working version to a transient version; a released version cannot be demoted. One may take the view that when a new version is derived from an existing transient version, the existing version should automatically be promoted to a working version; or that it should remain a transient version. Either option is valid depending on whether one would like to associate an added constraint with derivation of versions; that is, to require that new versions may be derived only from working versions.

Let us now consider the delete semantics for versions. First, even if a version to be deleted is not a leaf node of a version hierarchy, it is deleted; however, the record of it in the history of evolution of versions is maintained. For example, in Figure 12.1, version-3 may be deleted, regardless of whether it is a transient version or a working version. However, information about version-3 will continue to be maintained because version-4 has been derived from it. Second, if the only version of a versionable object is deleted, the versionable object is deleted also. For example, if all four versions in Figure 12.1 are deleted, the versionable object is deleted, along with the history of evolution of versions captured in the version hierarchy. Third, if a versionable object is directly deleted, it is deleted, along with all of its versions.

In object-oriented systems, an object may reference any number of other objects by embedding in it the identifiers of those objects. An object may reference a versionable object in one of two ways. One is to reference the versionable object as a generic object, and another is to reference specifically one of the versions of the versionable object. If an object references a specific version, it is said to be *statically bound* to the version. If an object reference the generic object, we say that the object is *dynamically bound* to the versionable object; the object is bound at run time to a *default version* of the versionable object. If the user specified a default version, it is used; otherwise, the system default is the most recent version. A generic object is an object in its own right; however, it maintains only information about the version hierarchy and the default version.

12.1.2 Messages

We will now illustrate how versions may be integrated into the core object-oriented data model. The approach we will adopt is to augment the basic syntax of the core object-oriented data model with limited extensions.

First, the **make-class** message may be extended with an additional keyword argument, versionable, as follows.

(**make-class** Classname **:versionable** TrueOrNil)

The keyword **:versionable** can have a value true or nil, indicating whether versions can be created for instances of the class.

When the user issues a **make** message, a generic object is created, as well as the first version of the versionable object. The new version is a transient version, and becomes the root of the version hierarchy for the versionable object. The optional keyword arguments of a **make-class** message supply attribute names and values for the version.

To derive a new version from an existing version, a **derive-version** message is sent to a VersionedObject, as follows.

(**derive-version** VersionedObject)

If VersionedObject is a transient version, it is promoted to a working version. The message also causes a copy to be made of the VersionedObject. The copy becomes a new transient version, and is assigned a new version number and an object identifier. If VersionedObject is a generic object, the message is redirected to the default version.

The application may explicitly promote a transient version to a working version by sending the **promote** message to a VersionedObject. Conversely, a working version can be demoted to a transient version by a **demote** message. In both the promote and demote messages, if the VersionedObject specified is a generic object, the message is redirected to the default version.

The default version number of a generic object can be changed with a **change-default-version** message.

(**change-default-version** VersionedObject [NewDefaultVersionNumber])

If the argument NewDefaultVersionNumber is specified, the default version number becomes fixed, and will not change even if new versions are created. It can be changed only with another **change-default-version** message. If the NewDefaultVersionNumber is not specified, the most recently created version number is used as the default.

The **delete-object** message is used to delete a version or a generic object. If the message is sent to a generic object, the entire version hierarchy is deleted. If a **delete-object** message is sent to a version, the version is deleted. If the version is a version from which no other versions have been derived, the history of the version is deleted as well. If the version is the only version of the versionable object, the generic object is also deleted. If the **delete-object** message is sent to a version that has other derived versions, however, the history of the version is not deleted.

To fetch, update, or delete versions based on a QueryExpression, the **select**, **change**, and **delete** messages shown in Chapter 3 can be used, without any changes in their syntax or semantics. These messages cause all versions of the specified class, irrespective of their version numbers, to be examined. As we will show in the next section, the system maintains system attributes, version-number and version-type (transient or working) for versionable objects. This means that the application can include these system attributes in the QueryExpression.

12.1.3 Implementation

When the application creates a versionable object, the system creates a generic object, along with the first version, for the versionable object. A generic object is essentially a data structure for the version-derivation hierarchy of a versionable object. A version is of course an object, and thus has a unique object identifier. A generic object is a data structure that the system automatically creates and maintains. However, it is also treated as an object, and is assigned an object identifier. A generic object and versions it describes belong to the same class; however, a generic object has a special flag that distinguishes it from a version.

A generic object maintains the following information:

(1) version count

(2) next-version number

(3) default version number

(4) user default switch

(5) the version-derivation hierarchy

The version count is the number of existing versions of the versionable object. The next-version number is the version number to be assigned to the next version of the versionable object that will be created. It is incremented after being assigned to the new version. The default version number is the version to be selected to resolve a dynamically bound reference to the generic object. The user default switch indicates whether the default version was specified by the user.

The version hierarchy is a tree of version descriptors, one for each version of a versionable object. The version descriptor includes

(1) the version number of the version

(2) object identifier of the version

(3) children

The children attribute is a list of references to the version descriptors of all versions directly derived from the version.

Further, each version of a versionable object contains three system-defined attributes, in addition to all user-defined attributes. The application may read, but update, any of these attributes. Further, the application may include any of these attributes in the Boolean QueryExpression of a query.

(1) version number

(2) version type

(3) object identifier of its generic object

The version number is needed simply to distinguish a version of a versionable object from other versions of the same versionable object. The version type indicates whether the version is a transient version or working version. This information is maintained, so that the system may easily reject an attempt to update a working version. The generic object identifier is required, so that, given a version, any other versions of the versionable object may be found efficiently.

From the above discussion, to support versions of simple objects, three system-defined attributes are necessary: version number, version type, and the object identifier of the generic object. Further, for a versionable object, the system needs to generate a generic object. The generic object must be examined and updated when a new version is derived, so that the system may keep track of the most recent version and update the version hierarchy for the generic object. Of course, all this overhead applies only to versionable objects. Versioning incurs fairly low processing overhead; however, only fairly large objects should be versioned so that the storage overhead may be amortized.

12.1.4 Query Processing

Evaluation of queries against versionable objects presents a somewhat interesting problem. The version number attribute may be used in the QueryExpression to find all or any specific versions of versionable objects, or to find only the user-default or the most recent versions of versionable objects that satisfy the QueryExpression. The first type of queries presents no difficulties; either all versions are sequentially scanned or a subset of them may be searched using a secondary index on some attribute of the class. It is the second type of queries which presents implementation and performance difficulties, because information about the user-default or the most recent version of a versionable object is stored in the generic object, rather than in individual versions. The following is a proposal for supporting it.

If the entire class must be scanned (either because there is no secondary index that may be used or because the query includes no predicates that can reduce the logical search space), we may fetch each generic object, find the identifier of the user default or the most recent version, whichever is necessary, and then fetch the version. If, however, there is an appropriate secondary index to quickly reduce the search space to a small set (smaller than the set of all generic objects) of qualifying versions, to isolate only the default or most recent versions from the set, we need to do the following for each version in the set:

(1) fetch the version

(2) find the version number of the version

(3) fetch the generic object of the version (using the generic object identifier stored in the version)

(4) find the default or most recent version, whichever is necessary, of the versionable object

(5) compare the version number found on step 2 with that found on step 4, and if they match, output the version fetched on step 1.

A straightforward approach to eliminate this inefficiency is of course to keep information about the default or most recent version of a versionable object in the versions. However, it will require updating this information in all versions of a versionable object, each time a new version is created or when the user changes the default version. Of course, if new versions are not created frequently and the number of versions for a versionable object is very small, this approach would be acceptable. Otherwise, the only reasonable approach seems to be to reduce the disk I/O penalty by physically clustering versions with their generic object.

12.1.5 Schema Evolution

There are two possible schema changes involving versions (ORION does not support either of these). One changes a versionable class to a non-versionable class; and the other changes a non-versionable class to a versionable class. These changes are both what we called *hard changes* in Chapter 5, that is, they both require updates to the database.

Let us examine the consequences of changing a versionable class to a non-versionable class. First, generic objects have no meaning for a non-versionable class, and all existing generic objects of the class must be dropped. Second, once the generic objects are deleted, any objects that currently reference the generic objects will then end up with dangling references. Third, there is the difficult issue of determining which of the versions for each of the versioned object should be retained; perhaps only the user-specified default version, or the most recent version, or even all of the versions should be kept. Fourth, the system-defined attributes for versioned objects lose their utility once the objects become instances of a non-versionable class, and should really be dropped from the existing versioned objects.

Changing a non-versionable class to a versionable class also presents problems. First, a generic object must be created for each of the existing instances of the class. Second, each of the existing instances of the class must be expanded with the system-defined attributes for versions.

12.1.6 Authorization

It is useful to extend the notion of implicit authorizations we explored in Chapter 8, to versions. A versionable object consists of more than one version, and a user who has a certain type of authorization on a versionable object may be regarded as implicitly having the same authorization on all versions belonging to the versionable object. This can not only reduce storage needed to maintain authorizations on versions, but also facilitate the granting of authorizations.

One reasonable way to extend the notion of implicit authorizations to versions and to integrate it into the authorization model developed for the core object-oriented data model is to introduce additional authorization object types to the Authorization Object Schema *(AOS)*. Figure 12.2 is the *AOS* of Chapter 8 augmented with new authorization object types related to versions (in a rectangle). The new authorization object types are setof-generic objects, generic object, and setof-versions.

Figure 12.3 illustrates an Authorization Object Hierarchy (*AOH*) for a database which contains versioned objects. In this example, two generic objects have been created in the database and each generic object is related to two version objects. The nodes generic-object[1] and generic-object[2] in the *AOH* represent the two generic objects in the database. A W authorization on generic-object[1] allows the user to modify the generic object (i.e., to change the default version number) and will also imply authorization on the two version objects referenced by generic-object[1]. An authorization on the *setof-generic-objects*[Auto] node will imply the same

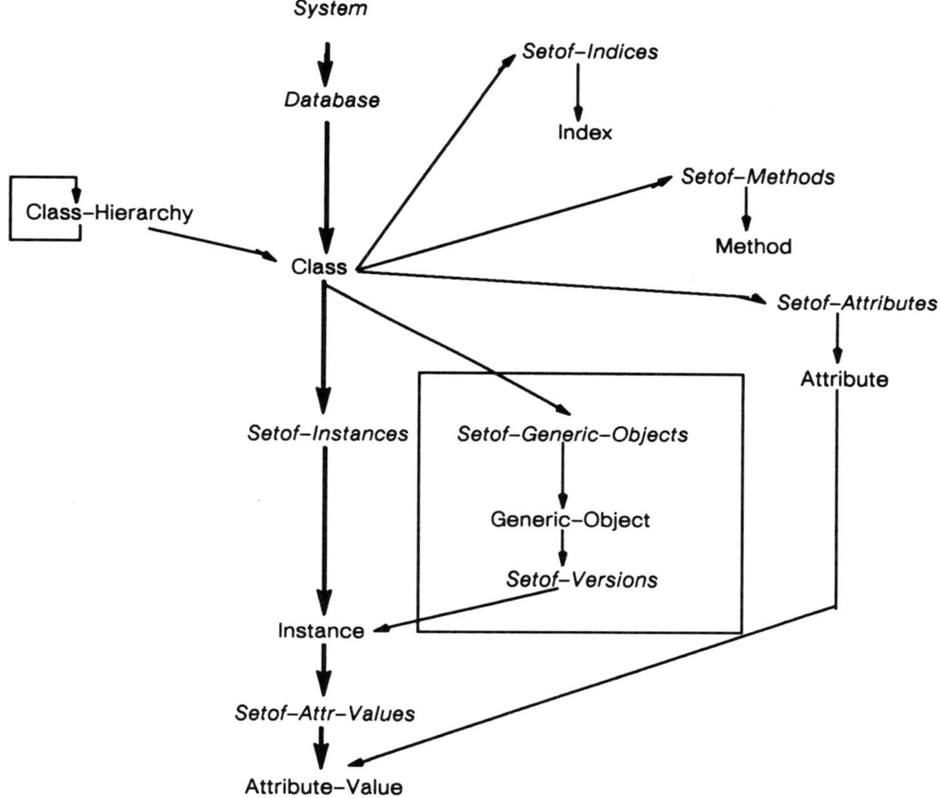

Figure 12.2
Authorization Object Schema (AOS) Extended with Versions

authorization on all of the generic objects of the class Auto. An authorization on the *setof-versions*[1] node, referenced by the generic-object[1] node, will imply the same authorization on the two version objects referenced by generic-object[1]. In this way, we can specify object-level authorizations over a potentially large number of instances using a single explicit authorization.

A W authorization on the node *setof-versions* (see the *AOS* of Figure 12.2) is also an authorization to create a new version, of the specific generic object, from an existing version of the instance. For example, if a user wishes to derive a new version from instance[6] in the *AOH* of Figure 12.3, the user must have a W authorization on *setof-versions*[2].

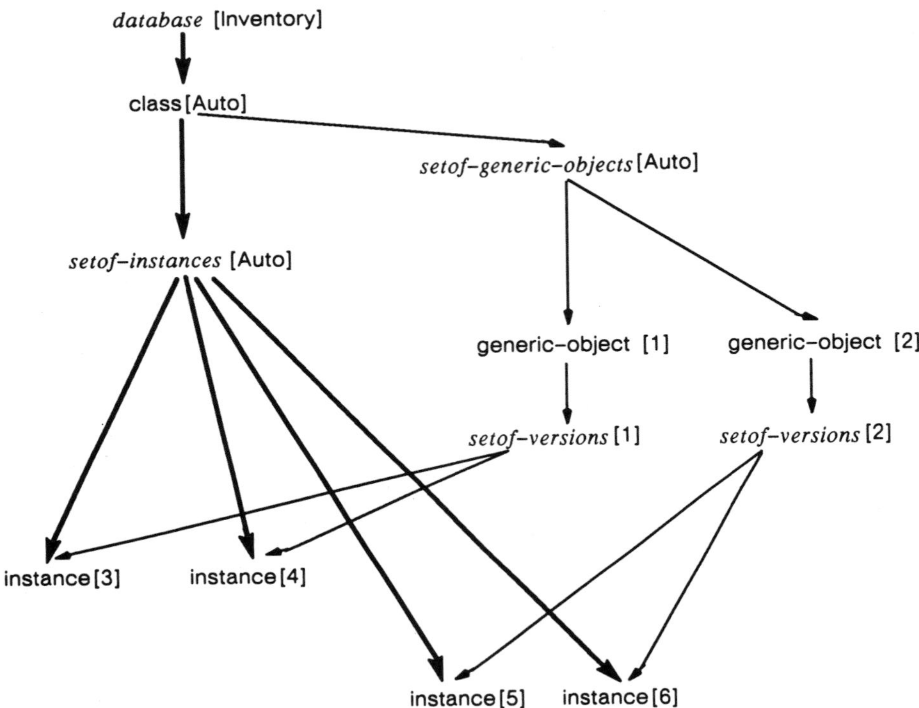

Figure 12.3
An Example AOH Including Versions

12.2 Composite Objects

A composite object is a part hierarchy of objects. Composite objects are similar to the complex objects implemented in an engineering database system called XSQL which was prototyped at IBM by extending IBM's SQL-based relational database system. Further, composite objects are similar to nested relations. However, at this time, ORION is the only object-oriented database system which supports composite objects as part of its data model. The notion of composite objects we will present in this section is an extension of that supported in ORION.

12.2.1 Semantics

In conventional object-oriented languages and systems, an object may have references to several other objects; however, the references do not have special semantics, other than referential integrity. As we discussed in Chapter 2, a useful relationship that we may attach to the references is the part-of relationship. This is the basis of constructing a part hierarchy of objects. An object may have n references, that is, references to n objects. The part-of relationship may be imposed recursively on all or some subset of these references. Once the system captures the part-of relationship among a collection of related objects, it has the basis for allowing queries on part hierarchies and for automatically enforcing integrity constraints that may be associated with the part-of semantics. We will call a reference augmented with the part-of semantics a *composite reference*. As we saw in Chapter 2, there are four meaningful types of composite reference.

(1) exclusive dependent composite reference

(2) exclusive independent composite reference

(3) shared dependent composite reference

(4) shared independent composite reference

The objects related through composite references form a composite object; a composite object then is a *part hierarchy* of component objects. One type of part hierarchy is a *physical part hierarchy* in which all composite references are exclusive; an object may be a component of at most one object in a physical assembly of parts. A different type of part hierarchy is a *logical part hierarchy* which may contain shared composite references; the text file for a chapter of a book may be a logical part of several books.

An object may have at most one exclusive composite reference to it; and an object which has an exclusive composite reference to it can have no other composite reference to it. However, an object may have any number of conventional references to it, which we call *weak references*, regardless of whether it has any exclusive composite reference to it. Further, an object may have any number of shared composite references to it, provided of course that it has no exclusive composite reference to it.

An object which has a dependent composite reference to it is deleted if its parent, that is, the object which has the dependent reference to it, is deleted; or if the reference itself is deleted. An object with an independent reference to it is not affected by the deletion of its parent object. If an object has both a dependent reference and an independent reference to it, it is deleted if the parent object with the dependent composite reference is deleted or the dependent reference is deleted; the object with an independent reference will now end up with a dangling reference.

That an object x references another object y really means that y is the value of an attribute A of x. The objects x and y of course are instances of some classes, say, X and Y, respectively; and the class Y is the domain of the attribute A of the class X. Then the part-of relationship on a reference from an object x to an object y is a property of the attribute of x whose value is y. That is, we can define an attribute of a class as a *composite attribute* if it has the part-of relationship.

12.2.2 Messages

Now we will make the discussion of the previous section concrete by showing how the syntax for the core object-oriented data model may be extended to include composite objects.

Class Definition
To support the extended semantics of a composite reference, we extend the syntax for attribute specification in the class definition with four types of keyword arguments, as follows:

```
(AttributeName      [:share SharedValue]
                    [:composite TrueOrNil]
                    [:exclusive TrueOrNil]
                    [:dependent TrueOrNil]
```

The keyword **composite** when set to True specifies that the reference is a composite reference. If the keyword **exclusive** is also True, the composite reference is an exclusive composite reference. If the keywords **composite** and **dependent** are both True, the reference is a dependent composite reference.

Below we provide two examples. The first is a physical part hierarchy; and the second a logical part hierarchy.

Example 1:

Let us consider a Vehicle composite hierarchy. We require that a vehicle part may be used for only one vehicle at any point in time; however, vehicle parts may be re-used for other vehicles. The definition for the class Vehicle is as follows (for simplicity we omit the definitions of all domain classes):

```
(make-class Vehicle
    :superclasses nil
    :attributes ((Manufacturer    :domain Company)
                 (Body            :domain AutoBody
                                  :composite true
                                  :exclusive true
                                  :dependent nil)
```

```
        (Drivetrain        :domain AutoDrivetrain
                           :composite true
                           :exclusive true
                           :dependent nil)
        (Tires             :domain ( set-of AutoTires)
                           :composite true
                           :exclusive true
                           :dependent nil)
        (Color             :domain String)))
```

Since all composite attributes in the class Vehicle are exclusive references, a set of vehicle components (Body, Drivetrain, and Tires) may be used for only one vehicle. However, since the exclusive references are independent, the components can be reused for other vehicles, if the vehicle which they constitute is dismantled later. The vehicle components may exist even if they are not part of any vehicle.

Example 2:

Let us now consider electronic documents. Suppose that a document consists of a title, authors and a number of sections. A section in turn is composed of paragraphs. A document may share entire sections or section paragraphs with other documents. Annotations may be added to documents; however, they are not shared among different documents. Further, documents may contain images that are extracted from files. The following are the definitions of two of the classes involved, Document and Section:

```
(make-class Document
    :superclasses nil
    :attribute ((Title             :domain string)
                (Author            :domain (set-of string))
                (Content           :domain (set-of Section)
                                   :composite true
                                   :exclusive nil
                                   :dependent true)
                (Figures           :domain (set-of Image)
                                   :composite true
                                   :exclusive nil
                                   :dependent nil)
                (Annotations       :domain (set-of Paragraph))
                                   :composite true
                                   :exclusive true
                                   :dependent true))
```

```
(make-class Section
    :superclasses nil
    :attribute ((Content        :domain (set-of Paragraph)
                                :composite true
                                :exclusive nil
                                :dependent true))
```

The attribute Content, defined as a set, is a shared composite reference. Other documents may share any element in this set (i.e., any section). A section exists, if it belongs to at least one document. Similarly, the class Section has a Paragraph shared composite reference. A paragraph may be shared among different sections (of possibly different documents). For a paragraph to exist, there must be at least one section containing it and thus a document containing it. In the case of Annotations we assume that a given annotation is used in only one document, thus the reference is exclusive. The attribute Figures is defined as an independent composite reference, since the existence of Images does not depend on the documents containing them.

Instance Creation

The following message is used to make an instance a part of one or more composite objects at the time of creation of that instance:

```
(make Class    :parent      ((ParentObject.1  ParentAttributeName.1)
                             (ParentObject.2  Parent AttributeName.2)
                             .......
                             (ParentObject.M  Parent AttributeName.M ))
               :Attribute.1  value.1
               :Attribute.2  value.2
                      .......
               :Attribute.N  value.N).
```

The keyword **parent** is associated with one or more pair (ParentObject.i ParentAttributeName.i), where ParentObject.i with the attribute ParentAttribute-Name.i is to reference the instance being created. If ParentAttributeName.i is a composite attribute, the new instance becomes part of ParentObject.i. Further, if ParentAttributeName.i is a dependent composite attribute, then the existence of the new object will depend on ParentObject.i.

When more than one pair (ParentObject.i ParentAttributeName.i) is specified such that ParentAttributeName.i is a composite attribute, then the instance being created is simultaneously made a part of all the specified objects. However, these attributes must be shared composite attributes.

Next, if an already existing object is made a part of a composite object through an exclusive reference, the system must check if there are no other composite references to that object. Similarly, if the object is made a part through a shared reference, the system has to ensure that there is no exclusive reference to that object.

We may define several operations on composite objects. These operations are used to determine the components, children, parents, and ancestors of an object. Most of these operations are rather obvious, and will not be illustrated here.

12.2.3 Implementation

Given a component of a composite object, it is often necessary to determine its parents or ancestors. Further, the system needs to determine efficiently the parents or the roots of a given component of a composite object to efficiently support locking, versions, and authorization of composite objects. We need to maintain in each component of a composite object a list of *reverse composite references*, that is, object identifiers of the parent objects. Although it is often useful for the system to be able to determine directly the roots of a composite object for a given component object, it is better to keep such information in each component; the reason is that the roots of a composite object may change when composite objects are created in a bottom-up fashion. Further, the reverse pointers should be kept in each component object, rather than in a separate data structure. This approach eliminates a level of indirection in accessing the parents of a given component, and simplifies deletion and migration of objects; however, it causes the object size to increase.

The number of reverse composite references in a component object is equal to the number of parent objects. A reverse composite reference actually consists of a couple of flags in addition to the object identifier of a parent. One flag indicates whether the object is a dependent component of the parent; while the other flag indicates whether the object is an exclusive component of the parent.

12.2.4 Schema Evolution

The notion of composite objects gives rise to two new types of schema change beyond those we discussed in Chapter 5 for the core object-oriented data model. One type of change is the deletion of a composite attribute. Another is the addition or removal of the part-of semantics from a composite attribute.

The deletion of a composite attribute affects the semantics of four of the schema changes discussed in Chapter 5.

(1) Drop an attribute A from a class C.
This operation causes all instances of the class C to lose their values for attribute A. If A is a dependent composite attribute, objects that are referenced

through A are deleted. The attribute must also be dropped from all subclasses that inherit it.

(2) Change the inheritance (parent) of an attribute (inherit another attribute with the same name).
Depending on the origin of the old and new attribute, this operation may cause the old attribute to be dropped. If the attribute dropped is a dependent composite attribute, this operation is identical to (1) above.

(3) Remove a class S as superclass of a class C.
If this operation causes class C to lose a composite attribute A, objects (of other classes) that are recursively referenced by instances of C and its subclasses through A are deleted according to (1).

(4) Drop an existing class C.
If the class C has one or more dependent composite attributes, objects referenced through the attributes are dropped. All subclasses of C become immediate subclasses of the superclasses of C.

Let us now explore meaningful changes from one type of attribute to a different one. The changes may be one of two types: removing a constraint from a composite attribute, and adding a constraint to a composite attribute. The following are the changes that remove a constraint.

(1) Change a composite attribute to a non-composite attribute.

(2) Change an exclusive composite attribute to a shared composite attribute.

(3) Change a dependent composite attribute (either exclusive or shared) to an independent composite attribute.

(4) Change an independent composite attribute (either exclusive or shared) to a dependent composite attribute.

The following changes add a new constraint to a composite attribute. Let us suppose that the class C is the domain of an attribute A of a class C', and that A is to be changed.

(1) Change a non-composite attribute to an exclusive composite attribute.
There must be no composite (either shared or exclusive) references to instances of the class C which are referenced by instances of the class C'.

(2) Change a non-composite attribute to a shared composite attribute.
There must be no exclusive composite references to instances of the class C which are referenced by instances of the class C'.

(3) Change a shared composite attribute to an exclusive composite attribute.
There can be at most one shared reference to instances of the class C which are referenced by instances of the class C'.

12.2.5 Authorization

In systems which support composite objects, it is desirable to include composite objects as a unit of authorization, regardless of whether a composite object is a collection of a small number of large objects or a large number of small objects. If a composite object is a unit of authorization, the user (who created the composite object or who has the grant authorization on it) needs to grant authorization on the composite object as a single unit, rather than on each of the component objects. Further, when a composite object is accessed, the system needs to check only one authorization (for the entire composite object), rather than authorizations on all component objects.

Therefore, as we have shown already for versions, we will consider extending the notion of implicit authorizations to composite objects. An authorization on a composite object should imply the same authorization on each of the component objects. Again, a reasonable approach to extend the model of authorization for the core object-oriented data model to include composite objects is to introduce additional types of authorization objects. Figure 12.4 is the Authorization Object Schema extended with authorization object types for composite objects, including setof-composite-objects, composite-object, and setof-composite-attribute-values. Figure 12.5 illustrates the Authorization Object Hierarchy *(AOH)* for a database which contains a composite object.

An authorization on a composite class C implies the same authorization on all instances of C and on all objects which are components of the instances of C. For example, let us consider a composite class hierarchy consisting of the classes Vehicle, Autobody, and AutoDrivetrain. If a user is granted a Read authorization on the class Vehicle, the user implicitly receives the same authorization on all instances of Vehicle, and all instances of Autobody and AutoDrivetrain which are components of the instances of Vehicle. We note, however, that the authorization on Vehicle does not imply the same authorization on all instances of Autobody and AutoDrivetrain, since not all instances of Autobody and AutoDrivetrain may be components of Vehicle. Further, because of negative authorizations, a new authorization issued on a component class may conflict with an authorization on the class which is implied by a previously granted authorization. In this case, the authorization subsystem must reject the new authorization.

As mentioned already, an authorization on a composite object implies the same authorization on each component of the composite object. If an instance is a component of more than one composite object, a user can receive more than one implicit authorization on that instance. For example, let us consider the composite objects in Figure 12.6. If a user receives a Read authorization on the composite object rooted at Instance[j], then the user implicitly receives a Read authorization on Instance[o']. If the user is later granted a Read authorization on the composite object rooted at Instance[k], the user again receives an implicit authorization on Instance[o'].

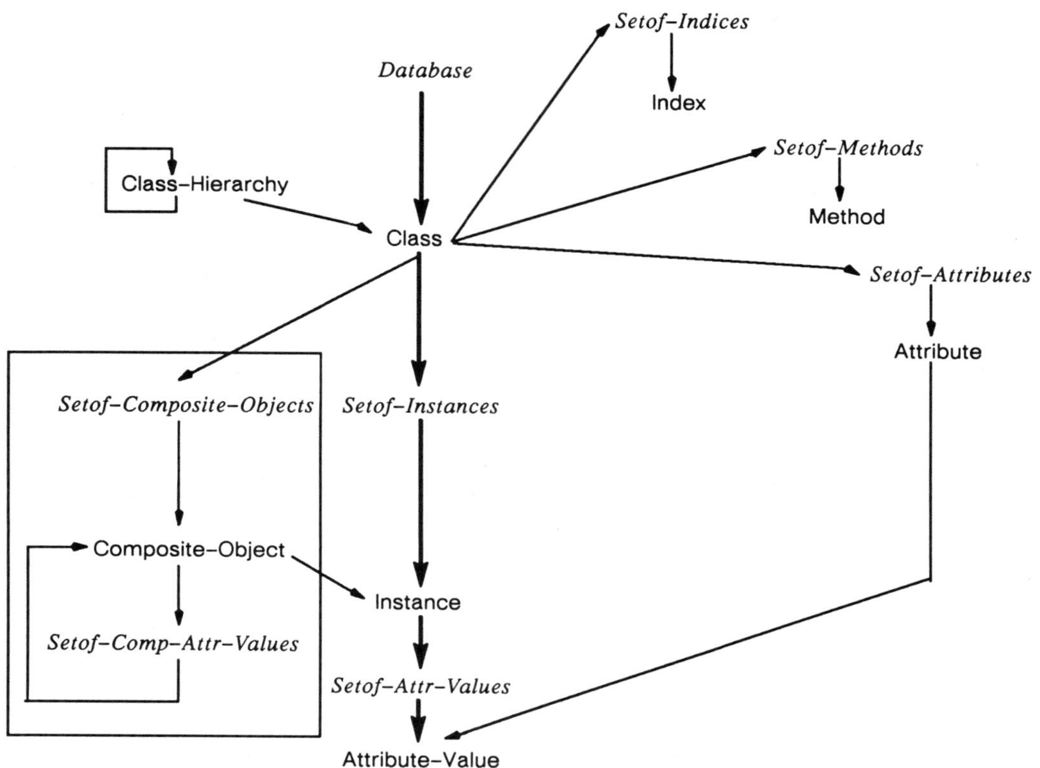

Figure 12.4
Authorization Object Schema (AOS) Extended with Composite Objects

Negative authorizations give rise to conflicts among implicit authorizations on objects which are components of more than one composite object. For example, if the user is granted a negative Read authorization on the composite object rooted at Instance[k] in Figure 12.6, it will conflict with the (positive) implicit authorization the user received from Instance[j]. In this case, the negative authorization can be granted only if the Read authorization on the composite object rooted at Instance[j] is a weak authorization (and therefore it can be overridden).

If an object O is a component of n composite objects, and an authorization is granted on one of the composite objects, the authorization subsystem must ensure that the new authorization does not conflict with any of the authorizations on O which are implied by the current authorizations on the composite objects. If there is no conflict, the resulting authorization on O is the strongest of all the implied authorizations on O. For

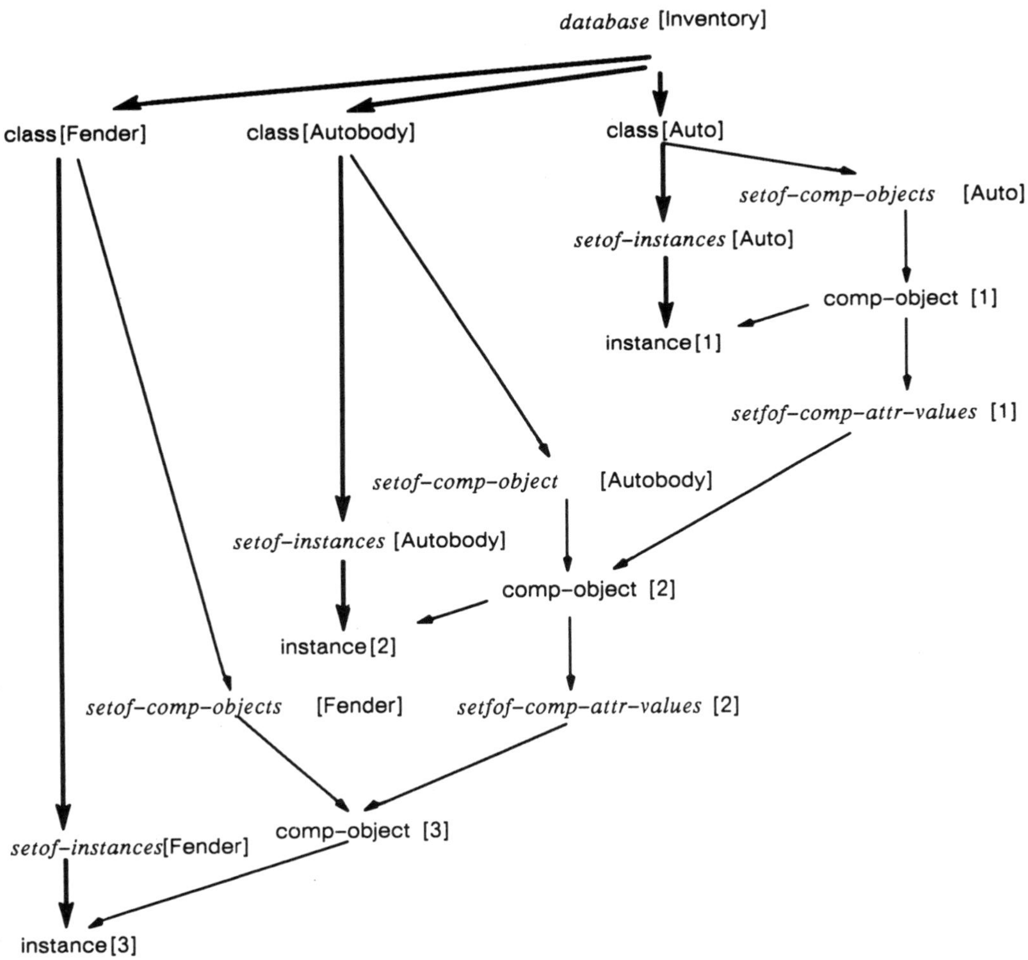

Figure 12.5
An Example AOH with Composite Objects

example, if a user receives a strong R authorization from Instance[j] and a strong W authorization from Instance[k], the authorization implied on Instance[o'] is a strong W authorization, which in turn implies a strong R authorization. Similarly, if a user receives a strong negative R authorization from Instance[j] and a strong negative W authorization from Instance[k], the authorization implied on Instance[o'] is a strong negative R authorization, which implies a strong negative W authorization.

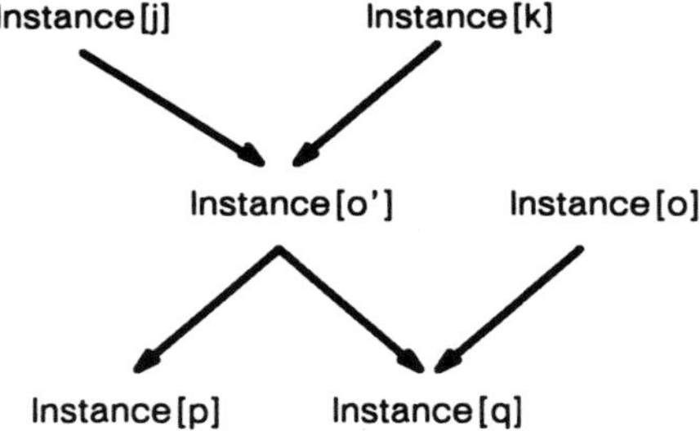

Figure 12.6
Implicit Authorizations for a Common Component

12.2.6 Concurrency Control

In Chapter 11 we reviewed the concept of implicit locking on a database granularity hierarchy; an explicit lock on a node of a granularity hierarchy implies the same lock on all direct and indirect descendant nodes. We can apply the concept of implicit locking to a composite object hierarchy. Of course, a composite hierarchy is entirely different from a database granularity hierarchy. However, the notion of implicit locking serves the same purpose, that is, it can significantly reduce the number of explicit locks that must be set and maintained in the system lock table.

To extend the conventional locking protocol to composite objects, we need to extend the database granularity hierarchy by introducing a composite object as a unit of locking. Figure 12.7 shows the extended database granularity hierarchy. Further, we need to introduce the protocol that an explicit lock on a composite object implies the same lock on every component object of the composite object.

The notion of a composite object as a unit of locking (lockable granule) means that a collection of objects that belong to more than one class is locked as a single unit. In

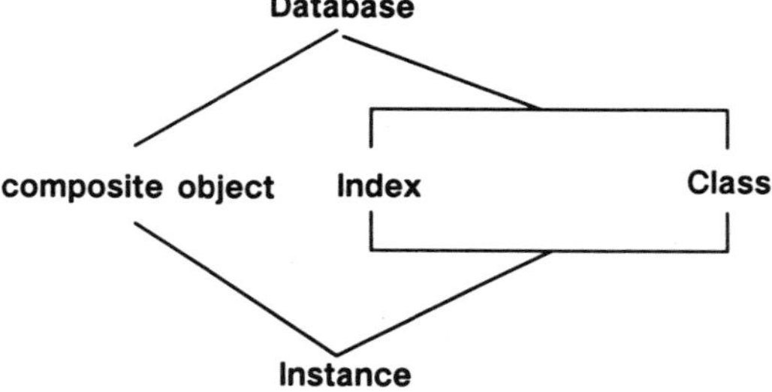

Figure 12.7
Database Granularity Hierarchy Extended with Composite Objects

database systems which do not recognize a composite object as a lockable granule, explicit locks must be set either on all the individual component objects or on all the classes to which the component objects belong. The problem with locking all component objects is that the system must maintain a potentially large number of locks in the lock table. The problem with locking all classes of the component objects of a particular composite object is that the locks on the classes may prevent access to other composite objects that are based on the same composite class hierarchy, even if they do not share any component object with the composite object currently being accessed.

We would like the locking protocol on composite objects to satisfy three objectives. First is to support implicit locking of all component objects. Second is to allow different transactions to concurrently access composite objects that are based on the same composite class hierarchy, but that do not share any component objects. Third is to allow transactions to access composite objects, while different transactions directly access instances of any component class of a composite class hierarchy on which the composite objects are based.

An intuitive, but incorrect, protocol is as follows. To lock an entire composite object, the root class of the composite class hierarchy is locked in IS, IX, S, SIX or X mode; and, if the root class is locked in IS, IX, or SIX mode, the root object of the composite object is locked in S, X, or X mode, respectively. Further, the component classes are also locked in IS, IX, S, SIX, or X mode, respectively. However, the component objects of a composite object are only implicitly locked; that is, they are not locked. To lock a class, which is a component class on a composite object hierarchy, independently of the composite object hierarchy, the class should be locked in IS, IX, S, SIX or X mode.

Unhappily, this simple protocol is incorrect. Suppose a transaction T1 has set an X lock on a composite object. This means that an IX lock has been set on each of the component classes of the composite object hierarchy. Then another transaction T2 attempts to update some instances of one of the component classes independently of the composite object hierarchy. T2 will set an IX lock on the class, and then X locks on instances of the class to be updated. However, unless the identifier of the root object of a composite object is stored in the component objects, there is no way to prevent transaction T2 from setting X locks on those component objects that the transaction T1 has implicitly locked in X mode.

We need three new lock modes to make the protocol correct: ISO, IXO, SIXO, corresponding to the IS, IX, and SIX modes, respectively. The compatibility matrix of Figure 12.8 completely defines the semantics of all lock modes we have in order to support both granularity locking and composite object locking for composite objects with exclusive references. As shown in the compatibility matrix, the key idea to correct the protocol is to force the ISO mode to conflict with the IX mode, and IXO requested mode

current mode	IS	IX	S	SIX	X	ISO	IXO	SIXO
IS	✓	✓	✓	✓	No	✓	No	No
IX	✓	✓	No	No	No	No	No	No
S	✓	No	✓	No	No	✓	No	No
SIX	✓	No	No	No	No	No	No	No
X	No	No	No	No	No	No	No	No
ISO	✓	No	✓	No	No	✓	✓	✓
IXO	No	No	No	No	No	✓	✓	No
SIXO	No	No	No	No	No	✓	No	No

Figure 12.8
Compatibility Matrix for Granularity Locking
and Composite Object Locking for Exclusive References

and SIXO modes to conflict with both the IS and IX modes. Then to lock a composite object, the root class is locked, as before, in IS, IX, S, SIX, or X mode. However, each of the component classes of the composite object hierarchy is now locked in ISO, IXO, S, SIX, or X mode, respectively.

The protocol allows multiple users to read and update composite objects having the same root class, as long as they update different composite objects. However, if there is even one reader via the composite object hierarchy, there can be no direct updaters of instances of component classes. Further, if there is even one direct reader of instances of a component class, there can be no updaters via the composite object hierarchy.

The following illustrates the locking protocol for accessing composite objects, and for directly accessing instances of a component class of a composite object hierarchy.

(1) Select vehicle composite objects such that . . .
(a) lock vehicle class object in IS mode
(b) lock the selected instances of vehicle in S mode
(c) lock the component class objects in ISO mode

(2) Update all vehicles or their components such that . . .
(a) lock vehicle class object in IX mode
(b) lock the selected instances of vehicle in X mode
(c) lock the component class objects in IXO mode

(3) Select all doors such that . . .
  (a) lock the door class object in IS mode
  (b) lock the selected door instances in S mode

(4) Update all doors such that . . .
  (a) lock the door class object in IX mode
  (b) lock the selected door instances in X mode

The protocol developed thus far is only applicable to physical part hierarchies, that is, composite objects with only the exclusive composite references. To extend the protocol for shared composite references, we need to introduce three additional lock modes for the component class of shared references: ISOS (intention shared object-shared), IXOS (intention exclusive object-shared), and SIXOS (shared intention exclusive object-shared), which correspond to the ISO, IXO, and SIXO for component classes with exclusive references. Figure 12.9 shows the compatibility matrix for the expanded set of lock modes.

Let us consider the composite objects in Figure 12.10, where component object Instance[c] and Instance[c'] belong to the same class C; Instance[w] and Instance[w'] belong to a class W; and Instance[i], Instance[j], and Instance[k] belong to classes I, J, and K, respectively. The following examples illustrate the revised locking protocol.

(1) Update the composite object rooted at Instance[i]
  (a) lock class I in IX mode.
  (b) lock composite object Instance[i] in X mode.
  (c) lock class C in IXO mode.

(2) Access the composite object rooted at Instance[k]
  (a) lock class K in IS mode.
  (b) lock composite object Instance[k] in S mode.
  (c) lock class C in ISOS mode.
  (d) lock class W in ISO mode.

(3) Update the composite object rooted at Instance[j]
  (a) lock class J in IX mode.
  (b) lock composite object Instance[j] in X mode.
  (c) lock class C in IXOS mode.
  (d) lock class W in IXO mode.

This protocol allows several concurrent readers and writers on a component class of exclusive references, and several readers and one writer on a component class of shared references. Therefore, examples 1 and 2 are compatible, while example 3 is incompatible with both 1 and 2. This protocol also suffers from the restriction that if there is even one reader (writer) via the composite class hierarchy, there cannot be any direct readers or writers via the instances of component classes, or vice versa.

requested mode

current mode	IS	IX	S	SIX	X	ISO	IXO	SIXO	ISOS	IXOS	SIXOS
IS	√	√	√	√	No	√	No	No	√	No	No
IX	√	√	No	No	No	No	No	No	No	No	No
S	√	No	√	No	No	√	No	No	√	No	No
SIX	√	No	No	No	No	No	No	No	No	No	No
X	No	No	No	No	No	No	No	No	No	No	No
ISO	√	No	√	No	No	√	√	√	√	√	√
IXO	No	No	No	No	No	√	√	No	√	√	No
SIXO	No	No	No	No	No	√	No	No	√	No	No
ISOS	√	No	√	No	No	√	√	√	√	No	No
IXOS	No	No	No	No	No	√	√	No	No	No	No
SIXOS	No	No	No	No	No	√	No	No	No	No	No

Figure 12.9
Compatibility Matrix for Granularity Locking and Composite Object Locking for Exclusive and Shared References

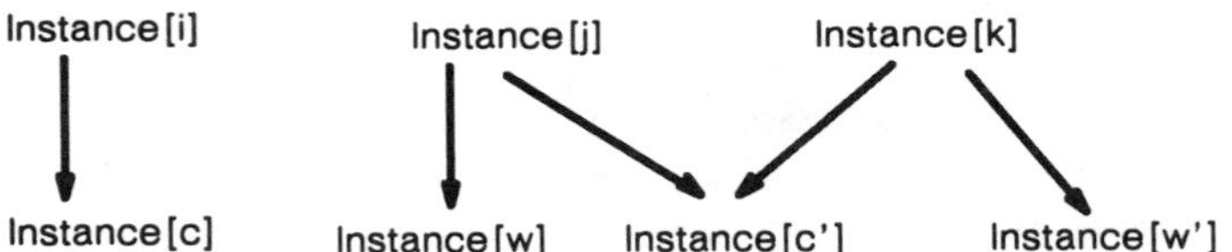

Figure 12.10
Example Composite Objects

The protocol we just presented is appropriate largely for conventional short-duration transactions. Unfortunately, it may not be suitable for long-duration transactions. For long-duration transactions, it may be better to lock individual component objects as needed. An appropriate locking protocol for long-duration transactions is still a research issue.

12.2.7 Versions

The semantics of composite references also necessitate changes to the model of versions of simple objects. The major difficulty in extending the model of versions of simple objects to a model of versions of composite objects lies in extending the semantics of a composite reference between a pair of instance objects to that between a pair of generic objects and between an instance object and a generic object. We will take the view that the semantics of a composite reference apply to a pair of generic objects, and that they transfer to one pair of versions of the respective generic objects.

The following set of rules captures the semantics of versions of composite objects. Let us consider a pair of classes C and D, and suppose C has a composite attribute A whose domain is D, and both C and D are classes for versionable objects.

Rule CV-1: The existence of a composite reference from a generic object g-c of the class C to a generic object g-d of the class D means that any number of versions of g-c may have the same composite reference to g-d.

Rule CV-2: A version may have at most one composite reference to it, if the reference is exclusive; or any number of composite references to it, if they are all shared references. A generic object may have more than one exclusive composite reference to it, only if all references are from objects that belong to the same version hierarchy. However, it may have any number of shared composite references to it.

As a consequence of Rule CV-2, when a version c-i of the class C is copied to derive a new version c-j, and c-i has an exclusive reference to a version d-k (rather than a generic object g-d) of the class D, the new version will have the same exclusive reference that the initial version has (as shown in Figure 12.11a). The reference in the new copy is set to the generic object g-d of the referenced version (as shown in Figure 1b). However, if the reference is a dependent composite reference, it is set to nil.

Rules CV-1 and CV-2 together imply that different versions of the same generic object g-c may have composite references to different versions of the generic object g-d, as long as each version of g-d is referenced through one exclusive composite reference or only shared composite references. Figure 12.12 illustrates this.

Rule CV-3: The existence of a composite reference from a version c-i of a generic object c-g to a version d-j of a generic object d-g implies a composite reference from c-g to d-g.

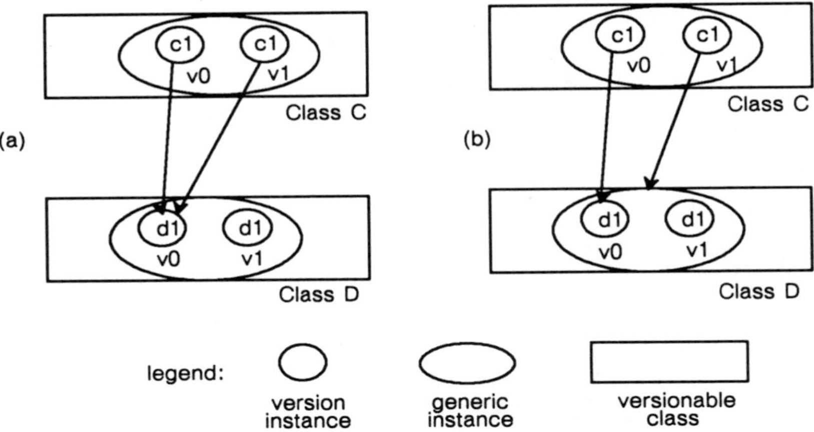

Figure 12.11
Deriving a New Version of a Composite Object

Rules CV-2 and CV-3 together prevent versions of different versionable objects, say, O' and O", from having exclusive composite references to different versions of the same versionable object O.

Rule CV-4: When a generic object g-c is deleted, all generic objects to which it has exclusive references are recursively deleted. Further, if a generic object is deleted,

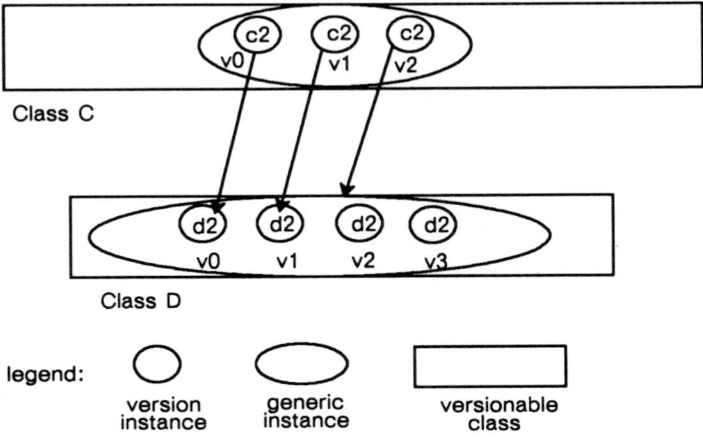

Figure 12.12
Versioned Composite Objects

all its versions are deleted; and if the last remaining version of a generic object is deleted, the generic object is also deleted.

Rules CV-2 and CV-4 together imply that the deletion of a version causes a recursive deletion of all versions statically bound to it through dependent references; however, it does not cause any generic object referenced to be deleted.

In this section, we discussed versions of composite objects, and authorizations on composite objects. At this time, the issue of authorizations on versions of composite objects has not been addressed in open literature. We leave it to the reader as a potentially interesting exercise.

Recommended Readings

A large part of this chapter is taken from [KIM87] and [KIM89d]. The readers interested in additional readings on versions may find [KATZ86] and [CHOU86] to be good starting points for a literature search. Both describe sophisticated models of versions which also have largely been implemented. Further, [KIM88c] and [KIM89d] provide starting points for a literature search on the semantics and implementation of composite objects in an object-oriented database system; [LORI83] and [KIM88c] discuss in detail the semantics and implementation of the complex-object extensions to relational database systems.

[RABI89] provides a background for the discussion of authorization for versions and composite objects. [GARZ88] and [KIM89d] discuss a locking protocol for composite objects; [KIM89d] describes implementation issues for schema evolution on composite objects and versions of composite objects.

13 Integrating Object-Oriented Programming and Databases

As we have seen, a number of semantic data modeling concepts, that is, relationships, are inherent in object-oriented concepts cast in object-oriented programming languages. This means that object-oriented programming languages are a good basis for extending as application programming languages for data-intensive applications, such as those found in computer-aided design and engineering, artificial intelligence, and office information systems. Programmers using object-oriented languages are already acclimated to the data modeling concepts, and as such they need not learn and use a programming language and a separate database language to program data-intensive applications. The current practice is to embed a database language, such as the relational language SQL, in conventional algorithmic programming languages such as FORTRAN, COBOL, and PL/1. Because of the serious mismatch in the data model and data structures in the two types of language, application programmers must program the conversion between the two data models and data structures.

To extend a programming language to a database programming language, the programming language must be extended with database primitives, and the database system must be designed and implemented to support the requirements of the programming language. The programming language needs to be extended with constructs to express queries, integrity specification (including transactions), access authorization, access methods, versions, and so on; this is necessary for the database programming language to make full use of the capabilities of the underlying database system. In previous chapters we have shown database extensions to programming languages.

The database system must also be designed to meet the requirements of programming language systems. The current database systems fetch page frames from the disk into the page-buffer pool, copy objects from the page-buffer pool, send them to the workspace of the application that requested them. The applications populate the workspace by calling database systems for objects one at a time, and, after updates to objects in their workspace, send them back to the database systems for persistent storage. Because of the mismatch in the data models and data structures between the applications and the database system, objects must undergo mapping as they are transferred between the applications and the database system. The mapping is programmed into the applications.

Unfortunately, mapping of the objects between the applications and the database systems is necessary, even if the applications are written using one integrated database programming language. The reason is that two different formats are needed for objects: in-memory format, and disk format. The in-memory format for objects is necessary to allow the objects to be directly manipulated in the programming language. The disk format differs from the in-memory format; it is designed for storage and retrieval efficiency, and, in the case of a structure, references embedded in constituent objects need to be converted between absolute addresses in memory and relative addresses on disk. Further, dynamic schema evolution, if deferred update of existing instances is used as in ORION, requires dynamic screening or padding of the values of dropped attributes before sending the objects to the applications.

Further, data-intensive applications, such as interactive simulators or expert systems, often perform extensive computations on a large number of in-memory objects. As discussed above, current database systems send to and receive from an application one object at a time; the performance penalty for each call to the database system is rather high. Further, current database systems maintain page frames in a rather limited number of page buffers for possible reaccess by the applications. In general, however, a page buffer contains not only the objects that an application has requested, but also useless neighboring objects. Therefore, the total number of objects in the page-buffer pool that an application may reaccess is rather limited. Finally, current database systems have no control over the objects once they have been placed in the workspace of the applications; that is, the database systems do not evaluate queries against them, do not provide concurrency control over shared access to them, and do not enforce database integrity over them.

To address the above problems, a database system must be architected to manage not only the page-buffer pool but also the workspace. In this way, the database system can exercise its full power over both the in-memory objects and the disk page frames. The database system will then perform the translation of the format of the objects as the objects move between the page-buffer pool and the workspace. Further, it may keep the in-memory objects in the workspace for access by other applications; this may significantly help to minimize the need for a database system to access the disk.

Many of the currently operational object-oriented database systems have integrated an object-oriented programming language and a database system, that is, to extend a programming language with database support. GemStone and AllTalk extended Smalltalk with database support; ORION and Statice provide database support for object-oriented extensions to LISP; and Vbase integrated an object-oriented superset of C with a database system. In this chapter we will focus our discussion on the architectural concepts and data structures necessary to give the application programmers the illusion and the performance of an infinitely large virtual memory for their objects. The discussion will be based on the issues and solutions implemented in ORION.

13.1 In-Memory Object Management

ORION uses a dual-buffer management scheme, in which the available database buffer space is partitioned into a page buffer pool and an object buffer pool (workspace). To access an object, the page that contains the object is brought into a page buffer, and then the object is located, retrieved, and placed in an object buffer. ORION supports data structures for efficiently managing objects in the object buffer pool, and addresses issues that arise from the fact that the object buffer pool and the database may contain different copies of the same object during a transaction. Applications can directly access the objects in the object buffer pool, and the transaction management feature of ORION ensures database consistency (concurrency control and crash recovery) for these in-memory objects. In this section, we describe the data structures ORION has implemented to manage in-memory objects, that is, objects in the object buffer pool. The impacts of dual buffering on the architecture of a database system, and the solutions implemented in ORION will be discussed in the next section.

13.1.1 Object Buffering

Figure 13.1a shows a high-level block diagram of the ORION architecture. (The architecture of ORION will be discussed in detail in Chapter 14; however, to illustrate the dual-buffering scheme, we need to introduce some aspects of the ORION architecture in this chapter.) The message handler receives all messages sent to ORION objects. The storage subsystem provides access to objects, both on in the page buffer pool and the object buffer pool. The transaction subsystem provides a concurrency control and recovery mechanism; as in conventional database systems, concurrency control uses a

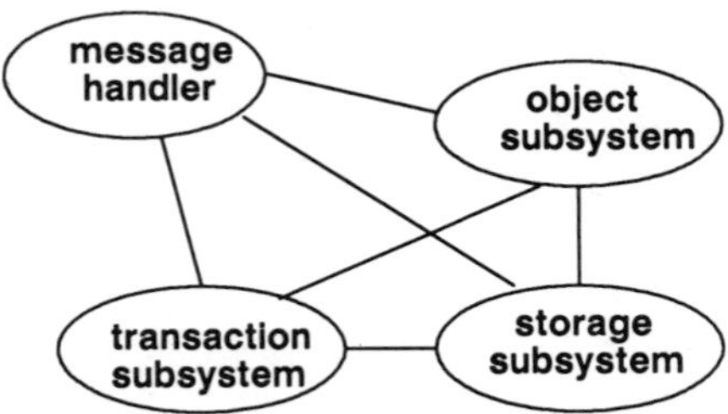

Figure 13.1a
ORION Architecture

locking protocol, and a logging mechanism is used for recovery from system crashes and aborts.

The storage subsystem consists of the access manager and the storage manager, as shown in Figure 13.1b. The storage manager manipulates objects in their disk format in the page buffer pool, and performs the transformation between the disk format and the in-memory format; while the access manager manages objects their in-memory format in the object buffer pool. The access manager controls the transfer of objects between the object buffer pool and the page buffer pool.

The ORION page buffer manager is similar to the buffer manager in conventional database systems. It manages a pool of page frames and implements a page replacement algorithm. The page buffer pool serves as a staging area for regular (small) objects as well as the buffer area for caching portions of long multimedia objects.

To manage objects in the object-buffer pool, the object-buffer manager maintains a virtual-memory address table (*resident object table or ROT*). Multiple applications may concurrently access objects in a single physical object-buffer pool. An application can accumulate objects in the object-buffer pool by creating new objects or sending object requests to the database system. Upon receiving a request to access an object through its unique identifier (UID), the object-buffer manager searches the ROT. If the object is not registered in the table (i.e., an object fault occurs), it must be retrieved from the database, placed in an object buffer, and registered in the ROT.

The most frequent operation on the ROT is looking up the location of an object. Since the ROT can grow to a substantial size, a hash table is used to speed up associative searches based on UIDs. The key of the hash table is the UID, and the value is a pointer to the descriptor for the object associated with the UID (to be discussed shortly). Insertions and deletions of the ROT entries are two other frequent operations that are necessary for supporting object swapping. Sometimes a collection of objects in the buffer pool must be accessed: for example, when the modified objects need to be flushed to the database to commit a transaction, or when the contents of the object-buffer pool are invalidated because of changes to the database schema.

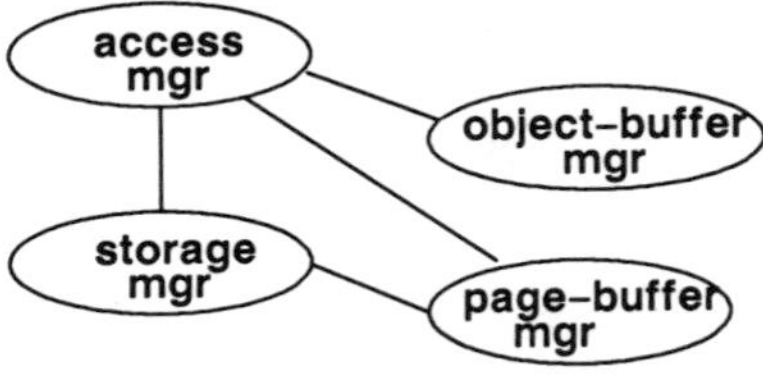

Figure 13.1b
ORION Storage Subsystem

Buffer management for objects in the object-buffer pool is inherently more complex than that for pages because of the variability of object sizes. Placement of a newly retrieved object is a nontrivial task, since a free block of memory with at least the size of the object must be found. Fragmentation of the buffer pool becomes more severe as objects of different sizes are swapped in and out of memory. Expensive compaction of the object-buffer pool may be required from time to time. The difficulty of object buffering is further compounded by the fact that objects in the buffer pool are directly accessible to the application. It is difficult, if not impossible, to keep track of all the outstanding object references (memory pointers) in the application program. Adding the fix/unfix protocol to the application interface would make the interface too cumbersome. This makes it necessary to rely on a garbage collection technique to reclaim space occupied by inactive objects.

13.1.2 Resident Object Descriptors

When the application requests an object, ORION returns a pointer to a descriptor of the object in the object buffer pool, rather than a pointer to the object. This is also the approach taken in the Large Object-Oriented Memory (LOOM) system developed at Xerox Palo Alto Research Center; however, the ORION object descriptor consists of several fields in addition to those used in LOOM, because of consideration for the performance and integrity of the database in a multiple concurrent-user environment. (The rest of this chapter will make this clear.) The descriptor, called the resident object descriptor (ROD), is illustrated in Figure 13.2a. The ROD is an intermediate data structure between the ROT and the actual object. The pointer-to-object field in

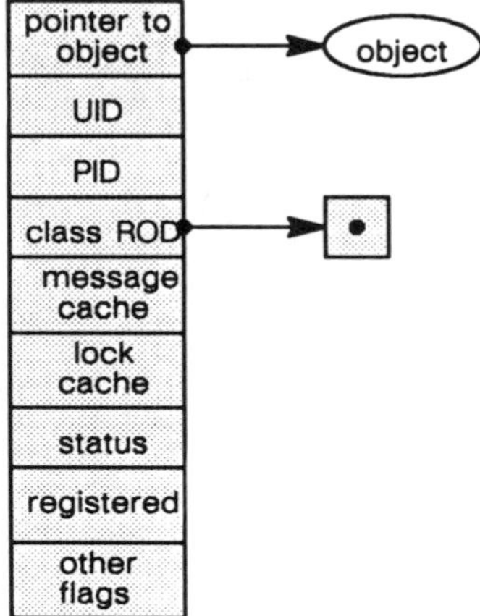

Figure 13.2a
ROD Structure

the ROD contains a pointer through which the contents of the object can be accessed. The UID field contains the UID of the object; the PID field contains the physical address of the object on disk; and the class-ROD is the pointer to the ROD of the class object of which the object is an instance. The status field is used to indicate if the object is changed. The registered field is used to indicate whether the ROT contains a pointer to the ROD. The other fields of the ROD, message-cache and lock-cache, are used to speed up message passing and concurrency control; their use will be discussed later.

ORION uses the ROD as a compromise between two somewhat conflicting goals that need to be satisfied for locating in-memory objects. On one hand, one would like to pass back the actual object (actually a pointer to the object) when a user requests it through a UID. On the other hand, one needs to retain the ability to swap out any object in memory when such a need arises, for example, when the main memory is flooded with too many old objects. However, without direct hardware support, there is no easy way to catch a direct reference to a swapped-out object and take appropriate actions, as in a paged virtual memory system.

An object may be swapped out when it is not referenced in any active transaction, or when the object buffer pool becomes full. Then the pointer (to the object) in the ROD is changed to nil. The memory pointer to the ROD in the ROT is also removed, so that the ROD itself can be garbage collected when there are no more outstanding pointers to it. There are situations where a ROD may be created before the object is brought into memory. For example, the result of a query is a set of RODs. There is no need to bring all the objects into memory since some of them may not be accessed at all. Under this situation, the access manager will create the RODs at query time, but fetch the objects only on demand. When an object is fetched, the access manager creates RODs for all references it has to other objects, and replaces these references with memory pointers to their corresponding RODs. As shown in Figure 13.2b, some

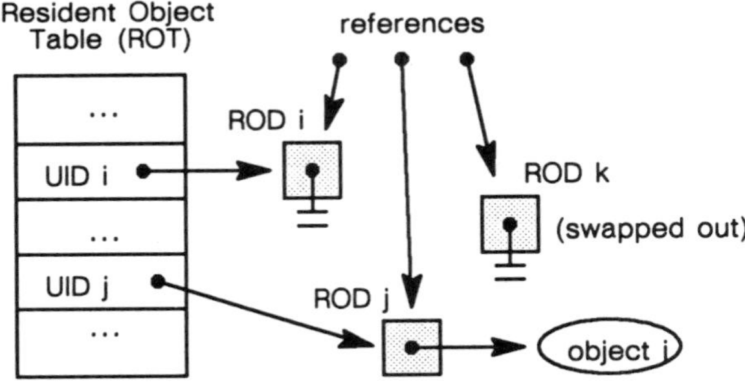

Figure 13.2b
Object Buffering

objects may have a ROT entry and a ROD that points to an in-memory copy of the object. Queried objects which have not been brought in have a ROT entry and a ROD containing a nil pointer. Finally, there are objects that reside only on disk and have no in-memory data structures associated with them.

The ROT is initially empty. The first time an object is accessed by a user, the object buffer manager detects that the object is not in the table and the access manager brings it in from the database. The access manager creates a ROD for the object and has the object buffer manager register it in the ROT with the UID as the key. The access manager passes a pointer to the ROD to the user, who can then directly access the contents of the object through the ROD. When another request comes in for the same object, the object buffer manager will locate the ROD (through the ROT) and pass back a pointer to the ROD. As shown in Figure 13.3, object y is referenced by both objects x and z through the same ROD.

The object buffering and ROD manipulation discussed above are all transparent to the users. A user simply sends a message to an object and expects a return message as in any object-oriented system. The objects that a user sees are actually pointers to RODs. To process a message sent to an object, the message handler first examines the ROD and have the object read in from the database, if necessary.

When the access manager receives a request to fetch an object based on its UID or ROD, it calls first the object buffer manager to see if the object is already in the object buffer pool. If it is, the access manager returns a pointer to the object's ROD. Otherwise, it directs the storage manager to determine the PID of the object by hashing into UID-PID table for all objects in the database (this is different from the ROT), fetch the

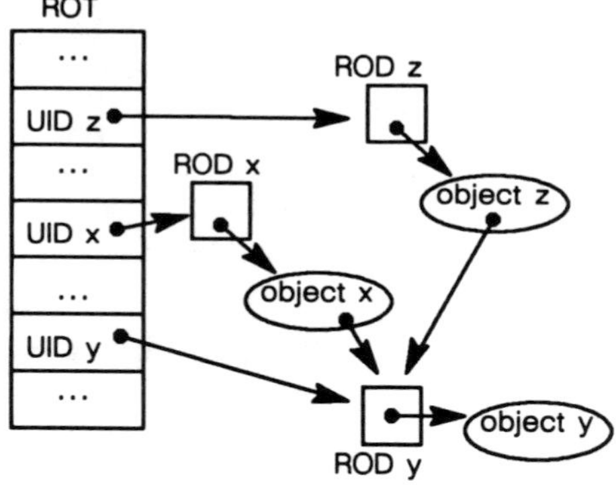

Figure 13.3
Concurrent References to an Object

page containing the object, isolate the object within the page, and transform the object from its disk format to the in-memory format. Finally, the access manager calls the object buffer manager to place the transformed object in the object buffer pool, and returns a pointer to the object's ROD. The PID of the object is recorded in the PID field of the ROD, shown in Figure 13.2a. This is to avoid the UID-to-PID translation overhead, when the object has to be flushed (written) to disk, or fetched again after it has been swapped out. To insert new objects, the storage manager determines the PIDs of the objects so as to cluster instances of the same class in the same physical segment, registers the objects in the UID-PID hash table for all database objects.

Message Cache

The main data structure of the message handler is the message cache. The message cache is an array of valid messages. Each entry of the array holds message functions for a class. A message function simply dispatches a message: it contains no knowledge of how the message is implemented. The message-cache field in the ROD of an object contains a reference to an appropriate entry of the message cache.

Lock Cache

Unlike LOOM, ORION supports multiple concurrent transactions. This means that before the access manager can return the ROD pointer of an object to a requesting transaction, it must check whether another transaction is accessing the object in a conflicting mode. This check is relatively expensive, since the access manager must call the lock manager in the transaction subsystem, and the lock manager must search the lock table.

To avoid this overhead whenever possible, when the access manager first creates or retrieves an object from the database, it encodes in the lock-cache field of the object's ROD the mode of the lock which is set on the object. In this way, the access manager needs to call the lock manager only the first time the object must be locked, and when a read lock on the object must be upgraded to a write lock (i.e., the object was first retrieved from the database with a read lock, and now it must be updated). In all other situations, calls to the lock manager may be avoided.

13.2 Consequences of Object Buffering on the Database System Architecture

Dual buffering has significant consequences on the architecture of a database system. These have to do with the fact that an object may have two different copies during a transaction: one in the object buffer pool and another in the database. One consequence is obviously the need for a translator to transform an object between its disk format and the in-memory format. A second consequence is the need to invalidate the in-memory objects, when certain types of changes are made to the database schema. A third consequence is the need to screen the database copy of an object from the result of a query, if the object has an in-memory copy. Let us examine the latter two aspects.

13.2.1 Object Buffer Flushing

Applications accumulate objects in the object buffer pool by creating new objects, and fetching and updating objects from the database. The new objects and updated copies of objects need to be written to the database when the transaction which has created or updated the objects commits. Of course, the objects are transformed to their disk format before being written to the database. New objects are registered in the UID-PID hash table for database objects, and updated objects replace their old copies in the database.

Further, when changes are made to the database schema which add or drop an attribute from a class, instances of the affected class which reside in the object buffer pool become invalid and must be purged from the object buffer pool. Of the schema changes discussed in Chapter 5, the following invalidate objects in the object buffer pool.

(1) Add a new attribute to a class

(2) Drop an existing attribute from a class

(3) Make a class S a superclass of a class C

(4) Remove a class S from the superclass list of a class C

(5) Drop an existing class

13.2.2 Query Processing

The access manager applies search predicates specified in a query to instances of a class. The ORION dual-buffering scheme complicates the implementation of a predicate-based access of objects. The two copies of the same object have the same identifier, but may differ in contents. Under an architecture which supports dual buffering, there are two fundamental approaches for processing a predicate-based access. One, which we will call a *dual-buffer evaluation scheme*, is to evaluate the predicates on a class twice: once against the objects of the class in the object buffer pool, and then against those objects of the class in the database whose copies are not in the object buffer pool. Another, which we will call a *single-buffer evaluation scheme*, is to flush (move) the new and updated objects in the object buffer pool to the database, transforming them into the disk format, and then to evaluate the predicates against the database.

Let us discuss the two options in more detail. Consider the situation shown in Figure 13.4. Objects X, Y, and Z, all of which are instances of the same class, have been placed in the object buffer pool, and X and Y have subsequently been updated and a

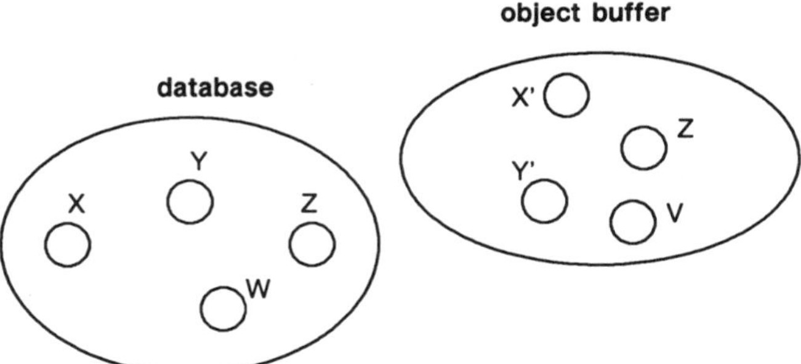

Figure 13.4
Dual-Buffer Query Evaluation

new instance V created. We can see that predicates should not be evaluated against X and Y in the database, since updated copies of the objects, X' and Y', exist in the object buffer pool. Also if Z satisfies the predicate, it should not be brought into the object buffer pool, since a copy already exists in the object buffer pool. Further, in the case of a deletion, if X' or Y' satisfies the predicate, its older copy, X or Y, must also be deleted.

The dual-buffer evaluation scheme may proceed in a number of different ways. One reasonable algorithm is as follows, assuming that the access request is confined to a single class C.

(1) Evaluate the predicates against the instances of class C in the object buffer pool, generating a set O of object identifiers that satisfied the predicates.

(2) Evaluate the predicates against the instances of class C in the database, generating a set D of object identifiers that satisfied the predicates. On this step, instances with copies in the object buffer pool are not evaluated again.

(3) The result of the access request is the union of the sets O and D.

We note that on step 2 above the predicates need be evaluated against only those objects in the object buffer pool that have been marked as new or updated, since objects that have not been updated after their retrieval from the database have already been evaluated on step 1. When objects are flushed to the database, copies of the updated objects are sent to the access manager and applied to the database. The update flags for the new or updated objects in the object buffer pool are then reset (cleared).

The single-buffer evaluation scheme proceeds as follows, again assuming that objects that satisfy predicates on the attributes of a single class C are to be determined and retrieved.

(1) Select those objects of class C in the object buffer pool that have been marked as new or updated since their retrieval from the database, and force copies of them to the database. This will make the two copies of each new or updated object identical.

(2) Evaluate the predicates against objects of class C in the database, generating a set D of object identifiers that satisfied the predicates. D is the set of all objects to be retrieved.

(3) Eliminate from D those objects of class C that are in the object buffer pool. Retrieve into the object buffer pool only those objects in the resulting set D'.

One major problem with the dual-buffer evaluation scheme is that the objects in the object buffer pool are in a different storage format from that used for objects in the database. This necessitates two different implementations of object search and predicate evaluation algorithms. This also makes it necessary to support efficient access paths for the objects in the object buffer pool, so as to avoid sequential searches of all objects. The shortcoming of the single-buffer evaluation scheme is of course that updates must be flushed to the database, and that objects must be transformed from their in-memory format to the disk format for predicate evaluation. Because ORION is implemented in LISP, the overhead incurred in object transformation in a LISP environment led to the dual-buffer evaluation scheme for ORION: under a different environment, the single-buffer evaluation scheme may be superior.

Recommended Readings

This chapter is largely taken from [KIM88b]. [KAEH81] presents the object-buffer management techniques first used in the LOOP system; these techniques have become the basis for subsequent efforts to integrate object-oriented programming languages with database systems. [COPE84] articulated the problems of impedance mismatch between applications and database systems. [WEIS89] provides a fairly detailed account of memory management in OZ+. [MAIE86] describes the approach adopted in GemStone to integrate Smalltalk with a database system; while [MELL89] discusses techniques used to expedite message passing in Alltalk. [ANDR87] discusses the integration of a programming language and database in Vbase.

[TRAI82, EFFE84, CHOU85] discuss buffer management in conventional database systems. The issues and solutions discussed in these papers should be contrasted with those necessary for object-buffer management.

14 Architecture

A database system, regardless of whether it is object-oriented or not, may run either on one processor or a network of processors. A database on a network in turn may be managed by one or more nodes (processors) on the network. A network-based database system in which the entire database is managed by one node of the network is called a *client/server database system*: a dedicated server manages the entire database, and all other nodes (called clients) communicate with the server to access the database on behalf of the applications that run on them. A network-based database system in which the database is managed by more than one nodes on the network such that the physical placement of the database is transparent to the users of the database system is called a *distributed database system*.

Most of the object-oriented database systems that are operational today are client/server systems. ORION is the only distributed object-oriented database system that is operational. The client/server architecture offers a few advantages. One is of course that it provides a relatively easy means for the users of 'diskless' workstations to manage their data. It allows fast access to objects in the object buffer pool, and makes those objects persistent as necessary. Another is that it is considerably easier to implement than a fully distributed object management system in which each computer can potentially manage a part of the shared persistent database. This is the reason most efforts, such as GemStone, Encore/ObServer, IRIS, O2, and one version of ORION, have adopted the client/server architecture.

However, the client/server architecture has a few obvious, and serious, disadvantages. The server is the single-point of failure, and access to the persistent database requires network communications. The communication overhead between the clients and the server is perhaps the most serious disadvantage. Both the objects and control information must be exchanged between the clients and the server, in general over the net. The clients must send for objects to populate their object buffer pools, and send dirty objects back to the server to make them persistent. However, the client/server architecture provides satisfactory performance for applications that tend to accumulate a large number of objects in the object buffer pool and repeatedly access a large subset of them.

A fully distributed version of ORION is currently operational, and the AVANCE system being prototyped at the University of Stockholm is designed to be a distributed object-oriented database system; there are some distributed Smalltalk systems and object-oriented storage systems. It required major efforts to extend uniprocessor relational systems System R and INGRES to distributed systems R* and INGRES*, respectively. Exactly the same set of architectural issues which researchers have explored for distributed relational database systems arises for distributed object-oriented database systems. These issues include distributed query optimization and processing, distributed transaction management (concurrency control and recovery), update synchronization in the presence of failures (site crash and communication failure), database distribution (database partition and replication), load balancing, etc. Solutions developed for distributed relational database systems apply directly to object-oriented database systems; as such, extending an object-oriented database system from a single-processor or a client-server architecture to a distributed architecture is mostly an engineering exercise.

Three different ORION prototypes are currently operational: ORION-1, ORION-1SX, and ORION-2. ORION-1 runs on a single computer; ORION-1SX is a client/server system; and ORION-2 is a distributed system. In this chapter, we will only describe the architecture of ORION-1 and ORION-1SX. The description of the architecture will also serve to tie together the discussions of the various architectural components of object-oriented database systems presented in previous chapters, such as query processing, transactioon management, in-memory object management, and so on.

14.1 Overview

Figure 14.1 illustrates the ORION-1SX configuration. The ORION-1SX clients are 'diskless' workstations, in the sense that they do not have a persistent database to manage. The server manages the shared database and control structures for the clients (e.g., lock table, page buffer pool). The client supports the ORION user interface through which applications may invoke object management services of ORION-1SX.

The ORION systems have been implemented in Common LISP on a Symbolics 3600 LISP machine, and have also been ported to the SUN workstation under the UNIX operating system. Therefore, ORION-1 runs on a SUN-3 or a Symbolics workstation, ORION-1SX and ORION-2 run on a local area network of SUN-3s or a network of Symbolics workstations.

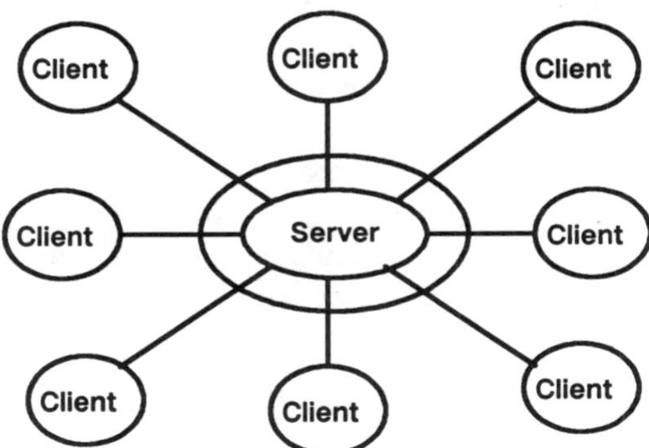

Figure 14.1
The ORION-1SX Configuration

Figure 14.2 shows the architecture of both ORION-1 and ORION-1SX in terms of the major subsystems that constitute the system. The message handler receives all messages sent to the ORION system. The object subsystem provides high-level data management functions, including query optimization, schema management, long data management (including text search), and support for versionable objects, composite objects, and multimedia objects. The transaction management subsystem coordinates concurrent object accesses and provides recovery capabilities, using locking and logging techniques, respectively. The storage subsystem manages persistent storage of objects and controls the flow of objects between the secondary storage device and main memory buffers.

In ORION-1 all subsystems reside in one computer. The ORION-1SX architecture is significantly different from ORION-1 in the management of shared data structures and distribution of these subsystems and their components (henceforth to be called a *module*). An ORION-1SX module may reside completely in the clients or in the server,

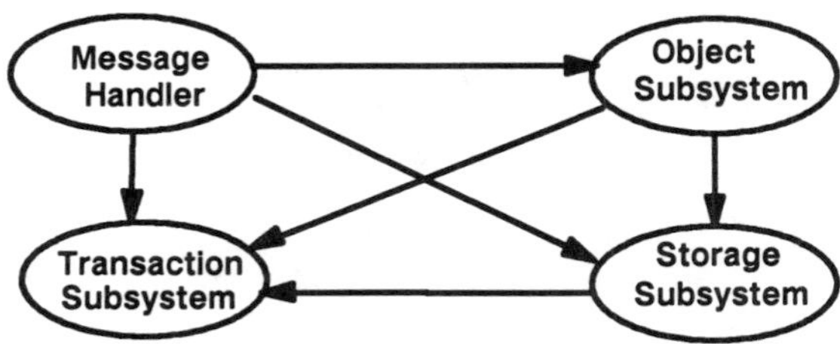

Figure 14.2
Functional Components of the ORION System

or some parts of the module may reside in the clients and the remainder of the module in the server. This architecture is the consequence of the separation of memory address spaces between the server and the clients, the dual-buffer management scheme, and the caching of objects and system structures.

Figure 14.3 is a high-level view of the architecture of ORION-1SX. The object subsystem and the message handler are placed completely in the clients. On the other hand, the communication subsystem, and parts of the transaction and storage subsystems are located in both the clients and the server. The communication subsystem is responsible for opening, closing, and controlling connections; receiving and delivering messages between client machines and the server machine.

14.2 Process Structure and Communication Subsystem

The architecture of ORION-1SX (just as any database system would be) is impacted by the underlying operating systems of the Symbolics workstations and Sun workstations. The Symbolics workstations support light-weight processes that share a common address space. The shared address space provides an efficient mechanism for accessing shared data from different processes on the same machine, such as the lock table main-

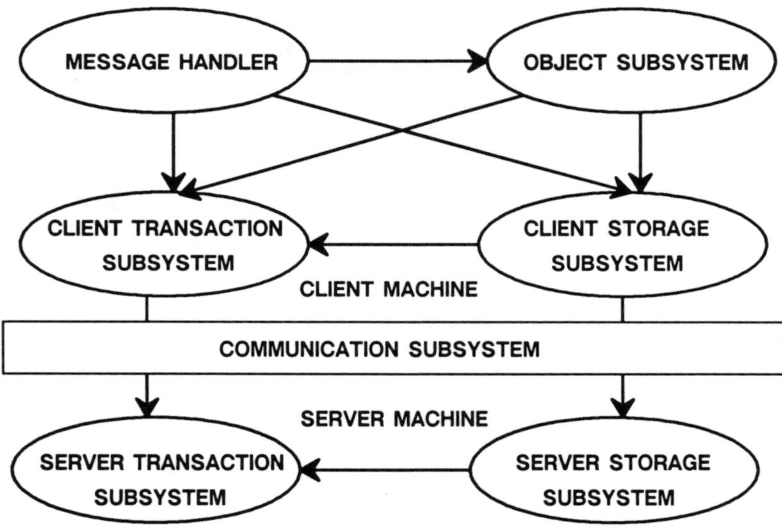

Figure 14.3
ORION-1SX Architecture

tained in the transaction subsystem. Thus inter-process communication is inexpensive; as such, it is convenient to create multiple server processes on the server machine. Further, the Symbolics *Generic Network System* makes it straightforward to associate each client process with a server process on the server machine. These considerations have led to the process structure shown in Figure 14.4. In this example, there are four client processes running on client machines A and B. Each client process is supported by a server process (which it invoked) on the server machine C. When a client transaction is suspended, for example due to a lock conflict, its supporting server process is blocked .

The Sun operating system, a derivative of the BSD 4.2 Unix operating system, supports an independent address space for each process. Although the shared memory facility of AT&T System V is also provided, it is inadequate for sharing complex data structures used by the ORION-1SX object server. The relatively high overhead of inter-process communication made it desirable to centralize all server functions in one server process to minimize the cost of accessing and maintaining shared data structures used by the server. Therefore, the ORION-1SX process structure for the Sun work-

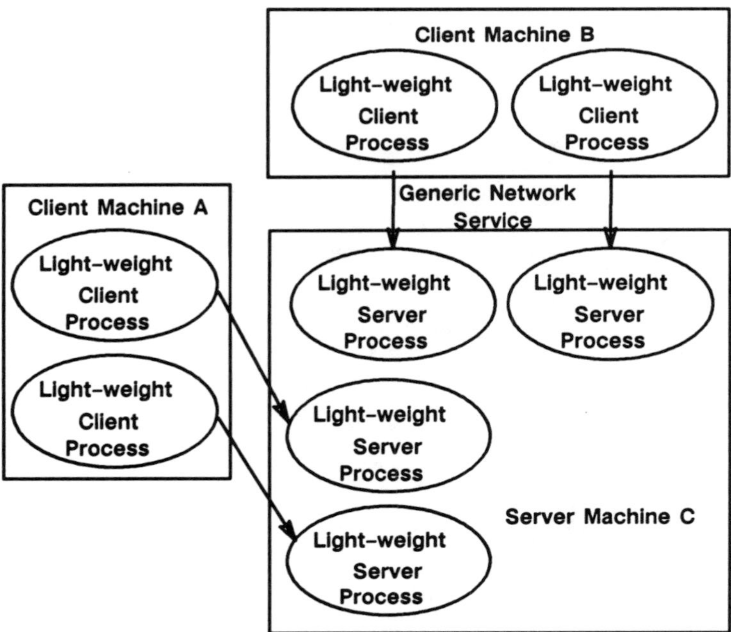

Figure 14.4
Process Structure on Symbolics Workstations

stations includes a single global server that supports all the client processes in the network. In the example shown in Figure 14.5, there are five client processes running on machines A, B, and C. All the client processes are supported by the same server process running on machine C. In contrast to the ORION-1SX server processes on Symbolics, the server on a Sun workstation schedules and services requests (remote procedure calls) in a round-robin fashion. A client transaction is suspended after queuing its current request in the server process.

In ORION-1SX, the communication protocol between a client and the server processes is the *remote procedure call.* When a client issues a request to the server, its thread of execution is blocked waiting for a response from the server. As far as the client is concerned, such a request is no different from an ordinary procedure call. Running concurrently with the client processes, the server process cycles through a loop to service incoming requests. After completing each remote request, the server process returns the result to the client process, which can then proceed with its computation.

Remote procedure calls, although conceptually simple and hence easy to use, are somewhat inadequate for a system with multi-casting and broadcasting; for example, two-phase commit or distributed query processing. Therefore, a different protocol is used for ORION-2.

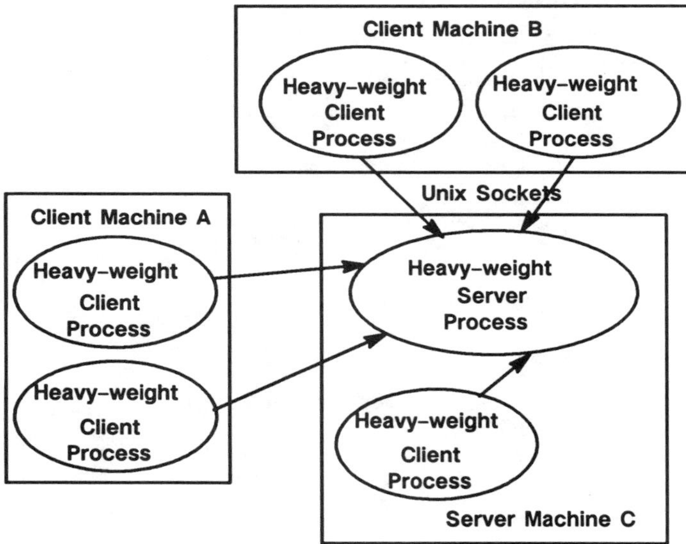

Figure 14.5
Process Structure on Sun Workstations

14.3 Object Subsystem

The object subsystem, illustrated in Figure 14.6, implements queries, schema evolution, version control, long data management, and support for composite objects. In ORION-1SX every module of the object subsystem is located in the client.

14.4 Transaction Subsystem

The ORION transaction subsystem provides mechanisms to protect database integrity while allowing the interleaved execution of multiple concurrent transactions. Transactions in ORION are *serializable*, which means that ORION completely isolates a transaction from the effects of all other concurrently executing transactions. The transaction subsystem consists of a number of major modules as shown in Figure 14.7. In ORION-1SX most modules of the transaction subsystem reside completely in the server. However, some parts of the transaction manager, and caches for locks and logs reside in the clients.

The lock manager maintains a lock table and a blocked transaction table, which indicate the locks each active transaction holds or is waiting for, respectively. The storage subsystem interacts with the lock manager to set locks on objects before retrieving or updating the objects. All locks (logical locks) acquired by a transaction are released when the transaction terminates (either commits or aborts). The locking techniques used in ORION are described in Chapter 11.

In ORION-1SX a lock manager was also defined in the client to cache locks in order to minimize calls to the server. When a lock is granted by the server lock manager, the client lock manager records the lock mode in a ROD lock slot of the object being locked . If the object is accessed again, the client lock manager checks the desired lock against the one recorded in the ROD. If the desired lock is less powerful than the one

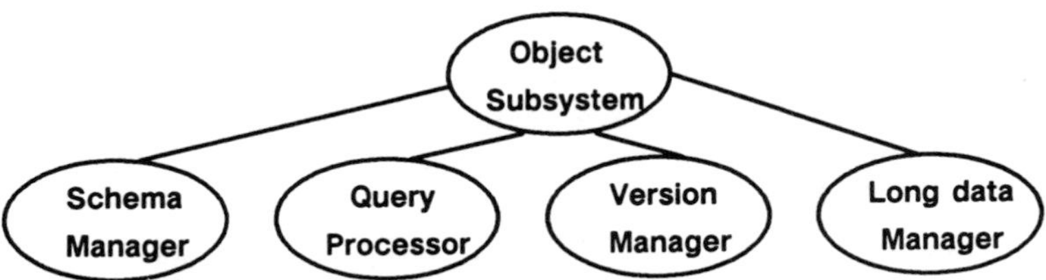

Figure 14.6
ORION Object System

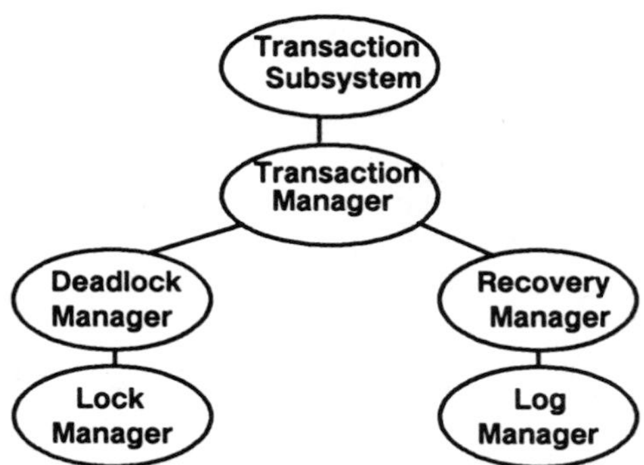

Figure 14.7
ORION Transaction Subsystem

recorded in the ROD, the server lock manager is not called. At the end of a transaction, the client transaction manager clears all cached locks.

The deadlock manager is responsible for deadlock detection and resolution. ORION uses a simple technique based on the use of timeouts. Each lock request is given a time limit for lock wait; and, if the request times out, the waiting transaction becomes a candidate for abort (only the action that caused the deadlock is backed out). The deadlock manager is a background process that is activated at prespecified time intervals when there are suspended transactions.

The log and recovery managers implement the atomicity property of a transaction. The log manager accumulates the log of changes to objects. The log is used to back out a transaction, or to recover from system crashes in the middle of a transaction which leaves the database in an inconsistent state. The recovery protocol is described in Chapter 11.

The transaction manager is responsible for generating transaction identifiers (TIDs), committing and aborting transactions, and running such special services as the deadlock detector, the disk garbage collector, etc. A TID is a unique identifier used to distinguish (e.g., during locking and logging) a transaction in the system, and as such they are defined in the server. The commit and abort operations are executed in both the client and the server in ORION-1SX.

A commit is started in the client by the user. The client transaction manager flushes objects modified by the transaction. Then the server transaction manager forces the log, flushes dirty pages, deallocates pages, destroys indexes, records end of transaction in the log, and removes locks acquired by the transaction (including cached locks). An abort is performed similarly.

14.5 Storage Subsystem

The storage subsystem, illustrated in Figure 14.8, provides access to database objects. It manages the allocation and deallocation of pages on disk, moves pages to and from disk, and finds and places objects in buffers. It also manages indexes on attributes of a class to speed up the evaluation of queries. The ORION buffer space is partitioned into a page buffer pool and an object buffer pool. Most of the modules of the storage subsystem reside in the server since their activities are related to the database on secondary storage. Some parts of the storage subsystem are placed in the clients to evaluate queries and to access objects in the object buffer pool.

14.5.1 Memory Management

Dual Buffering

As described in Chapter 13, ORION, as other systems designed to support programming language environments, uses a dual-buffer management scheme, in which the available database buffer space is partitioned into a page buffer pool and an object buffer pool. To access an object, the page that contains the object is brought into a page buffer, and then the object is located, retrieved, and placed in an object buffer.

The object buffer manager is the component of the storage subsystem which manages the object buffer pool. In ORION-1SX it is placed in the clients. The object buffer manager maintains a resident object table (ROT) to locate objects cached in the object buffer pool. ORION objects are placed in the object buffer pool when they are created or retrieved. A resident object descriptor (ROD) is an intermediate data structure between the ROT and the in-memory object.

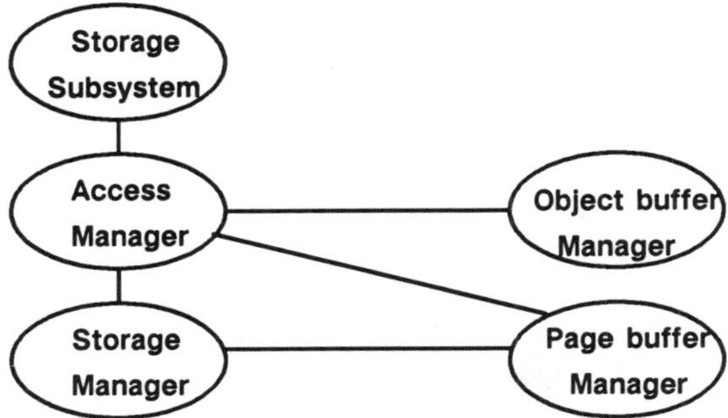

Figure 14.8
ORION Storage Subsystem

The page buffer manager, shown in Figure 14.8, is the component of the storage subsystem which manages the page buffer pool. It is similar to buffer managers in conventional database systems that follow the fix/unfix protocol to access pages. A page in the ORION system usually hold several objects. A page may be shared by concurrent transactions that retrieve objects from the page. The page buffer pool in ORION-1SX is placed in the server to allow sharing of pages among different client transactions.

The access manager, also shown in Figure 14.8, is responsible for creating, deleting, and accessing objects. It generates the unique identifiers (UIDs) of objects. It transforms objects from in-memory format to disk format (and vice versa), and controls the transfer of objects between the object buffer pool and the page buffer pool. Further, it searches the database (object buffer pool, page buffer pool and database disk) for objects that satisfy query search predicates. In ORION-1SX the access manager is split into the client access manager and the server access manager. The server access manager deals with objects in the disk format, and is responsible for generating UIDs and physical location identifiers for objects. In addition, it performs logging and index updates when it receives modified objects from the client storage subsystem. The client access manager performs object transformations and interacts with the object buffer manager to find cached objects.

Object Fetching and Flushing

The example in Figure 14.9 illustrates how an object is fetched from the server and cached in a client. When a transaction accesses an object A which is not in the object buffer pool, the client storage subsystem issues a fetch request to the server storage subsystem. The server storage subsystem, possibly after retrieving the object from disk, returns the requested object in the disk format. When the client storage subsystem receives the object, it transforms the object to the in-memory format and places it in the object buffer pool. Once the object is in the object buffer pool, the transaction can access the object.

Object flushing, necessitated by transaction commits and certain schema changes, requires steps similar to those for object fetching; except that data flows in the reverse direction. In the example shown in Figure 14.10, a modified object A is flushed from the client to the server. In the client, object A is first transformed to the disk format and then transmitted to the server. After receiving object A from the client, the server locates the page in which the old copy of object A resides. If the page cannot be found in the page buffer pool, it is fetched from disk. Finally, the new copy of object A replaces the old one in the page after the old copy is logged.

Cache Validation

An object which is cached in an object buffer of one client becomes invalid if a transaction of another client commits to the database an update to the object. In ORION-1SX a cached object is validated (invalidated) when it is accessed. When a lock on an

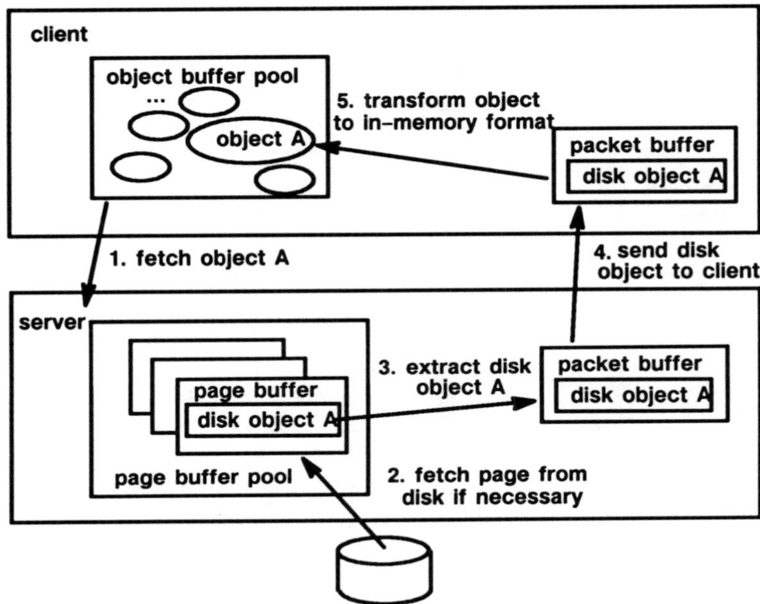

Figure 14.9
Object Fetch Example

object is requested, during an object fetch for example, the client checks if the desired lock is already cached in the ROD. If the lock is already cached, there is no need to call the server. Otherwise, the client requests a lock and validation of the object. The lock request is processed by the lock manager of the transaction subsystem in the server. Once the lock is granted, the object validation number (OVN) sent by the client is checked against that in the database. If they differ, the copy of the object in the client's object buffer is obsolete; hence the new copy in the database is returned to the client. If an object is returned, the client replaces the obsolete copy with the new one and caches the lock granted in the object's ROD. At the end of a transaction all locks granted on behalf of the transaction are released, and the locks cached in the RODs are also cleared.

If a class object in a client (i.e., object buffer pool) becomes invalid, all instances of the class that reside in the same client must also be invalidated. Invalidation of the instances is necessary since ORION-1SX (and ORION-1) supports schema evolution without a database reorganization or system shutdown. For example, suppose a transaction in client C1 fetches instance w1 of a class W, and then commits. A transaction in another client C2 drops attribute X from the class W, and then commits. Instances of

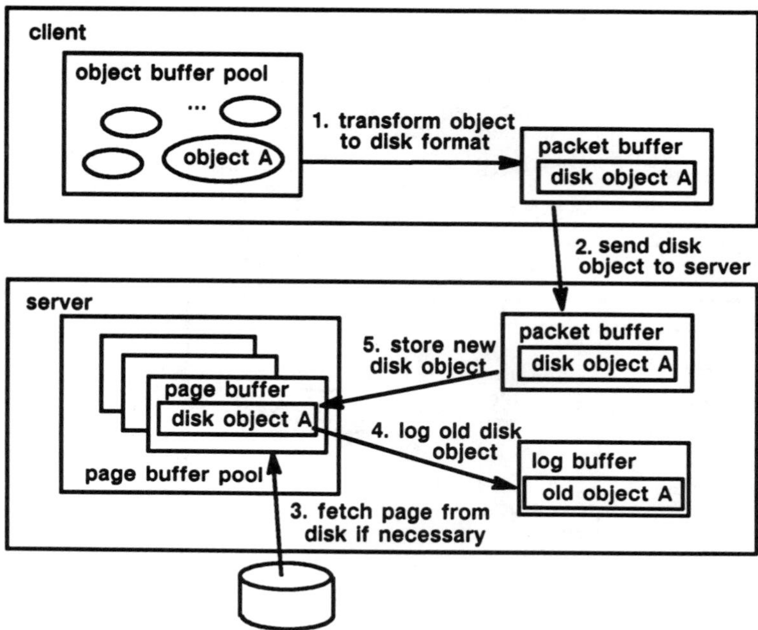

Figure 14.10
Object Flushing Example

W in the database contains a value for X. These instances are left untouched. When any of these instances are fetched from the database, the value for X is screened. Even when the copy of w1 in C1's object buffer pool contains the same validation number as the one in the database, the copy is invalid since it has an obsolete representation (i.e., the X value is not screened).

Before accessing any cached structure associated with a class (e.g., the message cache), the class object is validated even when the class object itself is not needed. In the previous example, suppose that a message is sent to the instance w1 in client C1 before the class object W is declared invalid. The class object W is validated before instance w1 is accessed. Since it is invalid, the instance w1 is removed from the object buffer pool. The object subsystem then fetches w1 from the server before performing the desired operation on w1.

ORION supports multimedia objects. A descriptor object is used to describe the disk location of the associated long data stored on pages. The long data are usually too large to place in their entirety in the object buffer pool. Instead, only pieces (i.e., pages) of a long data object are cached in the page buffer pool. For this reason, a page buffer pool is also defined in each client for exclusive use by the long data manager part of the object subsystem. For concurrency control purposes, long data pages are protected through locks on the descriptor object and by confining updates to the current pages (rather than the shadowed original pages). At the end of a transaction, the client flushes modified long data pages to the server page buffer pool but a copy is kept in the client page buffer pool.

If a copy of a page that was kept in the client page buffer pool is later referenced by the client, the validity of the page must be verified because the page may have been deallocated (i.e., due to the shadowing mechanism) and later allocated by the long data manager in another client. This validation of pages is accomplished using timestamps in the long data descriptor object and the client page buffer pool.

14.5.2 Secondary Storage Management

The primary function of the storage manager (shown in Figure 14.7) is disk space management (e.g., allocation and deallocation of segment and pages) and placement and tracking of objects in the disk format. It also implements class-hierarchy indexes (discussed in Chapter 9) for associative accesses to objects. The storage manager is located in the server machine to manage the disk.

The storage manager divides a raw disk into a set of partitions (analogous to cylinder groups in the UNIX file system) as shown in Chapter 9. Each partition consists of a number of segments; and each segment in turn consists of a number of blocks or pages. In Chapter 9, we also described the layout of pages.

14.5.3 Query Evaluation

One major task of the storage subsystem is the evaluation of query predicates against instances of classes. In Chapter 13, we showed that the use of dual buffering gives rise to two basic schemes for evaluating a query: the single-buffer evaluation scheme and dual-buffer evaluation scheme. These schemes were discussed in the context of a database architecture for a single processor. Let us now examine how these discussions may be extended to the client/server architecture.

First, let us consider a simple query whose evaluation requires access to instances of only one class. The single-buffer evaluation scheme applies straightforwardly to the client/server architecture; the object-buffer pool is associated with the client, and the page-buffer pool and database are associated with the server. The dual-buffer evaluation scheme requires some changes. In the dual-buffer evaluation scheme, it is desirable to avoid evaluating in the server objects already evaluated in the client. Unfortunately, it is expensive to pass a potentially long list of already evaluated objects to the server and then have the server search the list to determine if an instance has already been evaluated. A more reasonable approach is to evaluate every object in the server and only dirty objects in the client. The server sends the list of object identifiers of the objects which satisfied the query predicates. The client removes the object identifiers of dirty objects in the object buffer pool from the set of object identifiers returned by the server.

We now illustrate the dual-buffer evaluation of a simple query. Figure 14.11 shows two classes, each with two attributes. The Owner attribute of the class Automobile in each instance contains a reference to an instance of the class Person. Query 1 is a simple query, involving only instances of the class Automobile. The client first sends a request to the server to retrieve all Automobile instances with weight equal to 2000. This same operation is executed on dirty Automobile instances in the object buffer pool. The results are then merged as described earlier.

Let us now consider complex queries, that is, queries which must be evaluated against instances of a hierarchy of nested classes. Query 2 in Figure 14.11 is a simple example of a complex query. It must be evaluated against instances of both the class Automobile and the class Person. Consider an Automobile instance a-1, which is related to Person instance p-1 through the Owner attribute of a-1. It is possible for either one or both of the instances to be in the object buffer pool; further, they may or may not have been updated.

The single-buffer evaluation scheme for a complex query is straightforward. The dual-buffer evaluation scheme requires communication between the client and the server for each query processing step. However, only the object identifiers are transferred between the client and server, rather than the actual instances. ORION adopted this approach because of the overhead incurred in object transformation in a LISP environment.

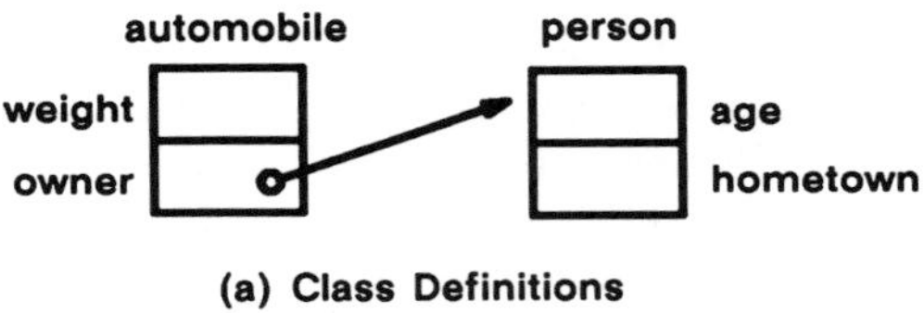

(a) Class Definitions

```
Query 1:    (select 'automobile '(= weight 2000))
Query 2:    (select 'automobile '(and (= weight 2000) (= owner age 29)))
```

(b) Queries

Figure 14.11
Query Examples

The ORION-1SX query optimizer selects the evaluation ordering of the classes of a complex query based on cost estimation. This evaluation ordering has some impact on the algorithm for executing a complex query. A complex query returns object identifiers of only the target class of the query. A complex query can be represented by a query graph, as shown in Chapter 6, where the target class is the root node. The simplest evaluation ordering is where the classes at the leaf nodes of the query graph are evaluated first, with evaluation of classes moving through the query graph, finally reaching the target class at the root node. This evaluation ordering is called reverse traversal. Reverse traversal is only one of the evaluation orderings supported in ORION-1SX. For expository simplicity, let us consider only this ordering in the following discussion.

The dual-buffer evaluation scheme for a complex query (assuming reverse traversal) proceeds as follows:

(1) The client evaluates one class of the complex query using the dual-buffer evaluation scheme for a simple query. The result of this evaluation is a set of object identifiers for qualified instances of the class.

(2) The dual-buffer evaluation scheme for a simple query is then used on the next class of the complex query. The set of object identifiers from step 1 are sent to the server (along with any other predicates on the next class) to evaluate the next class. The result of this evaluation is a set of object identifiers for qualified instances of the class.

(3) If step 2 was an evaluation of the target class of the query, the set of object identifiers from step 2 is returned as the result of the complex query. Otherwise, step 2 is executed iteratively until the target class is evaluated, with each iteration of step 2 supplying a set of object identifiers for evaluation of the next class.

Let us now step through the evaluation of query 2. Let us assume that the optimizer has chosen reverse traversal, that is, to first evaluate the Person class and then the Automobile class. First, the client requests the server to retrieve the object identifiers of all Person instances with age equal to 29. The client retrieves the object identifiers of dirty Person instances in its object buffer pool that qualify. The client merges the results as described earlier. The resulting set of Person object identifiers is then sent to the server, which in turn uses it to retrieve Automobile instances (with weight equal to 2000) that are owned by those persons in the set. The client executes this same retrieval on dirty instances in its object buffer pool, and, upon receiving the results from the server, merges the results from the server and the object buffer pool and generates the final query result.

Recommended Readings

The materials in this chapter are based significantly on [KIM90b]. The client/server architecture for other systems are described in the following papers: the ObServer architecture in [FERN88], the IRIS architecture in [FISH89], and the GemStone architecture in [BRET89].

[LIND80] provides a good discussion of the architectural issues in distributed database systems. The architecture of the distributed relational database system R* is provided in [LIND84], [LOHM85], and [MOHA86]. Distributed Smalltalk systems are described in [DECO86], [BENN87], and [McCU87]. [WIEB86] discusses an object-oriented distributed storage system. A first glimpse of the architecture of a distributed object-oriented database system is given in [JENQ90].

15 Survey of Object-Oriented Database Systems

A survey of the data models and architectures of currently operational object-oriented database systems and those under design reveal several interesting and rather surprising conclusions. Perhaps the most important, and pleasantly surprising, is that the core object-oriented concepts are indeed shared by almost all systems; that is, the data models supported include the notions of object identity, instances, classes, class hierarchy and inheritance, and message passing. Almost all systems support nested attributes and set-valued attributes; however, some systems support a more general notion of multi-valued attributes than others. The designers of most systems recognize the set-inclusion semantics for the domain of an attribute; that is, the domain of an attribute is the class hierarchy rooted at the user-specified class. All systems support persistence of objects, although a few different notions of persistence have been adopted with respect to explicit deletion of persistent objects. Most of the systems currently support a client/server architecture to support multi-user, workstation environments. Many of the systems also have attempted a seamless integration of a programming language and a database system by extending an object-oriented programming language with database commands, and by adding a layer between the applications and the database storage system to perform memory management and to negotiate the consistency of memory-resident objects and disk-resident persistent objects. Several systems support data models that are based on the DAPLEX functional data model; this perhaps should not be a surprise, considering the similarities between an object-oriented data model and the functional data model. Further, most systems support concurrency control, recovery, and transaction management; some do so through the features of underlying relational storage systems, while others provide these features directly. There are also strong indications that in the near future most systems will include multiple inheritance, versioning, queries, and multimedia data management; some systems already support some or all of these features.

In this chapter, we will provide a survey of representative operational object-oriented database systems. At this time we estimate that about thirty object-oriented database systems are under development around the world in commercial vendors, industrial research laboratories, and universities. The systems are in various stages of development and refinement; further, sufficient details about the architecture and data model, and the implementation status, are available in the public domain only for a relatively small number of these systems. Therefore, we will not attempt an exhaustive and detailed survey. For each system, we will highlight its most novel or noteworthy aspects, and summarize database features it currently supports. The primary objective of this chapter is to indicate the trends in the development of object-oriented database systems on the basis of the currently operational systems.

15.1 Commercial Systems

Presently, a few object-oriented database systems are commercially available. These include GemStone from Servio-Logic Development Corporation, Ontos (formerly Vbase) from Ontologic, Inc., and Statice from Symbolics, inc. G-Base from Graphael, Inc. was the first commercial offering which has been withdrawn from the market. The marketing of these systems has contributed much to the education of the potential customer base for object-oriented systems, and to the generation of interest in object-oriented databases in the database research community. CDC has recently formed a subsidiary to market MCC's ORION system. Several startup companies have recently sprung up and are now in various stages of readiness to offer their versions of object-oriented database systems; these companies include Object Design, Inc., Objectivity, Inc., and Object Sciences Corporation. Further, Innovative Systems Techniques is developing a system named Vision for use in investment analysis and other large statistical applications. In this section, we will provide brief overviews of three systems.

15.1.1 GemStone

GemStone supports a client/server architecture, in which a number of clients may connect with GemStone processes running on a central server. Currently, a VAX or a SUN workstation is used as the server; while IBM PCs, Apple Macintoshes, and Tektronix workstations are supported as client machines. GemStone was implemented initially in Pascal, and was reimplemented in C recently. Further, GemStone provides a C interface, C++ interface, and a Smalltalk interface for applications written in C, C++, and Smalltalk, respectively, to access GemStone. The programmatic interface to GemStone is called OPAL. This proprietary interface is a database extension to Smalltalk; that is, it extends Smalltalk with data definition and data manipulation capabilities for a database.

GemStone extends Smalltalk-80 into a database system. The GemStone data model is an extension of Smalltalk-80. It supports only single inheritance. However, it allows typing of attributes and classes. Further, GemStone supports set-valued attributes where the value of an attribute may be a set in which each element may in turn be a set, and in which the elements may be heterogeneous.

GemStone takes a rather different approach from most other systems with respect to persistence. The user cannot explicitly delete any object, as long as the object is referenced by any other object; a persistent object is automatically deleted only if it is no longer reachable from an object called a database root. A merit of this approach is that it prevents dangling references. This approach is consistent with that of Smalltalk.

GemStone is one of the more visible object-oriented database systems available today both in terms of the database features provided and contributions to research into object-oriented database architecture. GemStone supports concurrency control, recovery (recovery from both soft crashes and hard crashes), dynamic schema modification, transaction management, limited authorization, and queries. The GemStone approaches to queries and indexing, and concurrency control are unique.

GemStone takes the view that in general the notion of a class should be separated from the notion of the set of instances that belong to it; and in particular, the target of a query, and the unit of authorization, should be a collection of objects, rather than a class. This view is motivated primarily by the observation that if a user only wishes to work with a subset of all instances of a class, an index on the subset of instances should be somewhat less expensive to access than if an index is maintained on all instances of a class. GemStone supports a B+ tree index on a collection of objects. An index may be an equality index or an identity index. An equality index is one in which the key is a primitive value; while an identity index is one in which the key is the object identifier of some object. A GemStone query is essentially a single-target query along a class-composition hierarchy discussed in Chapter 6. A sequence of identity indexes and/or an equality index is used to evaluate nested predicates, as discussed in Chapter 9. GemStone currently does not do query optimization; that is, it requires the user to indicate in the query whether an index should be used.

GemStone has adopted a rather unique concurrency control technique which combines the pessimistic and optimistic concurrency control techniques. An optimistic concurrency control allows a transaction to proceed until it is ready to commit, but forces an abort of the transaction if it had any read-write or write-write conflict with any other concurrent transaction. An optimistic concurrency control is appropriate when conflicts among concurrent transactions are not likely; further, it does not give rise to deadlocks and it does not cause read-only transactions to be blocked or aborted. A pessimistic concurrency control is appropriate when conflicts are high, or when the duration of transactions is so long that the loss of work due to transaction aborts is significant. In GemStone, a pessimistic or optimistic concurrency control may be used for an entire transaction, or the two techniques may be used for different objects within one transaction. In this process, GemStone has made transactions non-serializable, and also requires the user to specify the method of concurrency control within a transaction.

For recovery from soft crashes, GemStone uses the shadowing mechanism, rather than the logging mechanism that most other systems use. For each user session (sequence of transactions), GemStone provides a copy of the object directory which maps an object identifier to the physical location of the object. Changes are made to the copy of the object directory, such that the object directory points to newly allocated pages for updated objects and newly created objects. When a transaction commits, the copy of the object directory essentially replaces the old object directory. If a transaction fails, the copy of the object directory is simply discarded.

GemStone is also one of the few systems, along with ORION and IRIS, which support dynamic schema modification. The GemStone approach is essentially a simpler version of that taken in ORION, since GemStone supports only single inheritance and does not allow objects to be explicitly deleted.

15.1.2 VBASE

VBASE is implemented in C, and runs on SUN workstations under 3.2 UNIX operating system. It is implemented in a client/server architecture. VBASE provides two programmatic interfaces: Type Definition Language (TDL), and C Object Processor (COP). TDL is a schema definition language for specifying types (classes), their properties (attributes) and operations (methods). COP is an object-oriented extension to the C language, and is a strict superset of C. VBASE application programmers use COP to program their applications and also to write methods. Both TDL and COP are proprietary languages; and for this reason, despite various interesting aspects of the languages, Ontologic, Inc. has recently decided to abandon the languages and adopt C++ as the basis of the programmatic interface to a future version of VBASE, namely, Ontos.

The treatment of types is the most novel aspect of VBASE. CLU has had strong influences on both TDL and COP. TDL is strongly typed; that is, all properties, arguments to the operations, return values from the operations are all defined in terms of their data types. Even an exception is treated as an instance of a type, an exception type. Just as any other type, an exception type may have properties and operations, and exception types may be organized as a type hierarchy. VBASE performs type checking at compile time whenever possible, that is, at the time methods and application programs written in COP are compiled. However, the users may optionally defer type checking to run time when necessary. Further, VBASE supports parameterized types; that is, the user may define an aggregate type, such as an array, whose elements in turn are typed objects. VBASE also allows the users to customize both types and properties of types. This is primarily to allow the users to tailor access methods to objects, especially those with special formats, such as a large block of unstructured text or graphics.

All objects known to VBASE become persistent, and they persist until the users explicitly delete them; VBASE programmers can program without being cognizant of whether they are persistent or not, just as though they program in any conventional, nonpersistent programming language.

One notable aspect of VBASE is that much of the system is designed and implemented in object-oriented style, that is, by explicitly taking advantage of the separation of the type specifications and their implementations. VBASE provides only a basic set of database features, including programmer-controlled clustering of objects, recovery, an SQL interface, and, at the time of this writing, a rudimentary support for concurrency control and access control. However, unlike most other systems, VBASE supports triggers by allowing methods to be included in the specification of properties and operations of a type.

The current version of VBASE supports only single inheritance. VBASE allows the value of a property to be a set of typed objects. Further, it allows a type to have private properties, as in C++; however, it does not support the notions of class attributes or meta types.

15.1.3 Statice

Statice is implemented in Common LISP to run on the Symbolics LISP machines. It uses a client/server architecture; although the system is not a distributed system, it can support multiple servers. The system is designed to seamlessly integrate a distributed LISP programming environment with a database system.

The Statice data model is largely based on the DAPLEX functional data model. It makes an explicit distinction between read-only attributes and read-write attributes. Statice, as in DAPLEX, supports inverse functions on attributes. For example, if the user defines a Vehicle class with an attribute Weight, the user may also define an inverse function on Weight. Then, the system can return a set of vehicles with a given weight. Statice supports multiple inheritance. Statice allows explicit deletion of persistent objects; however, if an object is deleted, Statice removes all references to that object, thereby preventing dangling references.

Statice provides a fairly rich set of database features, including transactions, concurrency control, recovery, a query language, query optimization, indexing, and multimedia data management. Statice uses page-level locking for concurrency control, and keeps a REDO log for recovery. The Statice transaction model is the conventional short-duration transaction model. The Statice query model includes queries on a single target class and multiple target classes; however, it does not take into account the class-hierarchy in a query that we discussed in Chapter 6. The Statice query language is a rather natural extension of the LISP syntax. Statice supports a conventional indexing technique to expedite query evaluation; it maintains a B*-tree index on an attribute or a combination of attributes of a single class that the user specifies. Statice also supports the storage and retrieval of multimedia data.

15.2 Industrial Research Prototypes

Presently, there are at least a dozen industrial research laboratories around the world in which object-oriented database systems are under construction. Many of these laboratories definitely plan to have their systems made commercially available in the near future, or at least available for internal use within their corporations. The IRIS project at Hewlett-Packard, the ORION project at MCC, and the O2 project at Altair, France, are the more advanced and visible efforts in industrial research laboratories. The ZEITGEIST project at Texas Instruments, and the Jasmin project at Fujitsu, Ltd., Japan, are other major efforts. Further, Digital Equipment Corp., Eastman-Kodak (the AllTalk project), Xerox (the Probe system), US West (the Vishnu project), and AT&T Bell Labs (the ODE project), among others, also have object-oriented database efforts. Let us examine some of these.

15.2.1 IRIS

The IRIS system is implemented in C and PASCAL, and runs on the HP 68000 workstation. IRIS provides object management services to C programs and LISP programs through a C-interface and a LISP-interface to IRIS. Further, the users may access IRIS through an object-oriented extension of SQL, called OSQL, or a graphical editor. The IRIS object manager currently runs on top of a relational storage system, called HP-SQL, which is very similar to the RSS storage subsystem in IBM's SQL/DS. There are plans to modify the relational storage system to support additional database features.

The IRIS data model is based on the DAPLEX functional data model. An attribute, called a function, may be single-valued or multi-valued (set-valued); a multi-valued attribute may have a heterogeneous set of objects as its value. As in the Statice data model, for each attribute, there may be defined an inverse attribute. Further, it supports multiple inheritance. IRIS takes the view that an object may have more than one type; the class and all its superclasses are the object's types.

IRIS allows explicit deletion of persistent objects; however, when an object is deleted, all references to the object are deleted to guarantee referential integrity. IRIS has adopted a rather unique semantics for a class deletion. If a class is deleted, instances of the class are not deleted; the instances simply lose that class as one of its types. Further, all attributes whose domains are the deleted class are deleted.

One elegant aspect of IRIS is the consistent use of a function formalism in its data modeling. An attribute or a method in a class is defined simply as a function on the class. A function may include a query expression. Further, a function, called a derived function, is defined as a function which invokes other functions. IRIS also uses derived functions to support a limited form of rules; conjunctive, disjunctive, and non-recursive rules. Although the rules IRIS supports are rather limited, IRIS is one of the few object-oriented systems which directly support rules.

IRIS supports a healthy list of database features. These include limited dynamic schema evolution, versions, a query language, and query optimization. Further, IRIS supports transactions, concurrency control, and recovery via HP-SQL. The IRIS model of versions is significantly influenced by the ORION version model. Unlike ORION, however, IRIS allows a non-versioned object to dynamically be changed to a versioned object.

One novel aspect of IRIS is the extensibility built into its architecture. IRIS enhances extensibility in two ways. One is its rule-based query translator, influenced by the Extra/EXODUS project. The IRIS query translator transforms a query tree into a suitable form for subsequent query optimization and evaluation. The query translator uses several sets of transformation rules; a transformation rule consists of a description of some aspect of the query tree and a corresponding algorithm for transforming the query tree. A rule-based query optimizer is an interesting topic of current research into extensible architecture for database systems. IRIS further enhances database extensibility by allowing the users to add foreign functions to the system; this is similar to the approach proposed for POSTGRES. A foreign function is a user-defined program, for example, a new access method, that extends the capabilities of the IRIS system. The IRIS query optimizer is designed to make use of the user-defined access methods.

15.2.2 O2

O2 is implemented in C and runs on SUN workstations under SUN OS 4.0. O2 is designed to support multiple object-oriented paradigms in a client/server environment. The O2 programmatic interface is embedded in C and Basic; the resulting languages are called CO2 and BasicO2, respectively. The object manager of O2 has been implemented on top of the Wisconsin Storage System (WiSS), essentially a simplified version of the RSS storage system in SQL/DS.

O2 has adopted a view of persistence that is somewhat more specialized from that of GemStone. A named object is persistent, and a component of a persistent object is also persistent. The user cannot explicitly delete a persistent object as long as it is referenced by another object; however, if an object is no longer reachable from any other object, the system automatically deletes it.

The O2 data model supports multiple inheritance. Further, O2 takes a more general view of the value of an attribute; it allows the value of an attribute to be a set of objects, a list of objects, or a tuple (a set of attributes) of objects.

In terms of database features, O2 currently supports only physical clustering of objects, concurrency control, and multimedia data, all through the facilities provided in WiSS. One of the notable aspects of O2 is that the system is designed to run differently in a development mode and a production mode. In a production mode, the run-time binding of methods allowed in a development mode is changed to function calls and access to named attributes is compiled into access to physical addresses of the attributes.

15.2.3 Jasmin

Jasmin has been developed in Fujitsu, Ltd., Japan. The object manager is implemented on top of an operational nested relational database system, also implemented in Fujitsu. The Jasmin data model is based on the DAPLEX functional data model, and is similar to the IRIS and Statice data models. It includes multiple inheritance.

Jasmin provides a programmatic interface called Jasmin/C, which is an object-oriented extension of C. One of the goals of Jasmin is the seamless integration of a programming language and a database system. Jasmin places emphasis on the support of triggers to enforce semantic integrity associated with user-defined classes.

15.3 University Research Prototypes

Currently, prototype object-oriented database systems are under development in several university laboratories. These include, among others, the ENCORE/ObServer project at Brown University; the POSTGRES project at the University of California at Berkeley; the Extra project at the University of Wisconsin at Madison; the OZ+ project at the University of Toronto; the AVANCE (formerly OPAL) project at the University of Stockholm, Sweden; the ROSE project at the Rensselaer Polytechnic Institute; and the Mneme project at the University of Massachusetts at Amherst.

The ENCORE/ObServer project has been an important university project in object-oriented databases; in particular, it was the first to offer important preliminary proposals on type (schema) evolution and concurrency control for long-duration transactions. Further, the POSTGRES project has played a leading role in extending relational databases with abstract data types and procedures, in effect bringing relational databases close to object-oriented databases.

15.3.1 ENCORE / ObServer

ENCORE / ObServer is implemented in C. ENCORE (Extensible and Natural Common Object REsource) is the front-end object manager, and ObServer (Object Server) is the back-end object server. ObServer runs on SUN workstations under UNIX; while ENCORE runs on SUN workstations and DEC machines under VMS. It is designed for cooperative computer-aided design environments.

The ENCORE data model includes multiple inheritance and multi-valued attributes. Further, like ORION, versions have been integrated into the data model. The ENCORE project, along with AVANCE, generated the first preliminary proposals for versioning not only instance objects but also types (classes).

ObServer stores multimedia data; further, it supports locking-based concurrency control, log-based recovery, and transactions. One of the noteworthy features of ObServer is the model of long-duration transactions that it supports to satisfy the requirements of cooperating users in computer-aided design environments. It introduces the notion of non-restrictive locks (also called soft locks in the literature). Both the share and exclusive locks are further distinguished in terms of whether they are restrictive, that is, whether they will block conflicting lock requests. Further, lock requests are accompanied by notification requests, so that the requestor of a lock, after acquiring the lock, may be notified if a subsequent requestor of a conflicting lock is blocked. The notion of a soft lock represents a point of departure from the conventional notion of transaction consistency. ObServer goes further by making uncommitted changes of one transaction visible to other transactions, and even allowing some changes to remain in the database even if the transaction that made the changes aborts. ObServer's concern for the requirements of long-duration transaction is also reflected in its technique for deadlock resolution. The ObServer deadlock detector simply removes one of the transactions in deadlock from the lock-wait queue, rather than forcing the transaction to abort; this approach is motivated by the desire to avoid losing work by aborting long-duration transactions.

ObServer supports physical clustering of objects. As in most other systems, objects belonging to the same class are clustered; further, an object may be clustered with other objects that it references. Further, unlike other systems, ObServer supports replication of objects for clustering purpose, and migration of objects from one physical cluster to another.

15.3.2 POSTGRES

POSTGRES is a sequel to the INGRES relational database system, which, along with System R from IBM's San Jose Research Lab (now Almaden Research Center), played a major role in ushering in the era of relational databases. For several years INGRES had been extended with a number of new features, most notably abstract data types, procedures, and triggers. POSTGRES is designed to incorporate these new features, along with complex objects, a type of recursive query, and management of historical data and versions.

The POSTGRES data model includes some basic object-oriented concepts. It includes a 'relation' hierarchy with multiple inheritance. Further, it introduces a 'procedure' as a valid type for an attribute of a relation; a procedure is a method. The value returned from a procedure may be the result of evaluating queries against other relations. An attribute of type procedure allows POSTGRES to support the aggregation concept (nested relations). The philosophy of the POSTGRES designers is to conservatively extend the well-founded relational model.

One of the noteworthy aspects of POSTGRES is the proposed support for historical data, besides versions. POSTGRES is one of only a few systems, along with Vision, designed to support the temporal dimension of data.

Another novel aspect of the POSTGRES design is the incorporation of advances in hardware technology into the database system architecture. In particular, the design uses optical disks as archival storage to store committed history data. This necessitates changes to the indexing technique; index entries for data that reside on magnetic secondary storage must be distinguished from those for data that have been archived on optical archival storage. Further, the use of archival storage, along with "stable" main memory for maintaining the tail of a log, results in a substantial simplification of the model of crash recovery.

For performance reasons, the design of POSTGRES calls for user-defined procedures to be precomputed and the result stored in the database. The stored result may become invalid when the schema or underlying database is updated. POSTGRES extends the current locking technique to support invalidation of precomputed procedures; it introduces a new mode of lock which is to be recorded in the data, rather than in the volatile lock table. POSTGRES further extends the locking technique to support detection of trigger conditions.

15.3.3 AVANCE

AVANCE (called OPAL earlier) is designed for use as a tool for office-applications development. The users of AVANCE program in the PAL language, which is a strongly typed programming language largely influenced by Simula, Smalltalk, and CLU. PAL includes multiple inheritance and parameterized types; further, it distinguishes private and public properties of a class. AVANCE is designed to support office application development.

AVANCE is designed to be a fully distributed object-oriented database system; at this time, however, AVANCE only runs on a single processor. It does not support a rich set of database features. However, the system supports object versions and transactions; in fact, to our knowledge, AVANCE is the only object-oriented database system that supports nested transactions. The AVANCE research resulted in an early proposal for versions of classes (versioning of classes has not been implemented). In AVANCE, a new version (of a class or an instance) is created in lieu of a direct update (of a class or an instance). One novel aspect of AVANCE is its use of a multi-version protocol for concurrency control.

15.3.4 OZ+

OZ+ is implemented in C and Turing Plus, and runs on SUN workstations under UNIX. The system, like AVANCE, is designed to facilitate the implementation of office applications and the modeling of office activities.

The OZ+ data model is noteworthy in its combination of the complex-object representation of objects and the actor model of communication among active objects. The data model supports single inheritance. The system is built on top of an existing relational database system, EMPRESS, for secondary storage management. The object manager layer implemented on top of the relational storage system manages in-memory objects that have been fetched from the database.

15.3.5 EXTRA

The EXTRA object manager is being constructed on top of the EXODUS extensible storage system. The storage technique used in EXODUS for long multimedia data has been adopted in ORION and IRIS. For the implementation of EXODUS, a new programming language called E was designed and implemented by extending C++. E contains a number of features appropriate for the implementation of a database system.

The EXTRA project plans to address issues of integrating a programming language and a database system on the basis of the E programming language efforts, and examine various issues in object-oriented database architecture, including rule-based query optimization.

The EXTRA data model is a rich amalgamation and extension of the data models of O2, GemStone, POSTGRES, GEM, and ORION. It includes multiple inheritance, composite objects, collections, and the set and array type constructors. A query language named EXCESS has also been designed. This project is a rather late entry into object-oriented databases; however, it is expected to make worthwhile contributions in the near future.

Recommended Readings

[RELE87, RELE88, SPAN89] provide brief accounts of the vendors and potential vendors of object-oriented database systems.

[MAIE86b] provides an early account of the design of GemStone, and [BRET89] updates it. [PENN87b] discusses the GemStone approach to schema evolution; [MAIE86a] describes the indexing techniques used in GemStone; and [PENN87a] describes the GemStone concurrency control techniques. [ANDR87] describes the design philosophy and programming language and database features of VBASE. [WEIN88] gives an overview of Statice. [CARU88] briefly discusses Vision. [GRAP86] is a rather brief product summary of G-BASE.

The description of IRIS in [FISH87] is updated in [FISH89]; a more detailed description of the design and implementation of the object manager of IRIS is provided in [LYNG87b]. The translation of a semantic query to equivalent relational queries is one of the basic tenets in the design of IRIS; this is described in [LYNG87a]. [DEUX90] summarizes the data model, user interface, and architecture of O2 in a single reference. [VELE89, DEUX90] provide an overview of the architecture of O2. The O2 data model is described in [LECL88]. [CHOU85] describes the design of WiSS, on which the O2 object manager has been implemented. [MAKI88] discusses the data model and language of Jasmin, along with a brief account of the Jasmin architecture. [MELL89] describes the architecture and message-passing implementation in Alltalk. Preliminary reports on the ODE and Mneme projects are given in [AGRA89] and [MOSS88], respectively. Reports on ZEITGEIST include [THAT86], [FORD88], and [PATH89].

The architecture of ENCORE/ObServer is discussed in detail in [HORN87]; [FERN88] provides the ObServer interface specification. An early version of the ENCORE data model is given in [ZDON86]. [SKAR86, SKAR87] discuss the ENCORE approach to versioning objects and types (classes). [SKAR89] describes the ObServer philosophy on concurrency control for long-duration transactions. The language and architecture of AVANCE are outlined in [AHLS85, BJOR88]. The AVANCE versioning and multi-version concurrency control schemes are described in [BJOR89]. OZ+ is described in [WEIS89]. The POSTGRES data model is discussed in [ROWE87], and the design of POSTGRES in [STON86b, STON87c]. The research that led to the data model and design of POSTGRES, namely, research into the issues of including abstract data types and procedures in relational database systems, is discussed in [STON83, STON84, STON86a, STON87b]. The EXTRA data model and query language are presented in [CARE88]; the architecture of the EXODUS extensible storage system on which EXTRA is being built is described in [CARE86]. The E programming language is discussed in [RICH87], and the rule-based query optimizer work is described in [GRAE87]. The philosophy and design overview of Mneme are given in [MOSS88]. [HARD87] introduces the ROSE system.

16 Directions for Future Research and Development

The area of object-oriented databases has come a long way during the past several years. After a few years of inevitable confusion, cynicism, and high expectations, the area has definitely settled down. As we saw in Chapter 15, there are already many operational object-oriented database systems, and the marketplace is expected to be rather crowded within the next few years. Despite this high level of research and development activities, there remain many technical and other challenges that must be met before object-oriented database systems can lay a solid claim as the standard next-generation database technology. These challenges include, in descending order of criticality in our view, standardization and formalization, performance improvement, migration path from conventional databases, database tools, additional database facilities, and extensible architecture.

16.1 Standardization and Formalization

There is a clear need to standardize an object-oriented data model and a corresponding programmatic interface language. It is encouraging that most systems already support a common set of core object-oriented concepts, and efforts are now underway to agree on some aspects of an object-oriented data model and architecture.

There is also a need to formalize and enhance some aspects of the core object-oriented concepts before a foundation for object-oriented databases can be laid. One aspect is the concept of inheritance and reusability. In view of the fact that the object-oriented approach is founded on reusability and extensibility, it is obviously desirable to discover ways to enhance reusability and extensibility. There has been an interesting debate about the relative merits of inheritance and delegation as a mechanism for information sharing. Further, some proposals have been made to increase reusability by decomposing a class hierarchy into two separate hierarchies: one for the behavior of objects and one for the implementation of objects.

Further, a query model, like the one described in Chapter 6, which is consistent with all the core object-oriented concepts will go a long way towards dispelling one of the current criticisms about object-oriented databases, namely, that object-oriented databases lack a theoretical foundation. The query model will have to account for the class hierarchy and the nested composition of a class; and it will have to be powerful enough to support operations equivalent to relational joins and set operations.

16.2 Performance Improvement

The transition from one generation of database technology to the next has made the programmers' tasks easier, but has always made the performance of database systems a major problem, and required considerable research and development efforts to increase the performance of the new generation databases to an acceptable level. This point is particularly true with the transition into the era of relational databases. The introduction of declarative queries in relational databases relieved application programmers of the tedious chore of programming navigational retrieval of records from the database. However, a major new component, namely the query optimizer, had to be added to the database system to automatically arrive at an optimal plan for executing any given query, such that the plan will make use of appropriate access methods available in the system. The transition to object-oriented next-generation database systems presents a set of challenges to meet the performance requirements of the next-generation database applications. In Chapters 9 through 14, we showed solutions to many of these challenges. Besides the elements of the architecture of object-oriented database systems we identified in those chapters for further research, we offer the following suggestions for additional research and engineering.

Object-oriented databases have been proposed as a platform for CAD/CAE/CASE/CAM applications and environments. To be sure, object-oriented database systems can satisfy the data modeling and performance requirements of many aspects of these applications. However, some of these applications pose seemingly impossible performance requirements to database systems, object-oriented or otherwise. They perform extensive computations on a large number of interrelated objects; they typically load all necessary objects in virtual memory first and then perform necessary computations on them. The computational paradigm of the conventional database systems is to deliver one object at a time to the application, and does not match that of these applications. Some object-oriented database systems have been designed to bring the full powers of database systems to bear on in-memory objects. However, they incur substantially higher performance overhead than some of these applications can tolerate, since the overhead incurred to access an in-memory object is still an order of magnitude higher than what is necessary for these applications, running without an underlying database system, to access an object in virtual memory by a few memory lookups. This performance gap must be significantly narrowed before object-oriented database systems can become a total integrating platform in CAD/CAE/CASE/CAM application environments.

There are a number of very frequent operations in any object-oriented system. Applications send messages to objects, by presenting the system with the logical identifiers of the objects. The system must be very efficient in determining and dispatching the corresponding methods. Further, the system must determine the physical location of the objects very fast; the objects may or may not be in memory. This in turn means that, if the objects are on disk, the mapping of the logical identifiers of the objects to their physical addresses must be done very fast. It is obviously important to identify very frequent operations in object-oriented database systems and optimize their performance; although microcoding is an option for some of them, it is not desirable since it will make the system less portable.

A somewhat tangential issue is the need for performance modeling, and a meaningful and common benchmark for object-oriented database systems. Relational database benchmarks, such as the Wisconsin benchmark, cannot really be used for object-oriented database systems, since operations supported in object-oriented database systems and relational database systems only partially overlap. For example, relational systems do not support operations based on concepts such as inheritance (class hierarchy), methods, object navigation (through unique object identifiers), nested objects (hierarchy of interrelated objects). Further, object-oriented database systems tend to be designed to support compute-intensive applications on in-memory objects in their in-memory data structure; relational systems have not fared well for such applications. The benchmark for object-oriented database systems should not only be meaningful for object-oriented databases, but also be useful in allowing a meaningful comparison with conventional database systems.

16.3 Migration Path from Conventional Databases

A system for managing a heterogeneous mix of databases is important as a migration path from relational databases to object-oriented databases, and is essential for object-oriented database systems to take root. One interesting line of research, related to distributed object management, is the object-oriented approach to the management of a heterogeneous mix of databases, in particular, a mix of object-oriented databases and conventional databases. It is highly desirable to allow the user to access a heterogeneous mix of databases under the illusion of a single common data model. For example, suppose that an Employee database is managed by a relational database system, a Product database is managed by a hierarchical database system, and a Company database is managed by an object-oriented database system. An object-oriented data model may be used as the common data model for presenting the schemas of these different databases to the user. The richness of an object-oriented data model makes it appropriate for use as the common data model for representing a broad range of data models. Further, since object-oriented design and programming promotes extensibility, it may be used for designing and implementing a system to manage a heterogeneous mix of databases which can accommodate the addition of new types of database.

16.4 Database Tools

The richness of an object-oriented data model is a mixed blessing. On the one hand, it makes it easier for the users to model their applications. On the other hand, the complexity of the object-oriented database schema, with the class hierarchy and class-composition hierarchies, significantly complicates the problems of logical database design and physical database design. Thus the need for friendly and efficient design aids for the logical design and physical design of object-oriented databases is significantly stronger than that for relational databases. In Chapter 9, we examined various alternatives for clustering objects in object-oriented databases, and the properties of class-hierarchy indexes and nested-attribute indexes and their use in expediting the evaluation of object-oriented queries. The current research into storage structures for non-first normal form relational databases is certainly relevant for the physical design of object-oriented databases. The framework for the evolution of an object-oriented database schema discussed in Chapter 5 is a first step toward the logical design of object-oriented databases.

A programmatic interface to a database system is too low level a tool for application development, and vendors of conventional database systems offer a number of additional tools as higher level interfaces to a database system to help non-programmers to develop applications. These interfaces include forms, menus, and graphics. The IRIS and O2 projects have developed first-generation graphical interfaces to their database systems to allow non-programmers to browse the database schema and issue queries. However, high-level user interfaces remain an area of research not only for object-oriented databases, but also for conventional databases.

16.5 Additional Database Features

Views

In relational databases, a view is defined as a "virtual relation" derived by a query on one or more stored relations. The relational operations join, select, and project may be used to define a view. Views have been used for data protection and as a shorthand for queries. A query may be issued against views just as though they were relations. Further, authorizations may be granted and revoked on views as on relations, allowing content-based authorization on stored relations. Views are also used as external schemas derived from an underlying schema.

Views are useful for object-oriented databases for similar reasons. Views may be used to specify logical partitioning of the instances of a class. Views may be used to define content-based authorizations in object-oriented databases; that is, views allow only the objects that satisfy specified authorization conditions to be made visible. The view mechanism may be used as one form of schema versioning to allow the users of a database to experiment with schema changes without introducing permanent changes to the contents of the database. To the best of our knowledge, no object-oriented database system supports views at this time; in fact, there has been no published account of research into views in object-oriented databases.

Deductive Capabilities

Object-oriented databases, deductive databases, and persistent programming have been areas of active research during the past several years. One common goal of these areas is the integration of programming languages with database systems. The objective of deductive databases is to integrate rules and traditional database of facts in support of complex reasoning which is not possible with queries against a traditional database. Much of the research has been focused on extending logic programming with database facilities. As we discussed in Chapter 13, programmatic interfaces of object-oriented database systems are often database extensions of object-oriented programming languages. A rule system has been interfaced to ORION, and IRIS presently provides a rudimentary support for rules. However, there is no object-oriented database system that can be regarded as a deductive database system. An object-oriented database system will become a deductive object-oriented database system once it can directly support rules and various reasoning concepts, such as truth maintenance and contradiction resolution. The current research is focused on extending an object-oriented database interface with rule specification and rule invocation. The issues of embedding various reasoning concepts, besides the forward and backward chaining of rules, directly in a database system have not been explored.

Semantic Modeling

One area of research, although rather tangential to object-oriented databases, is to augment the data modeling power of the core object-oriented concepts with semantic data modeling concepts. In Chapter 12, we provided a direction for this line of research. Besides versions and composite objects, there are additional semantic modeling concepts which may be important for some major applications. Just as versions and composite objects necessitated extensions and changes to the architecture of a database system, we expect that some of the additional semantic modeling concepts will have further impacts on the architecture of an object-oriented database system, including query evaluation, storage structures, and concurrency control.

Long-Duration Transactions

Another area of research which is also rather tangential to object-oriented databases is support for collaborative and interactive access to an integrated database in

CAD/CASE/CASE/CAM environments. The way in which the end users operate in these environments requires fundamental changes in the notion of database integrity and transactions. The conventional model of transactions is simply unacceptable in these environments where the duration of a transaction is long, lasting hours and days. The conventional model shields each transaction from the effects of all other concurrently running transactions. As such, when locking is used to control concurrency, once a transaction holds a lock on an entity, all other transactions requiring conflicting access to the entity are blocked; if optimistic concurrency control is used, a transaction which has been allowed to proceed to its commit point must be undone, if it had violated integrity. Further, if a transaction is to be aborted, all updates of the transaction must be undone. It is these aspects of the conventional transaction model which make it unacceptable for long-duration transactions. There have been a number of proposals for modeling long-duration transactions. However, more research is needed before a truly satisfactory model can be found which will remove the undesirable aspects of the conventional model of transaction and yet will ensure some notion of database integrity.

16.6 Extensible Architecture

Language-Independent Kernel

An important question that arises, in the absence of a common definition for object-oriented concepts, is then whether a different database system must be built for each different object-oriented data model, or if a number of applications based on 'similar' data models may use a common database system by embedding any necessary mapping in the applications to account for model incompatibilities among the applications.

One interesting observation about object-oriented databases is that a relatively small change in an object-oriented data model may require substantial changes in the architecture of a database system. The concept of a metaclass is a case in point. Although it is not very difficult to do a kludge mapping of metaclasses to an object-oriented data model, to directly implement metaclasses in an object-oriented database system will require fairly significant changes to a number of different components of the system. There may be a few other significant variations of and embellishments to the core object-oriented model which will impact the architecture of a database system that directly supports the core object-oriented data model.

One interesting approach to building object-oriented database systems is to define a storage-level subsystem, and use it as the kernel to support a large number of different object-oriented data models. A different higher level layer may be built on top of the common kernel to directly support a specific object-oriented data model. This will be an interesting and potentially fruitful area of research. Such efforts as DASDBS at the University of Darmstadt are aimed at defining a kernel for different higher level data models. The O2 project at Altair, HP's IRIS project, and the Mneme project at the University of Massachusetts at Amherst are also efforts to provide a common storage system for a number of different object-oriented language front-ends.

Supporting Semantic Extensions

Designers of database systems have traditionally shied away from capturing the semantics of data, largely because it has been very difficult to find consensus among users. One example is versions. There is no consensus on the semantics of any type of version: versions of a single object, versions of a composite object, versions of a class, and versions of a schema. The few systems which have implemented versions, namely, ORION and IRIS, have implemented their own models of versions. Since the semantics of versions tend to differ in varying degrees from installation to installation, a worthwhile approach may be to provide a layered architecture for versions. The lower level may support a basic mechanism for low-level version semantics that are common to various proposals; the higher level may be made extensible to allow easy tailoring of installation-specific version semantics. This approach should be explored not only for versions but also for other semantic modeling concepts.

Recommended Readings

This chapter is partially based on discussions on similar topics in [KIM90c] and [KIM90d].

An interesting comparison of inheritance and delegation, and classes and prototypes, is given in [STEI89]. [LaLO86] proposes the decomposition of a class hierarchy into two separate hierarchies.

[MAIE89] provides an interesting discussion of why conventional database systems are inadequate to meet the performance demands of CAD applications. [BRUM88] presents a performance model for a distributed object-oriented database system. [RUBE87] is a proposal for a benchmark for object-oriented databases.

There are two schools of thought on the management of heterogeneous databases. One is to integrate the schemas of the underlying databases into a single global schema under a single global data model [DAYA84]. Another is to simply present a schema for each of the underlying databases under a single global data model [LITW88].

[DESH88] discusses storage structures for nested relational databases. Initial results in user-friendly interfaces for object-oriented database systems are provided in [DEUX90].

Initial results in integrating object-oriented databases and rule-based deductive reasoning can be found in papers in [DOOD89]. The interfacing of ORION with a frame-based expert system shell is reported in [BALL88]. Good starting points for literature search in logic-based deductive databases are [BANC86, TSUR86].

Long-duration transactions, semantics and implementation issues, are discussed in [KIM84], [KATZ84], [BANC85], and [KORT88].

References

[ABIT84] Abiteboul, S., and N. Bidoit. "Non First Normal Form Relations to Represent Hierarchically Organized Data," in *Proc. ACM SIGACT-SIGMOD Symposium on Principles of Database Systems*, 1984, pp. 191-200.

[ACM83] ACM, *Proc. Databases for Engineering Applications*, Database Week, May 1983.

[AGRA89] Agrawal, R., and N. Gehani. "ODE (Object Database and Environment): The Language and the Data Model," in *Proc. ACM SIGMOD Intl. Conf. on Management of Data*, Portland, Oregon, June 1989, pp. 36-45.

[AHLS84] Ahlsen, M., et al. "An Architecture for Object Management in OIS," *ACM Trans. on Office Information Systems*, vol. 2, no. 3, July 1984.

[ALAS89] Alashqur, A., S. Su, and H. Lam. "OQL - A Language for Manipulating Object-Oriented Databases," in *Proc. 15th Intl. Conf. on Very Large Data Bases*, August 1989, Amsterdam, the Netherlands.

[ANDR87] Andrews, T., and C. "Combining Language and Database Advances in an Object-Oriented Development Environment," in *Proc. 2nd Intl. Conf. on Object-Oriented Programming Systems, Languages, and Applications,* Orlando, Florida, Oct. 1987, pp. 430-440.

[ATKI87] Atkinson, M., and P. Buneman. "Types and Persistence in Database Programming Languages," *ACM Computing Surveys*, vol. 19, no. 2, June 1987.

[BALL88] Ballou, N., et al. "Coupling an Expert System Shell with an Object-Oriented Database System," *Journal of Object-Oriented Programming*, vol. 1, no. 2, June/July 1988, pp. 12-21.

[BANC85] Bancilhon, F., W. Kim, and H. Korth. "A Model of CAD Transactions," in *Proc. Intl Conf. on Very Large Data Bases*, August 1985, Stockholm, Sweden.

[BANC86] Bancilhon, F., and R. Ramakrishnan. "An Amateur's Introduction to Recursive Query Processing Strategies," in *Proc. ACM SIGMOD Intl. Conf. on Management of Data*, Washington, D.C., 1986.

[BANC88] Bancilhon, F. "Object-Oriented Database Systems," in *Proc. ACM SIGACT-SIGMOD Symposium on Principles of Database Systems*, Austin, Texas, March 1988.

[BANC89] Bancilhon, F., S. Cluet, C. Delobel. "A Query Language for the O2 Object-Oriented Database System," Altair Technical Report: 35-89, August 1989.

[BANE87a] Banerjee, J., et al. "Data Model Issues for Object-Oriented Applications," *ACM Trans. on Office Information Systems*, vol. 5, no. 1, January 1987.

[BANE87b] Banerjee, J., W. Kim, H.J. Kim, and H.F. Korth. "Semantics and Implementation of Schema Evolution in Object-Oriented Databases," in *Proc. ACM SIGMOD Intl. Conf. on Management of Data,* San Francisco, Calif., May 1987.

[BANE88] Banerjee, J., W. Kim, and K.C. Kim. "Queries in Object-Oriented Databases," in *Proc. 4th Intl. Conf. on Data Engineering,* Los Angeles, Calif. Feb. 1988.

[BATO85] Batory, D., and W. Kim. "Modeling Concepts for VLSI CAD Objects," *ACM Trans. on Database Systems*, vol. 10, no. 3, Sept. 1985.

[BATO88] Batory, D., et al. "GENESIS: An Extensible Database Management System," *IEEE Trans. on Software Engineering*, vol. 14, no. 11, Nov. 1988.

[BAYE77] Bayer, R., and M. Schkolnick. "Concurrency of Operations on B-trees," *Acta Informatica,* vol. 9. pp. 1-21, 1977.

[BEEC88] Beech, D. "A Foundation for Evolution from Relational to Object Databases," in *Proc. Intl. Conf. on Extending Data Base Technology*, Venice, Italy, March 1988.

[BENN87] Bennet, J. "The Design and Implementation of Distributed Smalltalk," in *Proc. 2nd Intl. Conf. on Object-Oriented Programming Systems, Languages, and Applications,* Orlando, Florida, Oct. 1987, pp. 318-330.

[BERT89] Bertino, E., and W. Kim. "Indexing Techniques for Queries on Nested Objects," *IEEE Trans. on Knowledge and Data Engineering*, Oct. 1989.

[BILI85] Biliris, A. "Concurrency Control on Database Indexes: the mU Protocol," Technical Report: #85/014, Department of Computer Science, Boston University, December 1985.

[BIRT73] Birtwistle, G., et al. *Simula Begin*, Studentliteratur and Auerbach Publishers, Berlin, 1973.

[BJOR88] Bjornerstedt, A., and S. Britts. "AVANCE: An Object Management System," in *Proc. 3rd Intl. Conf. on Object-Oriented Programming Systems, Languages, and Applications,* San Diego, Calif., Sept. 1988.

[BJOR89] Bjornerstedt, A., and C. Hulten. "Version Control in an Object-Oriented Architecture," *Object-Oriented Concepts, Applications, and Databases*, (ed. W. Kim, and F. Lochovsky), Addison-Wesley, 1989.

[BLAS81] Blasgen, M., et al. "System R: An Architectural Update," *IBM Systems Journal*, vol. 20, no. 1, Jan. 1981, pp. 41-62.

[BOBR83] Bobrow, D.G.. and M. Stefik. *The LOOPS Manual,* Xerox PARC, Palo Alto, CA., 1983.

[BOBR86] Bobrow, D.G., et al., "CommonLoops: Merging Common Lisp and Object-Oriented Programming," in *Proc. 1st Intl. Conf. on Object-Oriented Programming Systems, Languages, and Applications,* Portland, Oregon, Oct. 1986.

[BRET89] Bretl, R., et al. "The GemStone Data Management System," *Object-Oriented Concepts, Applications, and Databases*, (ed. W. Kim, and F. Lochovsky), Addison-Wesley, 1989.

[BRUM88] Brumfield, J., J. Miller, and H.T. Chou. "Performance Modeling of Distributed Object-Oriented Database Systems," in *Proc. Intl. Symposium on Databases in Parallel and Distributed Systems*, Dec. 1988, Austin, Texas.

[CARE86] Carey, M., D. DeWitt, J.E. Richardson, and E.J. Shekita. "Object and File Management in the EXODUS Extensible Database System," *Proc. 12th Intl Conf. on Very Large Data Bases,* August 1986, Kyoto, Japan, pp. 91-100.

[CARE88] Carey, M., D. DeWitt, and S. Vandenberg. "A Data Model and Query Language for EXODUS," in *Proc. ACM SIGMOD Intl. Conf. on Management of Data*, Chicago, Ill., June 1988, pp. 413-423.

[CARU88] Caruso, M., and E. Sciore. "Meta-Functions and Contexts in an Object-Oriented Database Language," in *Proc. ACM SIGMOD Intl. Conf. on Management of Data*, Chicago, Ill., June 1988, pp. 56-65.

[CHEN76] Chen, P. "The Entity-Relationship Model: Toward a Unified View of Data," *ACM Trans. on Database Systems*, vol. 1, no. 1, Jan. 1976, pp. 9-36.

[CHOU85] Chou, H-T., et al. "Design and Implementation of the Wisconsin Storage System," *Software - Practice and Experience*, vol. 15, no. 10, October 1985.

[CHOU86] Chou, H.T., and W. Kim. "A Unifying Framework for Versions in a CAD Environment," in *Proc. Intl Conf. on Very Large Data Bases*, August 1986, Kyoto, Japan.

[CHOU88] Chou, H.T., and W. Kim. "Versions and Change Notification in an Object-Oriented Database System," in *Proc. Design Automation Conference*, June 1988.

[CODD79] Codd, E.F. "Extending the Relational Model to Capture More Meaning," *ACM Trans. on Database Systems*, vol. 4, no. 4, Dec. 1979.

[COPE84] Copeland, G., and D. Maier. "Making Smalltalk a Database System," in *Proc. ACM SIGMOD Intl. Conf. on Management of Data*, June 1984, pp. 316-325.

[COX84] Cox, B. "Message/Object Programming: An Evolutionary Change in Programming Technology," *IEEE Software*, Jan. 1984.

[CURR82] Curry, G.A. et al. "Traits: An Approach to Multiple-Inheritance Subclassing," in *Proc. the SIGOA Conf. on Office Automation Systems*, April 1982.

[CURR84] Curry, G.A. and R.M. Ayers. "Experience with Traits in the Xerox Star Workstation," *IEEE Trans. on Software Engineering*, vol. SE-10, no. 5, September 1984, pp. 519-527.

[DADA86] Dadam, P., et al. "A DBMS Prototype to Support Extended NF2 Relations: An Integrated View on Flat Tables and Hierarchies," in *Proc. ACM SIGMOD Intl. Conf. on Management of Data*, Washington, D.C., 1986, pp. 356-366.

[DANF88] Danforth, S., and C. Tomlinson. "Type Theories and Object-Oriented Programming," *ACM Computing Surveys*, vol. 20, no. 1, March 1988, pp. 29-72.

[DATE84] Date, C.J. *A Guide to DB2*, Addison-Wesley, 1985.

[DAYA84] Dayal, U., H. Hwang. "View Definition and Generalization for Database Integration in a Multidatabase System," *IEEE Trans. on Software Engineering*, vol. SE-10, no. 6, Nov. 1984, pp. 628-645.

[DECO86] Decouchant, D. "Design of a Distributed Object Manager for the Smalltalk-80 System," in *Proc. 1st Intl. Conf. on Object-Oriented Programming Systems, Languages, and Applications,* Portland, Oregon, Oct. 1986, pp. 444-452.

[DESH88] Deshpande, A., and D. Van Gucht. "An Implementation for Nested Relational Databases," in *Proc. Intl. Conf. on Very Large Data Bases*, 1988.

[DEUX90] Deux, O., et al. "The Story of O2," *IEEE Trans. on Knowledge and Data Engineering*, March 1990.

[DOOD89] *Proc. of 1st Intl. Conf. on Deductive and Object-Oriented Databases*, Kyoto, Japa, Dec. 1989, North-Holland.

[FERN88] Fernandez, M. *ObServer II Server Interface Specification, version 1.0*, Dept. of Computer Science, Brown University, Providence, Rhode Island, Dec. 1988.

[FISH87] Fishman, D., et al. "IRIS: an Object-Oriented Database Management System," *ACM Trans. on Office Information Systems*, vol. 5. no. 1, Jan. 1987, pp. 48-69.

[FISH89] Fishman, D., et al. "Overview of the IRIS DBMS," *Object-Oriented Concepts, Applications, and Databases*, (ed. W. Kim, and F. Lochovsky), Addison-Wesley, 1989.

[FORD88] Ford, S., et al. "ZEITGEIST: Database Support for Object-Oriented Programming," in *Proc. 2nd Intl. Workshop on Object-Oriented Database Systems*, Sept. 1988, Springer Verlag.

[GARZ88] Garza, J.F., and W. Kim. "Transaction Management in an Object-Oriented Database System," in *Proc. ACM SIGMOD Intl. Conf. on Management of Data*, Chicago, Ill., June 1988.

[GOLD81] Goldberg, A. "Introducing the Smalltalk-80 System," *Byte*, vol. 6, no. 8, August 1981, pp. 14-26.

[GOLD83] Goldberg, A. and D. Robson. *Smalltalk-80: The Language and its Implementation,* Addison-Wesley, Reading, MA, 1983.

[GRAE87] Graefe, G., and D. DeWitt. "The EXODUS Optimizer Generator," in *Proc. ACM SIGMOD Intl. Conf. on Management of Data*, San Francisco, Calif., May 1987.

[GRAP86] Graphael, Inc. G-BASE Product Summary, 1986, "Le Continental" Ave Descartes - B.P. 256 - 93153 Blanc Mesnil Cedex, France.

[GRAY78] Gray, J.N. *Notes on Data Base Operating Systems,* IBM Research Report: RJ2188, IBM Research, San Jose, Calif. 1978.

[GRAY81] Gray, J.N., et al. "The Recovery Manager of a Data Management System," *ACM Computing Surveys,* vol. 13, no. 2, June 1981, pp. 223-242.

[GRIF76] Griffiths, P.P. and B.W. Wade, "An Authorization Mechanism for a Relational Database System," *ACM Transactions on Database Systems,* vol. 1, n. 3, September 1976, pp. 242-255.

[GUIB78] Guibas, C., and R. Sedgewick. "A Dichromatic Framework for Balanced Trees," in *Proc. 19th Annual Symposium on Foundation of Computer Science*, 1978.

[HAMM81] Hammer, M., and D. McLeod. "Database Description with SDM: A Semantic Data Model," *ACM Trans. on Database Systems*, vol. 6, no. 3, Sept. 1981.

[HARD87] Hardwick, M. "Why Rose is Fast: Five Optimizations in the Design of an Experimental Database System for CAD/CAM Applications," in *Proc. ACM SIGMOD Intl. Conf. on Management of Data*, June 1987, pp. 292-298.

[HASK82] Haskin, R. and R. Lorie. "On Extending the Functions of a Relational Database System," in *Proc. ACM SIGMOD Intl. Conf. on Management of Data*, June 1982, pp. 207-212.

[HORN87] Hornick, M., and S. Zdonik. "A Shared, Segmented Memory System for an Object-Oriented Database," *ACM Trans. on Office Information Systems*, vol. 5, no. 1, Jan. 1987, pp. 70-95.

[HULL87] Hull, R., and R. King. "Semantic Database Modeling: Survey, Applications, and Research Issues," *ACM Computing Surveys*, vol. 19, no. 3, Sept. 1987, pp. 201-260.

[IBM81] SQL/Data System: Concepts and Facilities. GH24-5013-0, File No. S370-50, IBM Corporation, Jan. 1981.

[IEEE82] IEEE Computer Society, *Database Engineering*, special issue on Engineering Design Databases (ed. R. Katz), June 1982.

[IEEE84] IEEE Computer Society, *Database Engineering*, special issue on Engineering Design Databases (ed. R. Katz), June 1984.

[IEEE85] IEEE Computer Society, *Database Engineering*, special issue on Object-Oriented Databases (ed. F. Lochovsky), Dec. 1985.

[IEEE88] IEEE Computer Society, *Database Engineering*, special issue on Non-First Normal Form Relational Databases (ed. Z.M. Ozsoyoglu), Sept. 1988.

[JAES82] Jaeschke, G., and H. Schek. "Remarks on the Algebra on Non First Normal Form Relations," in *Proc. ACM SIGACT-SIGMOD Symposium on Principles of Database Systems*, 1982, pp. 124-138.

[JAGA88] Jagannathan, D., et al. "SIM: A Database System Based on the Semantic Data Model," in *Proc. ACM SIGMOD Intl. Conf. on Management of Data*, Chicago, Ill., June 1988, pp. 46-55.

[JENQ90] Jenq, P. D. Woelk, W. Kim, and W. Lee. "Query Processing in Distributed ORION," in *Proc. Intl. Conf. on Extending Data Base Technology*, Venice, Italy, March 1990.

[KAEH81] Kaehler, T. "Virtual Memory for an Object-Oriented Language," *BYTE*, pp. 378-387, August 1981.

[KATZ84] Katz, R., and S. Weiss. "Design Transaction Management," in *Proc. 21st Design Automation Conference*, Albuquerque, New Mexico, June 1984.

[KATZ86] Katz, R., E. Chang, and R. Bhateja. "Version Modeling Concepts for Computer-Aided Design Databases," in *Proc. ACM SIGMOD Intl. Conf. on Management of Data*, Washington, D.C., May 1986, pp. 379-386.

[KEEN85] Keene, S., and D. Moon. "Flavors: Object-Oriented Programming on Symbolics Computers," in *Proc. Common LISP Conference*, Boston, Mass., 1985.

[KIM84] Kim, W., D. McNabb, R. Lorie, and W. Plouffe. "A Transaction Mechanism for Engineering Design Databases," in *Proc. Intl. Conf. on Very Large Databases*, 1984, Singapore.

[KIM87] Kim, W., et al. "Composite Object Support in an Object-Oriented Database System," in *Proc. 2nd Intl. Conf. on Object-Oriented Programming Systems, Languages, and Applications*, Orlando, Florida, Oct. 1987.

[KIM88a] Kim, W., and H.T. Chou. "Versions of Schema for Object-Oriented Databases," in *Proc. Intl Conf. on Very Large Data Bases*, August-Sept. 1988.

[KIM88b] Kim, W., et al. "Integrating an Object-Oriented Programming System with a Database System," in *Proc. 3rd Intl. Conf. on Object-Oriented Programming Systems, Languages, and Applications*, San Diego, Calif., Sept. 1988.

[KIM88c] Kim, W., H. Chou, and J. Banerjee. "Operations and Implementation of Complex Objects," *IEEE Transactions on Software Engineering*, October 1988.

[KIMK88] Kim, K.C., W. Kim, and A. Dale. "Acyclic Query Processing in Object-Oriented Databases," in *Proc. 7th. Intl. Conf. Entity-Relationship Approach*, Nov. 1988, Rome, Italy.

[KIM89a] Kim, W. and F. Lochovsky. *Object-Oriented Concepts, Applications, and Databases*, (ed. W. Kim, and F. Lochovsky), Addison-Wesley, 1989.

[KIM89b] Kim, W., et al. "Features of the ORION Object-Oriented Database System," *Object-Oriented Concepts, Applications, and Databases*, (ed. W. Kim, and F. Lochovsky), Addison-Wesley, 1989.

[KIM89c] Kim, W., K.C. Kim, and A. Dale. "Indexing Techniques for Object-Oriented Databases," *Object-Oriented Concepts, Applications, and Databases*, (ed. W. Kim, and F. Lochovsky), Addison-Wesley, 1989.

[KIM89d] Kim, W., E. Bertino, and J. Garza. "Composite Objects Revisited," in *Proc. ACM SIGMOD Intl. Conf. on Management of Data*, Portland, Oregon, June 1989.

[KIM89e] Kim, W. "A Model of Queries for Object-Oriented Databases," in *Proc. Intl. Conf. on Very Large Data Bases*, August 1989, Amsterdam, the Netherlands.

[KIMK89] Kim, K.C., W. Kim, and A. Dale. "Cyclic Query Processing in Object-Oriented Databases," in *Proc. Intl. Conf. on Data Engineering*, Feb. 1989, Los Angeles, Calif.

[KIM90a] Kim, W., E. Bertino, and F. Rabitti. "A Query Language for Object-Oriented Databases," (unpublished manuscript).

[KIM90b] Kim, W. "Architecture of the ORION Next-Generation Database System," *IEEE Trans. on Knowledge and Data Engineering*, March 1990.

[KIM90c] Kim, W. "Architectural Issues in Object-Oriented Databases," *Journal of Object-Oriented Programming*, March/April 1990.

[KIM90d] Kim, W. "Object-Oriented Databases: Definition and Research Directions," *IEEE Trans. on Knowledge and Data Engineering*, June 1990.

[KORT88] Korth, H., W. Kim, and F. Bancilhon. "On Long-Duration CAD Transactions," *Information Science,* Oct. 1988.

[LAGU88] Laguna Beach Report on the Future Directions for Database Research, presented as a panel position paper at the *Intl. Conf. on Very Large Data Bases*, Long Beach, Calif., Sept. 1988.

[LaLO86] LaLonde, W., D. Thomas, and J. Pugh. "An Exemplar Based Smalltalk," in *Proc. 1st Intl. Conf. on Object-Oriented Programming Systems, Languages, and Applications*, Portland, Oregon, Oct. 1986, pp. 322-330.

[LANG86] Lang, K., and B. Pearlmutter. "Oaklisp: An Object-Oriented Scheme with First Class Types," in *Proc. 1st Intl. Conf. on Object-Oriented Programming Systems, Languages, and Applications,* Portland, Oregon, Oct. 1986.

[LECL88] Lecluse, C., P. Richard, and F. Velez. "O2, an Object-Oriented Data Model," in *Proc. ACM SIGMOD Intl. Conf. on Management of Data*, Chicago, Ill., June 1988, pp. 424-433.

[LIND80] Lindsay, B., et al. "Notes on Distributed Databases," in *Distributed Data Bases*, (eds. I. Draffen, and F. Poole), Cambridge University Press, 1980.

[LIND84] Lindsay, B., et al. "Computation and Communication in R*: A Distributed Database Manager," *ACM Trans. on Computer Systems*, vol. 2, no. 1., Feb. 1984, pp. 24-38.

[LIND87] Lindsay, B., J. McPherson, and H. Pirahesh. "A Data Management Extension Architecture," in *Proc. ACM SIGMOD Intl. Conf. on Management of Data*, San Francisco, Calif., May 1987, pp. 220-226.

[LISK81] Liskov, B., et al. *CLU Reference Manual, in Lecture Notes in Computer Science*, Springer Verlag, 1981.

[LITW88] Litwin, W. "From Database Systems to Multidatabase Systems: Why and How," in *Proc. 6th British National Conf. on Databases*, July 1988, pp. 161-188.

[LMI85] *ObjectLISP User Manual,* LMI, Cambridge, MA, 1985.

[LOHM85] Lohman, G., et al. "Query Processing in R*," *Query Processing in Database Systems*, (eds. W. Kim, D. Reiner, and D. Batory), Springer-Verlag, 1985.

[LORI83] Lorie, R. and W. Plouffe. "Complex Objects and Their Use in Design Transactions," *in Proc. Databases for Engineering Applications*, Database Week 1983 (ACM), San Jose, Calif., May 1983, pp. 115-121.

[LYNG87a] Lyngbaek, P., and V. Vianu. "Mapping a Semantic Database Model to the Relational Model," in *Proc. ACM SIGMOD Intl. Conf. on Management of Data*, San Francisco, Calif., May 1987.

[LYNG87b] Lyngbaek, P., et al. "Design and Implementation of the Iris Object Manager," in *Proc. Workshop on Persistent Object Systems: Their Design, Implementation and Use*, Scotland, August 1987.

[MAIE86a] Maier, D., and J. Stein. "Indexing in an Object-Oriented DBMS," in *Proc. Intl. Workshop on Object-Oriented Database Systems, Languages,* Pacific Grove, Calif., Sept. 1986.

[MAIE86b] Maier, D., et al. "Development of an Object-Oriented DBMS," in *Proc. 1st Intl. Conf. on Object-Oriented Programming Systems, Languages, and Applications,* Portland, Oregon, Oct. 1986, pp. 472-486.

[MAIE89] Maier, D. "Making Database Systems Fast Enough for CAD Applications," *Object-Oriented Concepts, Applications, and Databases*, (ed. W. Kim, and F. Lochovsky), Addison-Wesley, 1989.

[MAKI77] Makinouchi, A. "A Consideration of Normal Form of Not-necessarily Normalized Relations in the Relational Data Model," in *Proc. Intl Conf. on Very Large Data Bases*, 1977, pp. 447-453.

[MAKI88] Makinouchi, A., and H. Ishikawa. "The Model and Architecture of the Object-Oriented Database System JASMIN," working paper, Fujitsu, Ltd., Kawasaki, Japan, 1988.

[McCU87] McCullough, P. "Transparent Forwarding: First Steps," in *Proc. 2nd Intl. Conf. on Object-Oriented Programming Systems, Languages, and Applications,* Orlando, Florida, Oct. 1987, pp. 331-341.

[MELL89] Mellender, F., S. Riegel, and A. Straw. "Optimizing Smalltalk Message Performance," *Object-Oriented Concepts, Applications, and Databases*, (ed. W. Kim, and F. Lochovsky), Addison-Wesley, 1989.

[MEYE85] Meyer, B. "Eiffel: A Language for Software Engineering," Tech. Report, Dept. of Computer Science, University of California at Santa Barbara, Nov. 1985.

[MICA88] Micallef, J. "Encapsulation, Reusability, and Extensibility in Object-Oriented Programming Languages," *Journal of Object-Oriented Programming*, vol. 1, no. 1, April/May 1988, pp. 12-36.

[MILL88] Miller, J., J. Brumfield, and H. Chou. "Performance Modeling of ORION-2," MCC Technical Report: ACA-ST-073-88, 1988.

[MINS75] Minsky, M. "A Framework for Representing Knowledge," *The Psychology of Computer Vision*, (ed. P. Winston), McGraw-Hill, New York, 1975.

[MISS82] Missikoff, M. "A Domain-Based Internal Schema for Relational Database Machines," *in Proc. ACM SIGMOD Intl. Conf. on Management of Data*, May 1982, pp. 215-224.

[MISS83] Missikoff, M., and M. Scholl. "Relational Queries in Domain Based DBMS," *in Proc. ACM SIGMOD Intl. Conf. on Management of Data*, May 1983, pp. 219-227.

[MOHA86] Mohan, C., B. Lindsay, and R. Obermarck. "Transaction Management in the R* Distributed Database Management System," *ACM Trans. on Database Systems*, vol. 11, no. 4, December 1986, pp. 378-396.

[MOON86] Moon, D. "Object-Oriented Programming with Flavors," in *Proc. 1st Intl. Conf. on Object-Oriented Programming Systems, Languages, and Applications,* Oct. 1986, Portland, Oregon.

[MOON89] Moon, D. "The Common LISP Object-Oriented Programming Standard System," *Object-Oriented Concepts, Applications, and Databases*, (ed. W. Kim, and F. Lochovsky), Addison-Wesley, 1989.

[MOSS88] Moss, J.E., and S. Sinofsky. "Managing Persistent Data with Mneme: Issues and Application of a Reliable, Shared Object Interface," Technical Report: 88-30, Dept. of Computer and Information Science, University of Massachusetts, Amherst, Mass., April 1988.

[PATH89] Pathak, G., J. Joseph, and S. Ford. "Object eXchange Service for an Object-Oriented Database System," in *Proc. Intl. Conf. on Data Engineering*, Feb. 1989, Los Angeles, Calif.

[PAUL87] Paul, H., et al. "Architecture and Implementation of Darmstadt Database Kernel System," in *Proc. ACM SIGMOD Intl. Conf. on Management of Data*, May 1987, San Francisco, Calif., pp. 196-207.

[PECK88] Peckham, J., and F. Maryanski. "Semantic Data Models," *ACM Computing Surveys*, vol. 20, no. 3, Sept. 1988, pp. 153-190.

[PENN87a] Penney, J., J. Stein, and D. Maier. "Is the Disk Half Full or Half Empty?: Combining Optimistic and Pessimistic Concurrency Mechanisms in a Shared, Persistent Object Base," in *Proc. Workshop on Persistent Object Stores,* Appin, Scotland, August 1987.

[PENN87b] Penney, J., and J. Stein. "Class Modification in the GemStone Object-Oriented DBMS," in *Proc. 2nd Intl. Conf. on Object-Oriented Programming Systems, Languages, and Applications,* Orlando, Florida, Oct. 1987.

[PURD87] Purdy, A., D. Maier, and B. Schuchardt. "Integrating an Object Server with Other Worlds," *ACM Trans. on Office Information Systems*, vol. 5, no. 1, Jan. 1987.

[RABI88] Rabitti, F., D. Woelk, and W. Kim. "A Model of Authorization for Object-Oriented and Semantic Databases," in *Proc. Intl Conf. on Extending Database Technology*, Venice, Italy, March 1988.

[RABI89] Rabitti, F., E. Bertino, W. Kim, and D. Woelk "A Model of Authorization for Next-Generation Database Systems," *ACM Trans. on Database Systems* (submitted).

[RELE87] Release 1.0, August 1987, EDventure Holdings, Inc., 375 Park Ave., New York, NY.

[RELE88] Release 1.0, Sept. 1988, EDventure Holdings, Inc., 375 Park Ave., New York, NY.

[RICH87] Richardson, J., and M. Carey. "Programming Constructs for Database System Implementation in EXODUS," in *Proc. ACM SIGMOD Intl. Conf. on Management of Data*, San Francisco, Calif., May 1987, pp. 208-219.

[ROWE87] Rowe, L., and M. Stonebraker. "The POSTGRES Data Model," in *Proc. Intl. Conf. on Very Large Data Bases*, Brighton, England, Sept. 1987, pp. 83-95.

[RUBE87] Rubenstein, W., M. Kubicar, and R. Cattell. "Benchmarking Simple Database Operations," in *Proc. ACM SIGMOD Intl. Conf. on Management of Data*, San Francisco, Calif., May 1987, pp. 387-394.

[SCHA86] Schaffert, C., et al. "An Introduction to Trellis/Owl," in *Proc. 1st Intl. Conf. on Object-Oriented Programming Systems, Languages, and Applications,* Oct. 1986, Portland, Oregon.

[SCHM86] Schmucker, K. *Macintosh Library: Object-Oriented Programming for the Macintosh*, Hayden Publishing, Co., Hasbrouck Heights, N.J. 1986.

[SCHR88] Schrefl, M., and E. Neuhold. "Object Class Definition by Generalization Using Upward Inheritance," in *Proc. Intl Conf. on Data Engineering*, Feb. 1988, pp. 4-13.

[SELI79] Selinger, P.G. et. al. "Access Path Selection in a Relational Database Management System," in *Proc. ACM SIGMOD Intl. Conf. on Management of Data*, Boston, Mass., pp. 23-34, 1979.

[SHIP81] Shipman, D. "The Functional Data Model and the Data Language DAPLEX," *ACM Trans. on Database Systems*, vol. 6, no. 1, March 1981.

[SKAR86] Skarra, A., and S. Zdonik. "The Management of Changing Types in an Object-Oriented Database," in *Proc. 1st Intl. Conf. on Object-Oriented Programming Systems, Languages, and Applications*, Portland, Oregon, Oct. 1986.

[SKAR87] Skarra, A., and S. Zdonik. "Type Evolution in an Object-Oriented Database," in *Research Directions in Object-Oriented Programming*, (eds. B. Shriver and P. Wegner), MIT Press, Cambridge, Mass., 1987.

[SKAR89] Skarra, A., and S. Zdonik. "Concurrency Control and Object-Oriented Databases," *Object-Oriented Concepts, Applications, and Databases*, (ed. W. Kim, and F. Lochovsky), Addison-Wesley, 1989.

[SMIT77] Smith, J., and D. Smith. "Database Abstraction: Aggregation and Generalization," *ACM Trans. on Database Systems*, vol. 2, no. 2, June 1977, pp. 105-133.

[SNYD86] Snyder, A. "Encapsulation and Inheritance in Object-Oriented Programming Languages," in *Proc. 1st Intl. Conf. on Object-Oriented Programming Systems, Languages, and Applications*, Portland, Oregon, Oct. 1986, pp. 38-45.

[SPAN89] *Spang-Robinson Report*, John Wiley and Sons, 1989.

[STEF86] Stefik, M. and D.G. Bobrow. "Object-Oriented Programming: Themes and Variations," *The AI Magazine*, January 1986, pp. 40-62.

[STEI89] Stein, L., H. Liebermann, and D. Ungar. "A Shared View of Sharing - The Treaty of Orlando," *Object-Oriented Concepts, Applications, and Databases*, (ed. W. Kim, and F. Lochovsky), Addison-Wesley, 1989.

[STEM88] Stemple, D., private communication, Feb. 1988.

[STON76] Stonebraker, M. "The Design and Implementation of INGRES," *ACM Trans. on Database Systems*, vol. 1, no. 3, Sept. 1976, pp. 189-222.

[STON81] Stonebraker, M. "Hypothetical Data Bases as Views," in *Proc. ACM SIGMOD Conf. on Management of Data*, pp. 224-229, 1981.

[STON83] Stonebraker, M., B. Rubenstein, and A. Guttman. "Application of Abstract Data Types and Abstract Indices to CAD Data Bases," *in Proc. Databases for Engineering Applications*, Database Week 1983 (ACM), San Jose, Calif., May 1983.

[STON84] Stonebraker, M., et al. "QUEL as a Data Type," in *Proc. ACM SIGMOD Conf. on Management of Data*, Boston, Mass., June 1984.

[STON86a] Stonebraker, M. "Inclusion of New Types in Relational Database System," in *Proc. 2nd Intl. Conf. on Data Engineering*, Los Angeles, Calif., Feb. 1986, pp. 262-269.

[STON86b] Stonebraker, M., and L. Rowe. "The Design of POSTGRES," in *Proc. ACM SIGMOD Intl. Conf. on Management of Data*, Washington, D.C., May 1986.

[STON87a] Stonebraker, M., E. Hanson, and C.H. Hong. "The Design of the POSTGRES Rule System," in *Proc. Intl. Conf. on Data Engineering*, Feb. 1987, Los Angeles, Calif., pp. 356-374.

[STON87b] Stonebraker, M., J. Anton, and E. Hanson. "Extending a Database System with Procedures," *ACM Trans. on Database Systems*, vol. 12, no. 3, Sept. 1987.

[STON87c] Stonebraker, M. "The Design of the POSTGRES Storage System," in *Proc. Intl. Conf. on Very Large Data Bases*, Brighton, England, Sept. 1987.

[STRO86] Stroustrup, B. *The C++ Programming Language*, Addison-Wesley, Reading, Mass., 1986.

[STRO88] Stroustrup, B. "What is Object-Oriented Programming?," *IEEE Software*, May 1988, pp. 10-20.

[SYMB84] *FLAV Objects, Message Passing, and Flavors,* Symbolics, Inc., Cambridge, MA, 1984.

[THAT86] Thatte, S. "Persistent Memory: A Storage Architecture for Object-Oriented Database Systems," in *Proc. Intl. Workshop on Object-Oriented Database Systems*, Pacific Grove, Calif., Sept. 1986.

[THOM86] Thomas, S., and P. Fischer. "Nested Relational Structures," in *Advances in Computing Research III, The Theory of Databases*, (ed. P. Kanellakis), JAI Press, 1986, pp. 269-307.

[THUR89] Thuraisingham, M.B. "Mandatory and Discretionary Security Issues in Object-Oriented Database Systems," in *Proc. Object-Oriented Programming Systems, Languages, and Applications,* Oct. 1989, New Orleans, Louisiana.

[TIEM88] Tiemann, M. *User's Guide to GNU C++*, MCC Technical Report: ACA-ESP-099-88, March 1988.

[TOML89] Tomlinson, C., M. Scheevel, and W. Kim. "Sharing and Organization Protocols in Object-Oriented Systems," *Journal of Object-Oriented Programming*, Nov./Dec. 1989.

[TRAI82] Traiger, I. "Virtual Memory Management for Database Systems," *ACM Operating Systems Reviews*, vol. 16, no. 4, pp. 26-48, October 1982.

[TSUR86] Tsur, S., and C. Zaniolo. "LDL: a Logic-Based Data Language," in *Proc. 12th Intl. Conf. on Very Large Data Bases*, August 1986, Kyoto, Japan.

[VELE89] Velez, F., G. Bernard, V. Darnis. "The O2 Object Manager: an Overview," in *Proc. 15th Intl. Conf. on Very Large Data Bases*, Amsterdam, the Netherlands, August, 1989.

[WEIN88] Weinreb, D. et al. "An Object-Oriented Database System to Support an Integrated Programming Environment," in *IEEE Database Engineering Bulletin*, June 1988, vol. 11, no. 2 (ed. Roger King), pp. 33-43.

[WEIS89] Weiser, S., and F. Lochovsky. "OZ+: An Object-Oriented Database System," *Object-Oriented Concepts, Applications, and Databases*, (ed. W. Kim, and F. Lochovsky), Addison-Wesley, 1989.

[WIEB86] Wiebe, D. "A Distributed Repository for Immutable Persistent Objects," in *Proc. 1st Intl. Conf. on Object-Oriented Programming Systems, Languages, and Applications*, Portland, Oregon, Oct. 1986, pp. 453-465.

[WILL82] Williams, R., et al. "R*: An Overview of the Architecture," in *Improving Database Usability and Responsiveness*, (ed. P. Scheuermann), Academic Press, 1982.

[WOEL87] Woelk, D., and W. Kim. "Multimedia Information Management in an Object-Oriented Database System," in *Proc. Intl. Conf. on Very Large Data Bases*, Brighton, England, Sept. 1987, pp. 319-329.

[ZANI83] Zaniolo, C. "The Database Language GEM," in *Proc. ACM SIGMOD Intl. Conf. on Management of Data*, May 1983, pp. 207-218.

[ZARA85] Zara, R.V. and D.R. Henke. "Building a Layered Database for Design Automation," in *Proc. 22nd Design Automation Conf.*, 1985, pp. 645-651.

[ZDON86] Zdonik, S., and P. Wegner. "Language and Methodology for Object-Oriented Database Environments," *Proc. 19th Annual Hawaii Intl. Conf. on System Sciences*, Jan. 1986.

ORION Papers Published

Data Model

Banerjee, J., et al. "Data Model Issues for Object-Oriented Applications," *ACM Trans. on Office Information Systems*, vol. 5, no.1, January 1987.

Banerjee, J., W. Kim, H.J. Kim, and H.F. Korth. "Semantics and Implementation of Schema Evolution in Object-Oriented Databases," in *Proc. ACM SIGMOD Intl. Conf. on Management of Data,* San Francisco, Calif., May 1987.

Ballou, N., et al. "Coupling an Expert System Shell with an Object-Oriented Database System," Journal of Object-Oriented Programming, vol. 1, no. 2, June/July 1988, pp. 12-21.

Queries (Query Model, Language, Processing)

Banerjee, J., W. Kim, and K.C. Kim. "Queries in Object-Oriented Databases," in *Proc. 4th Intl. Conf. on Data Engineering,* Los Angeles, Calif., Feb. 1988.

Kim, W. "A Model of Queries for Object-Oriented Databases," in *Proc. Intl. Conf. on Very Large Data Bases*, August 1989, Amsterdam, the Netherlands.

Kim, K.C., W. Kim, D. Woelk, and A. Dale. "Acyclic Query Processing in Object-Oriented Databases," in *Proc. 7th. Intl. Conf. Entity-Relationship Approach*, Nov. 1988, Rome, Italy.

Kim, K.C., W. Kim, and A. Dale. "Cyclic Query Processing in Object-Oriented Databases," in *Proc. Intl. Conf. on Data Engineering*, Feb. 1989, Los Angeles, Calif.

Jenq, P. D. Woelk, W. Kim, and W. Lee. "Query Processing in Distributed ORION," in *Proc. Intl. Conf. on Extending Data Base Technology*, Venice, Italy, March 1990.

Access Methods

Kim, W., K.C. Kim, and A. Dale. "Indexing Techniques for Object-Oriented Databases," *Object-Oriented Concepts, Applications, and Databases*, (ed. W. Kim, and F. Lochovsky), Addison-Wesley, 1989.

Bertino, E., and W. Kim. "Indexing Techniques for Queries on Nested Objects," *IEEE Trans. on Knowledge and Data Engineering*, Oct. 1989.

Multimedia Data Management

Woelk, D., and W. Kim. "Multimedia Information Management in an Object-Oriented Database System," in *Proc. Intl. Conf. on Very Large Data Bases,* Brighton, England, Sept. 1987, pp. 319-329.

Transaction Management

Garza, J.F., and W. Kim. "Transaction Management in an Object-Oriented Database System," in *Proc. ACM SIGMOD Intl. Conf. on Management of Data*, Chicago, Ill., June 1988.

Authorization

Rabitti, F., D. Woelk, and W. Kim. "A Model of Authorization for Object-Oriented and Semantic Databases," in *Proc. Intl Conf. on Extending Database Technology*, Venice, Italy, March 1988.

Semantic Models

Chou, H.T., and W. Kim. "A Unifying Framework for Versions in a CAD Environment," in *Proc. Intl Conf. on Very Large Data Bases*, August 1986, Kyoto, Japan.

Chou, H.T., and W. Kim. "Versions and Change Notification in an Object-Oriented Database System," in *Proc. Design Automation Conference*, June 1988.

Kim, W., et al. "Composite Object Support in an Object-Oriented Database System," in *Proc. 2nd Intl. Conf. on Object-Oriented Programming Systems, Languages, and Applications*, Orlando, Florida, Oct. 1987.

Kim, W., and H.T. Chou. "Versions of Schema for Object-Oriented Databases," in *Proc. Intl Conf. on Very Large Data Bases,* August-Sept. 1988.

Kim, W., E. Bertino, and J. Garza. "Composite Objects Revisited," in *Proc. ACM SIGMOD Intl. Conf. on Management of Data*, Portland, Oregon, June 1989.

Performance Modeling

Brumfield, J., J. Miller, and H.T. Chou. "Performance Modeling of Distributed Object-Oriented Database Systems," in *Proc. Intl. Symposium on Databases in Parallel and Distributed Systems*, Dec. 1988, Austin, Texas.

Architecture

Kim, W., et al. "Integrating an Object-Oriented Programming System with a Database System," in *Proc. 3rd Intl. Conf. on Object-Oriented Programming Systems, Languages, and Applications,* San Diego, Calif., Sept. 1988.

Kim, W., et al. "Features of the ORION Object-Oriented Database System," *Object-Oriented Concepts, Applications, and Databases*, (ed. W. Kim, and F. Lochovsky), Addison-Wesley, 1989.

Kim, W. "Architecture of the ORION Next-Generation Database System," in *IEEE Trans. on Knowledge and Data Engineering*, March 1990.

General

Kim, W. "Object-Oriented Database Systems: Mandatory Rules and Prospects," *Datamation*, Jan. 1990.

Kim, W. "Architectural Issues in Object-Oriented Databases," *Journal of Object-Oriented Programming*, March/April, 1990.

Kim, W. "Object-Oriented Databases: Definition and Research Directions," in *IEEE Trans. on Knowledge and Data Engineering*, June 1990.

Index

The MIT Press, with Peter Denning as general consulting editor, publishes computer science books in the following series:

ACM Doctoral Dissertation Award and Distinguished Dissertation Series

Artificial Intelligence
Patrick Winston, Founding editor
Michael Brady, Daniel Bobrow, and Randall Davis, editors

Charles Babbage Institute Reprint Series for the History of Computing
Martin Campbell-Kelly, editor

Computer Systems
Herb Schwetman, editor

Explorations with Logo
E. Paul Goldenberg, editor

Foundations of Computing
Michael Garey and Albert Meyer, editors

History of Computing
I. Bernard Cohen and William Aspray, editors

Information Systems
Michael Lesk, editor

Logic Programming
Ehud Shapiro, editor; Fernando Pereira, Koichi Furukawa, Jean-Louis Lassez, and David H. D. Warren, Associate editors

The MIT Press Electrical Engineering and Computer Science Series

Research Monographs in Parallel and Distributed Processing
Christopher Jesshope and David Klappholz, editors

Scientific and Engineering Computation
Janusz Kowalik, editor

Technical Communication
Ed Barrett, editor